Living Across Worlds:
Diaspora,
Development and
Transnational Engagement

by
Ninna Nyberg Sørensen

IOM International Organization for Migration

CONTENTS

FOREWORD

The International Organization for Migration is pleased to present *Living Across Worlds, Diaspora, Development and Transnational Engagement*, a collection of research papers, directed by Ninna Nyberg Sorensen. Our Organization has been particularly committed over the last few years to proposing responses to the complex challenge of linking migration to development issues and this volume is part of this effort.

IOM's views on migration and development are derived from 55 years of experience helping governments to manage migration for the benefit of all. IOM emphasizes the pressing need to ensure that migration is integrated into development planning agendas at national and international levels and that the voice and role of transnational players - individuals and organizations - are heard and taken into account.

While there is growing agreement at the international level that migration considerations need to be routinely factored into development planning and that migration policies need to become more "development friendly", there are still gaps in defining the effects of migration on development. The aim of this collection is to show through selected case studies, the diversity of potential contributions of diasporas to the development of both their home and destination countries. The research presented in this volume shows how the conditions of migration and integration in the host societies can impact on diasporas' contributions to development and thus more globally how conditions under which migration takes place determine the development impact of migration.

This research allows us to "meet" with the diasporas, listen to their voices, enter their stories, get close to their concerns and aspirations, recognize the diversity of their motivations and discern the complexity of each personal migration path. Understanding the heterogeneity of strategies and circumstances hidden behind the word "diaspora" is a key element for developing policies that effectively engage diasporas for development. Policies failing to establish a working agenda and an effective partnership with diasporas are bound to generate very limited results.

The Research and Publications Unit of IOM views the collaboration of the organization with scholars involved in research throughout the world, as of great significance. IOM provides a platform for expression and exchange of views between researchers and policy makers, represented by IOM's membership, composed of 120 member states in 2007.

This publication is part of IOM's research and policy programme on migration and development, which comprises a large number of events and research papers on the subject. IOM publishes numerous documents on migration and development within the Migration Research Series and the International Dialogue on Migration Series, all available on IOM's website (www.iom. int).

The organization and in particular the Research and Publications Unit, would like to express its gratitude to Ninna Nyberg Sorensen, the director of the publication and to all authors who contributed to this volume, Manuel Orozco, Fiona Wilson, Simon Turner, Pia Steen, Nauja Kleist, Peter Hansen, Luis E. Guarnizo and Karsten Paerregaard.

While directed to a diverse audience of policy makers and academics, we expect that this volume will also interest social partners, non governmental actors, media as well as those transnational individuals who through their own stories of migration, live both "here" and "there".

Living Across Worlds:
Diaspora, Development and Transnational Engagement[1]

- *An Introduction*

Ninna Nyberg Sørensen

At the turn of the 21st century, globalization has reached most corners of the world. The transnational system that underpins current processes of globalization has led to increased mobility of capital, goods and information, and despite attempts to control, curtail or stem human mobility, global chains of interaction between migrants and family members left behind have lengthened and spread considerably. Increased mobility has led to a growing complexity of migratory movements, manifested in a substitution of "old" migration destinations with new ones, a growing class diversification and informalization of migration, a feminization of particular flows, and the phenomenon of "mixed flows" making the conventional distinction between forced and voluntary migration increasingly difficult. In the tension between transnational flows of people and states, new forms of control mechanisms and policies are emerging, and the scope and constituency for policy discussions around the migration-development nexus are broadened. The studies presented in this book critically examine some of these tensions.

Against the background of increases in human mobility, the cognate notions of globalization, diaspora and transnationalism have gained currency as means of making sense of migrant and refugee practices and the long-term, long-distance, connections maintained between family members, communities and states across international borders. From these new theoretical points of departure, notions of push-pull factors, remittances and conspicuous consumption, brain drain and return/repatriation have gradually been complemented with explorations of the complexity of migratory experiences, social remittances, human capital potential, and diaspora and transnational networks.

Throughout history, migration and development have been conceptualized as intimately interlinked. At a structural level, the linkage has been attributed to imbalances in levels of development between different communities, nation states or regions. Neo-classical equilibrium approaches have explained migration as either a function of wage-level differentials, employment opportunities, or human safety, thereby understanding human mobility as a way of maximizing resources and minimizing risks. Structuralist and Marxist approaches have focused attention on explicating migration in a global, capitalist context in which the development of "uneven development" is understood as a result of colonialism and (neo-)imperialism. Making a crude generalization, one may say that both approaches have viewed "development" quite instrumentally, although on very different grounds. In the first case, migration has been seen as beneficial to development: the movement of people from poor to rich countries is counteracted by a movement of money and consumer goods from rich to poor countries, whereby the global distribution of resources is equilibrated. This way of thinking underlies much current remittance policy debate. In the second case, migration has generally been understood as negatively effecting local development: migration deprives local communities of their most productive members; former producers convert into consumers; and migrant investments are generally not productive but rather channeled into conspicuous consumption that leads to further inequality. Traces of this way of thinking can be found in current brain drain concerns (for an overview, see Schuerkens, 2005; Spaan et al., 2005; Van Hear and Sørensen, 2003).

Rather than presuming such homogenizing outcomes of complex migratory processes, the individual contributions to this book explore the multiple – and sometimes contradictory – transnational flows and diaspora formations of past and present migrations. The case studies show that remittances of different kinds, the return of migrants with novel experiences or lifestyles acquired abroad, the establishment of investment, trade and intellectual links, as well as wider socio-cultural links between diaspora associations and developing countries may indeed potentially benefit development, especially if policy becomes informed by a set of new conceptualizations, including the understanding that migration is as much about the people who stay behind as it is about those who move across international borders (Levitt and Sørensen, 2004).

In exploring the dispersion, diasporization and transnationalization of populations across geographic regions and continents, migration studies have re-emerged as a vibrant area of research. Accompanying such explorations is growing recognition that globalization is uneven in its scope and effects. There are winners and losers, those who are included while others are excluded, those who are engaged and those who are marginalized, those gaining skills and recognition by mobilizing their existence and those becoming deskilled and perhaps further marginalized in the process. Despite a shift from a rather pessimistic to a more optimistic assessment of the role of migration in development processes, current research suggests that global migration, only in some cases and under certain circumstances, sets in motion processes that engage people in global, diasporic or transnational networks. The actual link between migration and development thus remains an empirical question to be studied in concrete situations. And even if migration in itself rarely seems to be able to induce the broader social, economic and political changes needed to advance progress in most developing countries, we still need to ask what can be learned from migrants' attempts to overcome structural barriers to development.

Despite important empirical and theoretical contributions from a growing number of studies applying a transnational lens, we still know too little about the *determinants of transnational engagement*. What, for example, makes people develop diasporic identifications and engage in transnational activities? To what extent are such identifications and engagements influenced by the form and conditions of movement, the context of reception and incorporation in destination countries, the status and standing of diasporas within them, and the attitude of source country governments towards their populations abroad? Another set of questions in need of further exploration evolves around the degree to which choice or compulsion in movement shape the subsequent influence of diasporas. Who has the power to initiate and sustain global flows, who are denied spatial mobility and, by implication, social mobility in transnational social space?

While particular transnational migration experiences have been extensively examined on a case basis, there is still a dire need for comparative research into the factors that determine whether migrant and refuge diasporas integrate into their countries of destination, return to the source countries, or engage in transnational practices that embrace both source and destination countries and/or the wider diaspora. The nature of destination societies and the place of diaspora groups within them are likely to shape profoundly the capacity of individuals and diaspora organizations to influence the homeland. But does marginalization encourage or discourage transnational engagement? Are the dynamics the same no matter what social, political, economic, cultural or religious forms such engagements take? And how do differences of wealth, power, class, ethnicity, gender and generation within diasporas shape the form and scope of transnational activities and their influence?

The present collection of studies aims to cast light on these complicated questions in a broader comparative perspective. As agued by Kennedy and Roudometof (2002), most of the academic literature on transnationalism has been based on the experience of the so-called "new" post-1945 migration into the USA and has concentrated on issues related to migrant diasporas and transnational nation-state building. The strong interest in the relationship between international migration and the development of nation states, and in particular Western nation states, has in the past 30 years tended to revolve around the negative impact of foreigners on the destination countries and the problem of integration. As international migration has become subject to greater control and increasing numbers of migrants concomitantly have been forced to travel and live in undocumented ways, research has also focused on the ability of migrants to negotiate the legal, social and economic barriers they encounter because of their precarious legal status (Sørensen and Olwig, 2002). Both research foci have been most thoroughly investigated in studies of migration between Mexico and the United States, which, due to several historic and geographical circumstances, is probably too specific to serve as ground for broader theorizations (see Orozco, this volume).

On a similar note, Sean Carter has argued, that recent work dealing with issues of diaspora has failed to pay sufficient attention to the geographic specificities of particular diasporas. Although spatial metaphors abound in analyses, the significance of geography is denied and often left un-interrogated. As a result, the "reterritorializing elements of diasporic practices" are discounted (Carter, 2004: 55). In order to respond to this challenge, studies included in this volume not only reflect on the specificities of particular migrant and refugee diasporas but also on the specificities of particular places, spatial practices and the production of social space that follows from cross-border movement and transnational engagement.

GLOBALIZATION, DIASPORA AND TRANSNATIONAL MIGRATION

The growing complexity of international migration has been both prompted and facilitated by globalization. Apart from the growing disparity in the levels of livelihood possibilities and human security, other factors contribute to the current magnitude, density, velocity, and diversity of human population movements. These include improved transportation, communication and information technology; the expansion of transnational social net-works and diaspora formations; and, at times, the emergence of a commercial and often criminal industry devoted to facilitating human movement across international borders. However, while the cornerstone of globalization has been an increase in the international flow of trade, capital, information and services, the right to freedom of movement – especially for poor migrants, refugees and asylum seekers – has been severely curtailed. Migrant workers and people in flight, although mobile by definition, are actually among those excluded from the freedom and benefits of borderless globalization (Jordão, 2001). The increasing number of migrants, as well as the containment of oth-ers, therefore reflects the limitations of globalization.

Within the social sciences, work on the relation between the global and the local has focused attention of the restructuring and extension of net-works of flows and their articulation with spaces of different scales (Castells, 1996, Smith, 2001), leading, among other things, to the concept of transna-tional social space (Pries, 2001). Another body of research has focused at-tention on diaspora (Clifford, 1994; Cohen, 1997; Van Hear, 1998; Safran, 1999; Vertovec, 2000; Axel, 2001), and on what distinguishes diasporas and the sometimes tricky issue of accountability and transparency of diaspora po-litical networks (Østergaard-Nielsen, 2006). Work on transnationalism (Glick Schiller et al, 1992; Smith and Guarnizo, 1998) has generally been linked to transmigration (Basch et al, 1994; Rouse, 1991; Kearney, 1995; Portes et al, 1999; Mahler. 1998). Gains from these approaches include an abandoning of "methodological nationalism", the assumption that the nation-state is the logical, natural container within which social life takes place (Wimmer and Glick Schiller, 2003). Another gain stems from a redirection of the analytical focus from place to mobility and from the bipolar view of "place of origin" and "place of destination" to the movements involved in sustaining mobile or cross-border livelihoods (Sørensen and Olwig, 2002).

These interrelated bodies of work reflect a growing understanding of global inter-connectedness and that people on the move are able to sustain and extend social life into widespread networks of relations including both source and destination countries. The literature also emphasizes stratifica-tion in the degree of mobility. "Nowadays we are all on the move", Bauman writes, but the fluidity of contemporary society has very different meanings for "the tourist" – or the highly mobile executive traveller - than for "the vaga-bonds" (e.g. undocumented travellers working at the bottom of the labour market) (Bauman, 1998).

Work on globalization, diaspora and transnationalism nevertheless differs in the key assumptions made about the role of the state in the produc-tion of meaning, identity and social outcomes. Whereas the perspective of globalization is largely decentred from specific national territories (Kearney, 1995), work on diaspora and transnationalism depicts economic, political and socio-cultural processes and relations as anchored in, while also tran-scending, more than one nation state, and thereby understands the nation state and transnational practices as mutually constitutive social formations (Smith, 2001).

The concepts and theoretical assumptions guiding globalization, diaspora and transnational studies moreover have different genealogies. Work on the nature of globalization has tended to privilege economic over cultural, social and political processes. Diaspora studies have primarily been concerned with identity and history, and transnational studies have tended to focus on the social ties and networks that link contemporary migrants or refugees to the communities or nation states of their birth. As a consequence, migrants' transnational practices have been understood to dissolve fixed assumptions about identity, place and community, whereas diasporic identity-making has been understood to evolve around attempts to "fix" and closely knit identity and community (see Simon Turner, this volume). In addition to reflecting different theoretical and disciplinary approaches – globalization studies being informed by geography, economy and political science; diaspora studies being primarily informed by the humanities and concerned with the issue of identity; and transnational studies being primarily informed by the social sciences and concerned with the relationship between people and states – this division in approach and interest has obscured the fact that it is exactly in the duality of "transgression" and "fixation" that migrant diasporas' transnational engagement may contribute to development.

It is the contention of this book that a renewed focus on diaspora and the new types of social formations created within transational social space can offer a new point of departure in research and policy debates around the migration-development nexus. At the same time, such a "new" point of departure needs to be historically anchored. Whereas the bulk of contemporary migration studies habitually view migration as a recent phenomenon linked to the globalization of capitalism, several of the empirical studies included in this volume show how diasporic identifications and contemporary transnational practices have historical antecedents. This is evident in Fiona Wilson's re-reading of the early determinants of Mexican migration to the US and the subsequent production of a new transnational social space spreading "modernity" to small towns in Mexico. In Karsten Paerregaard's analysis of Peruvian migration to such diverse settings as the US, Europe and Japan, earlier migration histories of contemporary migrants are seen to influence the choice of destination as well as their current transnational engagements. As such, the concepts of diaspora and transnational social space take into account the specific geopolitical circumstances that precipitate contemporary migratory movements.

In addition to historical sensitivity, the theoretical approaches adopted by the authors included in this volume involve a different set of questions and take into consideration a different set of factors than those traditionally considered by policymakers. Conceptualizing the migration experience as taking place within transnational social space moves the analysis beyond those who actually migrate to those who do not necessarily move but are connected to migrants through the networks of social relations they sustain across borders. This insight is important, because it reveals that the so-called "development impact" of migration is not solely related to return. Because people who stay behind are connected to migrants through social networks, they are exposed to a constant flow of economic and social remittances on a regular basis (Levitt, 1999), which might change their identities, world views and aspirations. Similarly, locating migrants within transnational social fields makes clear that incorporation into a new state and enduring attachments to the countries of origin are not necessarily binary opposites (Levitt and Sørensen, 2004). The economic, political and cultural practices of migrant populations are not merely a function of the opportunity structures in migrant receiving states. While more inclusive structures – which in principle allow for migrant incorporation – may weaken homeland ties, they may also facilitate mobilization around homeland developmental concerns (see Pia Steen, this volume).

THE CONTRIBUTIONS

The contributions to the volume consist of a number of case studies that detail various aspects of the concerns outlined above. They include migration from as diverse source areas as Central America, South America, the Caribbean, the Horn of Africa and the Great Lakes Region to as diverse destinations as the United States, various European countries, Central and South America, Japan and the Middle East. This broad geographical outlook allows for a broader analysis of diaspora formation, the production of transnational social space, the determinants of transnational engagements and, ultimately, the possible positive and negative influences of such engagements on developing the countries and/or local communities within them.

The first two chapters give an overview and discussion of conceptual clusters surrounding notions of "diaspora" and "transnational social space". Manuel Orozco's chapter, "Conceptualizing Diasporas: Remarks about the Latino and Caribbean Experience" discusses contemporary definitions and conceptualizations of diaspora. Particular emphasis is placed on the extent to which definitions and conceptualizations of diasporas acknowledge the role of border redefinition in creating potential diasporas. In addition, the relevance or irrelevance of dispersion to the diasporic identification, and the imprecision in most conceptualizations of what constitutes diasporic linkages are discussed. Using case studies of Guatemalan, Guyanese, Mexican, Nicaraguan, and Salvadoran migrants in the United States, Orozco shows how diasporic involvement can range from the exclusive maintenance of family ties in the homeland to establishing political connections that may lead to acquiring positions of power. In this regard, four kinds of involvement are observed at the family, community, social and political level. Diasporas, however, do not emerge solely as a consequence of dispersion, common national ancestry, or simply any kind of connection. There is a process by which groups are motivated or influenced to become diasporas, Orozco argues. These include the level of community consciousness about the needs for a link with the homeland, whether the homeland government is encouraging diasporic identifications or links, the perception of emigrants by the society in the homeland, and, finally, the relationship between homeland and host governments. How such processes are played out among the different Central American migrant groups is then demonstrated.

By using the example of the early determinants of Mexican migration to the United States (1910s to 1940s), Fiona Wilson's chapter, "Mestisaje and Clothing: Interpreting Mexican-US Transnational Social Space", approaches the production of social space through Henri Lefebre's (1991) distinction between space as practiced, conceived and perceived. Studies of labour migration, Wilson argues, generally assume the first in the relatively straightforward spatial *practice* of migrancy. In contrast, a *conception* of space as national, abstract and homogeneous underlies the view of politicians and planners who pass and execute legislation affecting migration from one territory to another. But it is the third of Lefebvre's perspectives, the *perception* of social space, that is central to Wilson's argument. The ways social space is perceived are both more intimate and less tangible as distance and barriers to movement are no longer absolute but become elastic and negotiable. In the social space produced by historical back and forth movements between western central Mexico and the United States, migrants could work with and negotiate greater self consciousness as *mestizos* and Mexicans. Alongside migration, the spread and innovations of modernity in the countryside allowed people at home to also visualize themselves as "moving with the times". Although historical in scope, Wilson's analysis pinpoints that "policy" not only has a long history but also that much of what might be considered "policy relevant" from the Mexican case is still relevant today.

A second relevant theme is constituted around the issue of group formation and collective action. Simon Turner's contribution "Burundians in Belgium: Constructing, performing and contesting diaspora" sets out to analyse the contradictory processes of the making and unmaking of transnational communities and diasporic identities. The existence of several Burundian diasporas challenges conventional concepts of "diaspora" and "transnational community", Turner argues. While the existence of multiple Burundian diasporas can be explained to some extent by different arrival times – and thus different experiences of migrating for economic or political reasons – Turner shows that the seeming correlation between ethnicity (Hutu/Tutsi), time of arrival, and objective position in the country of destination is not simply born out of objective position in the diaspora. Rather, individual political manouvering in the transnational political field shapes diasporic networks and determines the contents of transnational practices. Burundian migrants in Belgium distinguish between three main waves of arrival: *les anciens* who arrived after the selective genocide in 1972, *les boursiers* who arrived as students throughout the 1980s (first the Tutsi elite, later also including Hutu students), and finally the refugees arriving after 1993. These groups harbour a great deal of animosity and suspicion towards one another, but there are also overlaps between the categories. While religious identities may provide an avenue to transcend animosities, distinct political identities nevertheless seem to be what drives these different waves to construct different Burundian diaspora communities. Different projects of long-distance nationalism, rather than attempts to re-unite and get beyond home-country based animosities, seem to be the dispersed and diverse Burundian diaspora's primary political project.

Quite a different outcome is observed by Pia Steen, who in her chapter "Spaces of democratic practice: Nicaraguans in San José, Costa Rica" analyses the determinants of Nicaraguan migrants' transnational engagement. Like other Central American diasporas, the Nicaraguan one is made up of a mixed flow of political exiles and economic migrants and therefore consists of differentiated and partly separated groups of people. But whereas the middle and upper class may not be representative for the diaspora as a whole, neither in terms of social profile nor in terms of numbers, they are significant because of their transnational engagement linking different parts of the diaspora together across class divides. The forms and determinants of these engagements map a new political culture among Nicaraguans in the diaspora, Steen argues, reflecting the merging of experiences from Costa Rica and what they brought along with them from Nicaragua. The experiences gained from these activities and the activities themselves might become valuable drivers in processes of democratization within and across borders. Apart from providing an excellent illustration of the blurred area between refugee-ness and migrancy, Steen's analysis shows how the changing political situation in post-conflict societies shapes the continuing flows in and out of Nicaragua many years *after* the conflict has officially ended, as well as the myriad forms of transnational participation migrants engage in.

A third important theme evolves around the issue of return. In his chapter "Revolving Returnees to Somaliland", Peter Hansen points to a seemingly united form of long-distance nationalism among migrants and refugees from northern Somalia, Somaliland. During Siad Barre's dictatorship, the Somali diaspora – especially those living and working in Saudi Arabia and the United Kingdom – participated in the organization and funding of an armed resistance movement. At present, the diaspora is heavily engaged in the Republic of Somaliland's struggle for international recognition, and it is called upon by local political authorities for both financial and lobbying purposes. The present relationship between diaspora members returning home and society at large is neither outright positive nor welcoming, nor is it especially problematic or conflict ridden. This, Peter Hansen argues, is basically due to the fact that "everybody" fled Somaliland at some point during recent history, and therefore few can claim higher moral grounds because they didn't leave. Does that make the inhabitants of Somaliland return migrants or repatriated refugees? Although such categories may be attached to many Somalilanders by international organizations such as IOM or UNHCR, Hansen argues that we can only understand current civic engagement in Somaliland politics, economy and social life by employing the concepts of mobile livelihood and circular migration. To underscore this point, six groups of circular migrants currently engaged in Somaliland society are distinguished, including returnees employed within the "development industry"; returnees involved in political and bureaucratic circles; circular migrants engaged in the private business sector; migrants returning to secure ownership or buy plots of land; people visiting Somaliland during their holidays, either to visit family members, to find a spouse, or to see if going back is a viable option; and finally, young Somalilanders who may either have come voluntarily to Somaliland to learn Somali culture or may have been sent back by their parents for "re-educational" purposes. Whatever the reason for being in Somaliland, the chapter shows, successful return is only possible to the extent that people maintain strong transnational links to the wider diaspora, possess important "diasporic capital" connecting them to local social networks as well as social and economic resources overseas, and hold foreign residence or citizenship papers that allow for continued mobility.

Contrary to the variety of individual return strategies presented by Peter Hansen, Nauja Kleist's contribution, "Somali-Scandinavian Dreaming: When 'the diaspora' returns to the dessert", takes issue with the planned collective return by a group of Somalilanders from Sweden, Denmark, Norway and the United Kingdom who are united in the umbrella association Somscan & UK Cooperative Association. This association constitutes a rather unusual hometown association, which aims at establishing a "Scandinavian-style" neighbourhood in a central Somaliland town, Burao. In cooperation with Somscan & UK, the Danish Refugee Council has managed to raise funding for a large grant from the EC High Level Working Group on Asylum and Migration to support the repatriation process – and to avoid that the return-ees drain Burao for scarce resources such as water. Still, the members of the association acknowledge that return is not a straightforward task. In her analysis of the process of establishing the new neighbourhood – as well as the conflicts erupting with IDP squatters already residing on these premises – Kleist foregrounds the complicated relations of power and social space that this arrangement has given rise to. By applying a gendered optic, the analysis also shows that conflict over return not only arises between returnees and locals, but also within transnational families. The dream of returning to So-maliland is seen as an expression of a gendered social order, where an ideal patriarchal family life can be realized. Such an option may be more attractive to men losing status in transnational social space than to women.

This leads us to a fourth area of concern included in the volume, namely the issue of transnational family life. Discourses on transnational family life have generally been framed in terms of gender relations within households or families. But, as shown in Ninna Nyberg Sørensen and Luís E. Guarnizo's contribution, "Transnational Family Life across the Atlantic: The Experience of Colombian and Dominican Migrants in Europe", state policies severely influence family-level gender politics. It is generally accepted that migration motivation and decision making is embedded in larger family con-cerns. However, assessments of the role that migrants play in promoting de-velopment in the source countries still take their point of departure in issues such as remittances, return and diaspora support *without* considering who migrates and who stays behind, under what circumstances, for what purpos-es, and with which consequences. In analyses of the feminization of particu-lar migration streams, the developmental impact is moreover often assessed in negative terms and as leading to spatially fractured family relations and even family breakdown. Sørensen and Guarnizo's analysis of transnational family life among Colombian and Dominican migrants in Europe shows a much more complicated picture in which transnational families – due to entry requirements – increasingly consist of family members of different na-tionalities. Fractured family relations moreover tend to precede rather than result from female migration. Finally, the analysis emphasizes how society's moral disciplining of transnational mothers and fathers varies. Since fathers are supposed to be *absent* anyway, their migration abroad is in many ways a continuation of this absentee role. The current migration of Latin American women to Europe therefore goes against the grain of organic notions of *present* mothers, domesticity and morality, and culturally coded narratives of "family values". This may explain the limited "outreach" from the Colombian and Dominican states towards domestic workers in Europe.

The volume's final contribution, "Adios Peru: Persistence and Variation in Peruvian Transnational Engagement", by Karsten Paerregaard, brings together several issues touched upon in the previous chapters. Paerregaard sets out to explore the migration experiences of eight Peruvians that in different ways elicit the circumstances that urge migrants to leave their country of origin. Particular emphasis is placed on the extent to which migrants' decision to emigrate is influenced by the social and ethnic status in Peru that have been thrust upon them because of the migration histories of their ancestors. Another important factor in society influencing the choice of destination and the migrants' current transnational engagement is related to previous migratory experience and economic and social status in Peruvian society. The chapter examines how migrants construct different notions of home in response to the context of reception in their new settings as well as to their previous migration experiences, and discusses the ideas of belonging that these constructions give rise to. Paerregaard concludes that Peruvian emigration is at variance with the migration practices described in the growing body of literature on transnational migration and that a model of transnational engagement that takes into consideration people's previous migratory experiences and applies a global view of contemporary migration practices is warranted.

The case studies included in the volume shed light on several emerging areas of research and policy debates related to diaspora, development and transnational engagement. Several common themes emerge, pointing towards a more encompassing understanding of what makes people engage in transnational migration and development in their home countries. Our main argument is that a future agenda for aligning migration and development concerns will benefit from seriously incorporating the complicated questions of diaspora and the production of transnational social space. The challenge is to figure out which transnational engagements hold positive and lasting development potential. Some of these themes and challenges are put together in the book's conclusion.

NOTE

1. The research network "Diaspora, development and conflict" has provided a rich intellectual environment for several discussions on the links between migration and development. I want to acknowledge and thank the Danish Social Science Research Council for the generous research and network grants that allowed four years of comparative research and the international workshop from which the contributions stem. Our work has also been supported by the Danish Council for Development Research, and funding for several other related activities was graciously provided by the Danish development agency "Danida". For making individual and group efforts into this book, I warmly thank the International Organization for Migration (IOM), Geneva. My thanks also go to the Danish Institute for International Studies (DIIS) for fellowships, assistantships and technical as well moral lifelines over the years. Department and network assistant Ane Toubro patiently and knowingly made the solid ground for our work, meetings and workshops. Former colleague Marie Bille provided language editing of the chapters originally written in "danglish" and "spanglish". Finally, I want to thank Nicholas Van Hear for taking part in the initial efforts to establish the network as well as for his contributions to several of the network's activities.

REFERENCES

Axel, B.
2001   "The nation's tortured body", *Violence,* representation and the for-
        mation of the Sikh diaspora, Duke University Press, Durham.
Basch, L., N. Glick Schiller, and C. Szanton-Blanc
1994   *Nations Unbound: Transnational Projects and the Deterritorial-
        ized Nation State,* Langhorne, PA, Gordon and Breach.
Bauman, Z.
1998   *Globalization: The Human Consequences,* Polity Press, Cambridge.
Carter, S.
2004   "The geopolitics of diaspora", *Area,* 37(1): 54-63.
Castells, M.
1996   *The Rise of the Network Society,* Blackwell, Oxford.
Clifford, J.
1994   "Diasporas", *Current Anthropology,* 9(3): 302-38.
Cohen, R.
1997   *Global Diasporas: An Introduction,* London, UCL Press
Faist, T.
2000   *The Volume and Dynamics of International Migration and Trans-
        national Social Spaces,* Oxford University Press, Oxford.
Glick Schiller, N., L. Basch, and C. Szanton Blanc (Eds)
1992   "Transnational perspective on migration", *Race, Class, Ethnicity,
        and Nationalism Reconsidered,* Annals of the New York Academy
        of Sciences 645, New York.
Kearney, M.
1995   "The local and the global: The anthropology of globalization and
        transnationalism", *Annual Review of Anthropology,* 24: 547-65.
Kennedy, P., and V. Roudometof (Eds)
2002   "Communities across borders", *New Immigrants and Transnation-
        al Cultures,* Routledge, London.
Lefebvre, H.
1991   *The Production of Social Space,* Blackwell Publishers, Oxford.
Levitt, P.
2001   *The Transnational Villagers,* University of California Press, Berkeley.
Levitt, P., and N.N. Sørensen
2004   "The transnational turn in migration studies", *Global Migration
        Perspectives,* No. 6: 2-13.
Mahler, S.J.
1998   "Theoretical and empirical contributions towards a research
        agenda for transnationalism", in M.P. Smith and L.E. Guarnizo
        (Eds), *Transnationalism from Below,* Transaction Publishers, New
        Brunswick.
Portes, A., L.E. Guarnizo, and P. Landolt
1999   "Introduction: Pitfalls and promise of an emergent research field",
        Ethnic and Racial Studies, 22(2): 217-37.
Pries, L. (Ed.)
2001   *New Transnational Social Spaces,* Routledge, London.

An Introduction

Rouse, R.
   1991   "Mexican migration and the social space of postmodernism", *Diaspora,* 1(1): 8-23.
Safran, W.
   1999   "Comparing diasporas: A review essay", *Diaspora* 8(3), winter.
Shuerkens, U.
   2005   "Transnational migrations and social transformations: A theoretical perspective", *Current Sociology,* 53(4): 535-553.
Smith, M.P.
   2001   *Transnational Urbanism: Locating Globalization*, Blackwell, Massachusetts.
Smith, M.P., and L.E. Guarnizo (Eds)
   1998   *Transnationalism from Below*, Transaction Publishers, New Brunswick.
Sørensen, N.N. and K.F. Olwig (Eds),
   2002   "Work and migration", *Life and Livelihoods in a Globalizing World*, Routledge, London.
Spaan, E., T. van Naerssen, and F. Hillman
   2005   "Shifts in the European discourses on migration and development", *Asian and Pacific Migration Journal*, 14(1-2): 35-69.
Van Hear, N.
   1998   *New Diasporas*, UCL Press, London.
Van Hear, N., and N.N. Sørensen (Eds),
   2003   *The Migration-Development Nexus*, International Organization for Migration, Geneva.
Vertovec, S.
   2000   *The Hindu Diaspora: Comparative Patterns*, Routledge, London.
Wimmer, A., and N. Glick Schiller
   2003   "Methodological nationalism, the social sciences and the study of migration", An essay in Historical Epistemology, *International Migration Review*, 37(3): 576-610.
Østergaard-Nielsen, E.K.
   2001   "Transnational political practices and the receiving state: Turks and Kurds in Germany and the Netherlands", *Global Networks*, 1(3): 261-282.
   2006   "Diasporas and conflict resolution – part of the problem or part of the solution?", *DIIS Brief March*, (www.diis.dk).

Conceptualizing Diasporas: Remarks About the Latino and Caribbean Experience

Manuel Orozco

ABSTRACT

In the last decade, the term diaspora has begun to emerge, first in migration studies, then in development studies. The present chapter attempts to contribute to this debate. Particular emphasis is placed upon the extent to which definitions and conceptualizations of diasporas acknowledge the role of border redefinition in creating (potential) diasporas, the relevance or irrelevance of dispersion to diasporic identification, and the imprecision of what constitutes diasporic linkages. Using case studies of Latinos in the United States today, it is shown that different contexts shape the emergence of a group as a diaspora. These include the level of community – and in particular elite and activist consciousness about the needs for a link with a homeland; whether the homeland government is encouraging diasporic identification or links; the perception of emigrants by the society in the homeland; and finally, the relationship between the homeland and host governments.

INTRODUCTION

In the last decade, the term diaspora have begun to emerge, first in migration studies, then in development studies. Once conceptualized as exile or forced dislocation from a "homeland", in the recent migration-development literature diaspora has increasingly been used to describe the mass migrations and displacements of the second half of the 20th century as well as to analyse the developmental "impact" of these migrants' cross-border activities.

This chapter attempts to contribute to the contemporary debate on what diasporas are all about and how we should understand them in our political society. Two lines of inquiry are suggested in this chapter. On the one hand, to analyse the extent to which widely accepted definitions and conceptualizations of diasporas ignore three empirical problems, namely the role of border redefinition in creating (potential) diasporas, the relevance or irrelevance of dispersion to diasporic identification, and the imprecision of what constitutes diasporic linkages. It is argued that we cannot assume that the notion of dispersion is sufficient, and in some cases even necessary, for the articulation of a diaspora. Moreover, the linkages that constitute or inform diasporic development must be tangible and influential, not merely symbolic. On the other hand, we need to pay firm attention to the material and political circumstances which are encouraging or inhibiting the growth of contemporary diasporas.

Using case studies of Latinos in the United States today, the chapter shows that four contexts shape the emergence of a group as a diaspora. These are (i) the level of community – and in particular elite and activist – consciousness about the needs for a link with a homeland, (ii) whether the homeland government is encouraging diasporic identification or links, (iii) the perception of emigrants by the society in the homeland, and, finally, (iv) the relationship between the homeland and host governments.

DIASPORAS

The association between diasporas and dispersion is unambiguous in perhaps the case of Jews or Greeks. Once, however, the notion of "diaspora" is applied to other religious or ethnic groups, "it becomes immediately apparent how difficult it is to find a definition that makes a clear distinction between a migration and a diaspora, or between a minority and a diaspora" (Chalian and Rageau, 1995: xiii).

How, then, might one clearly define or establish a concept of diaspora? Shain (1995), for example, uses the term to refer to a people with common national origin who reside outside a claimed or an independent home territory. Esman (1986) has defined a diaspora as a minority ethnic group of migrant origin which maintains sentimental or material links with its land of origin. These, and other, definitions of diaspora[1] share in common notions of a relationship between groups of people that are based on some form of national ancestry, and sometimes of dispersion.

These interpretations or descriptions of diaspora seem problematic. First, assuming the traditional notion of diaspora as related to dispersion leaves out all those groups which, by virtue of the formation of a nation state, were separated but not dispersed by territorial boundaries. Mexicans and the descendants of those living in northern Mexico before its annexation by the United States are one example. Numerous African groups in the post-colonial period provide other examples of separation without dispersion.

Second, these definitions assume that any group by virtue of their common national origin and scatteredness constitute a diaspora. However, this categorization may include groups who do not identify with what is regarded as the homeland. In other words, not all ethnicities who have a common national origin can be regarded, or regard themselves, as diasporas. Rather, by virtue of these and some other conditions such groups become a diaspora.

Third, the assumption about diasporas as groups that retain some meaningful link with perceived homelands is important but imprecise. The assumption depends on some abstract notion of a link or connection which is difficult to pin down. What act or acts are sufficient to constitute a linkage meaningful enough to be considered as diasporic? How much of a linkage is required to call a group a diaspora? And who is defining the connection – an individual, a community, an outside group, or all of them?

In contemporary transnational migrant communities, diasporic involvement can range from the exclusive maintenance of family ties in the homeland to establishing political connections that may lead to acquiring positions of power. In this regard at least four kinds of involvement can be observed at the family, community, social and political level. In most cases, migrants maintain family ties and some community and social connections with the homeland. Political exiles who struggle to return to their homeland and (re-)gain power are more eager to pursue political links with local constituencies. In these cases, however, the establishment of ties as an indicator of diasporic connection requires further specification. Thus, meaningful contact needs to be tied to another triggering or motivational variable.

As a preliminary definition, and in this context, Sheffer offers a more concrete definition of diasporas as a "socio-political formation, created as a result of either voluntary or forced migration, whose members regard themselves as of the same ethno-national origin and who permanently reside as minorities in one or several host countries. Members of such entities maintain regular or occasional contacts with what they regard as their homeland and with individuals and groups of the same background residing in other host countries" (Sheffer, 2003: 10-11).

By virtue of this reality, diasporas implicate themselves internationally through relationships with the homeland, other international entities, and host country governments and societies, thereby influencing various dynamics, including development.

FACTORS

Diasporas do not emerge solely as a consequence of dispersion, common national ancestry, or simply any kind of connection. There is a process by which groups are motivated or influenced to become diasporas. Orozco and de la Garza's case study research on Latinos and their links to their homelands indicate that four critical factors enable the formation of a group into a diaspora (de la Garza and Orozco, 2000). These are:

1. the level of community – and particularly elite and activist – consciousness about the need or desire for a link with the homeland,
2. the homeland's perceptions of emigrants,
3. the outreach policies by governments in the homeland, and
4. the existence of relationships between source and destination countries.

With reference to case material, each of these factors is elaborated below.

Homeland links
First, the community must experience a need or demand for values and interests from the homeland. Among national or ethnic migrant groups an appeal to the values or interests common to those of the ancestral homeland can occur. Such an appeal or demand will depend on whether a leader or members of the community (due to some experience with the homeland or with enforcing their values or identities) find it is to the best of their interest or identity to identify with the homeland. When exile groups, for example, look for the support of the migrant community they have found it necessary to appeal to values and interests of the homeland.

Even minorities, whose nexus with a homeland is rather symbolic or historically distant, may find it to their interest to appeal to common values with that homeland. This is for example the case of third generation Mexican-Americans or Mexican-Americans whose ancestry is rooted in California or Texas. Invoking the homeland can increase economic or political interests that benefit their own resources.

The formation of hometown associations (HTAs) is a concrete example of a demand for values and interests. HTAs are philanthropic migrant organizations created under the common cause to support the communities of origin though the transfer of donation and resources (Orozco, 2000; Goldring, 2003). HTAs develop political capital in the places of settlement, which in turn increases the reliance of the local migrant-sending community on the resources of these associations. Thus leaders of the HTAs can reap personal

Conceptualizing Diasporas: Remarks About the Latino and Caribbean Experience

benefits from links to both communities. In this regard some observers have seen HTAs as a personal investment for the HTA leaders; leaders may hope that they will take future lucrative leadership positions in their hometowns (Alarcon, 2000). Within that context, HTA leaders come to have more influence from abroad than they would have from their hometown (Zabin, 1998).

Mexican and Guyanese immigrant communities provide two examples of active hometown associations operating in the US. In the Guyanese case, an estimated 200 associations have been formed in the US. They carry out projects both in Guyana and in the places of settlement in the US and these projects often address issues such as education and health. One distinct characteristic of Guyanese HTAs is that they often are organized by religious or professional affiliation or formed in order to deal with a specific cause. Another characteristic is that they sometimes depend on membership's dues for fund sources, collecting a yearly average of under US$5,000. Guyanese HTAs have formed partnerships with the national Guyanese government, local municipalities, as well as non-profit organizations such as churches. Partnerships have also been formed with other Carribean groups (Orozco, 2003a).

Mexican HTAs are among the better known and studied. An estimated 600 Mexican HTAs are operating in over 30 US cities. Unlike Guyanese groups, they work with a specific geographical location or community. Fundraising efforts result in average yearly collections of under US$10,000, mostly collected through organized events in the US such as dances, raffles, or dinners. Around 80 per cent of Mexican HTAs have collaborated with other institutions towards projects in their hometowns (Orozco, 2003b). This articulation of an emigrant group to reconnect with the home country is indicative of a sense of diasporism. Such indications are perceived in the expression of a common and shared interest about the home country's needs and challenges.

Homeland perceptions of emigrants

Second, people in the homeland must have positive perceptions of their emigrants to create an incentive to link to "distant" brothers. Thus, the kind of perceptions a homeland has of their emigrants plays a critical role in motivating particular groups to link with their countries of origin. The way Latin American states think of their emigrants varies from country to country. Except for El Salvador, Central Americans living in the United States have historically been little known or recognized by their home countries. In Nicaragua, for example, a country whose emigrant population is more than 20 per cent the size of the total population, there has been only little official notice of a Nicaraguan diaspora.

Until recently, researchers attached to Nicaraguan universities did not study migration of Nicaraguans to the US or Costa Rica (the other major receiving country of Nicaraguans), nor did the government know much about the Nicaraguan diaspora. Yet, the diaspora's invisibility should not be taken at face value. In the early nineties, in Managua, Nicaraguans who visited or returned to their home country were called "Miami boys", an expression used to refer to them as different from both US and Nicaraguan native populations.

In Nicaragua, the opinion of Nicaraguans in the US is mixed. For a long time, many groups were very critical of Nicaraguans in Miami as they were associated with the ones who fought with Somoza and created the contra forces (Orozco, 2002). Other sectors of society looked upon the diaspora with indifference or barely noticed them, despite the fact that the country receives millions of dollars in remittances. More recently, however, a "heroic" view of immigrants, particularly those in Costa Rica, has emerged. These are regarded as hard working people who left their country in search of livelihood opportunities and are now facing hardship in a foreign land. Costa Rica is the destination for 50 per cent of Nicaragua's migrants and some 400,000 Nicaraguans are estimated to reside in Costa Rica. In contrast to Nicaraguans living in the US, those in Costa Rica come mainly from rural areas with lower incomes. An average of US$100 million dollars is sent from Costa Rica to Nicaragua each year. This trend is recent; 53 per cent of Nicaraguans residing in Costa Rica have been sending remittances for less than three years (Orozco, 2004a).

In the Salvadoran case, the diaspora in the United States is considered more positively by the homeland. Salvadoran migrants are generally regarded as those who left during the war and now are helping to rebuild the country from war and natural disaster through remittances and other material support. Guatemala, on the other hand, conforms to the general Central American tendency, with an attitude of ignorance and indifference towards Guatemalans abroad.

The Guatemalan situation is not static, however. Polarization has gradually diminished as the country attempts to heal its wounds from the civil war. Guatemalan organizations in the US (some of them in the South and Midwest) have recently shown an interest in working or returning to their home country (Popkin, 2003). One important example refers to Guatemalans residing in Oxnard, California, who maintain deep connections to the highlands of Guatemala.

Former Guatemalan exiles living in the United States – who have established themselves more or less permanently there – have temporarily returned to their country in a display of support for the peace process and a newly-emerging civil society (de la Garza and Orozco, 2000). Moreover, in 2004, during the newly inaugurated administration of Oscar Berger, a vice-minister of foreign affairs for migration and human rights was appointed in order to seek implementation of a policy of attention to the Guatemalan diaspora. However, there is still room for a more significant societal appreciation of the Guatemalan diaspora.

The Guatemalan and Nicaraguan cases thus suggest another factor, that may explain interest in external mobilization of migrants, namely the level of political polarization in the home country. Compared to other Central American countries, El Salvador experienced lesser levels of polarization after its civil war. The success of the peace accord provided an important incentive to Salvadoran émigrés to go back to help rebuild the country. Interestingly, however, as the returnees renew their local engagement, their ideological allegiances are reflected, thus expressing positions in the political continuum of Salvadoran affairs.

Nicaragua, on the other hand, continues to be polarized along the lines of *Sandinismo* versus *Somocismo*, and most Nicaraguans living in the United States are anti-Sandinistas. Because Miami-based Nicaraguans strongly believe that Sandinista control of Nicaragua remains very strong, their interest in mobilizing abroad to support Nicaragua has been limited, except when their direct political interests and financial considerations are at stake. Thus, when Miami Nicaraguans wanted their seized property returned, they used US pressure to help their cause. Nicaraguans living in Miami were also very influential in sending a message to their relatives in Nicaragua during the electoral campaign of 1996 (Orozco, 2002). Their message was that if presidential candidate Arnoldo Aleman did not win the election with their families' support, they would stop sending remittances. More recently, the *Sandinismo-Somocismo* divide was revived when former president Aleman was put in jail for corruption charges. The divide was mirrored in the United States with groups blaming the current administration of president Bolaños of betraying Liberal party values and of being too soft with the Sandinistas.

Government outreach policies

Third, positive homeland policies towards its emigrants may shape or enable the formation of a diasporic identity. Outreach programmes targeting those regarded as belonging to the nation, but who are living abroad, provide a positive incentive for forging a connection to or identifying with the homeland. Such homeland outreach policies have proven to be quite important in motivating and sustaining diasporic identifications and practices.

An example of such homeland policies is provided by the Salvadoran government towards their emigrants living in the United States. A recent study on Central American transnationalism suggested that "the Salvadoran government as compared to other governments in the region, both central as well as local, has a much more institutionalized response to international labor migration" (Andrade-Eeckoff, 2003: 35). Despite the limited resources available in a poor country like El Salvador, the government has sought to adapt to changing circumstances and promote policies towards their emigrant communities.

One of the first steps in that direction was the creation of a General Directorate within the Ministry of Foreign Affairs to address the Salvadoran community living abroad (DGACE). The directorate, created in January 2000, has been the main official link between the government and the Salvadoran diaspora. The Directorate justifies its existence by pointing to the continuing reality of migration and remittances of Salvadorans living outside El Salvador. The program addresses three areas: economic ties and integration; community and local development; and cultural and educational ties.[2]

This government office has been active in forging and maintaining relationships with the Salvadoran diaspora by working directly with consulates and the embassy, coordinating projects with other government agencies, visiting the diaspora and its leaders on a regular basis, and keeping the diaspora informed through an online publication *Comunidad en Acción* which reports on various activities and projects implemented by the diaspora as well as by the diaspora in collaboration with government or private entities.[3] The government outreach strategy has focused primarily on education and community outreach, but has not addressed political matters such as the right to vote abroad and broader representation of the community.

The government outreach efforts have also been met by other institutions. The media in El Salvador in particular has created an active strategy to keep the diaspora informed about home-country affairs as well as about events in the home country. Newspapers like *La Prensa Gráfica* and *Diario de Hoy* have a section on Salvadoran diaspora news ranging from political events to social issues, including topics like crime and conditions of the community. *La Prensa Gráfica*'s section, "Departamento 15", maintains a regular news section that also operates online.[4]

Relations between source and destination country

Fourth, the existence of continuous relations between source and destination countries has proven to be of importance to diaspora formation. Such relations may provide the means for the identification of a historical memory and identification with the homeland and some sense of connectedness with it. This issue has been critical in the aftermath of civil wars in Central America, leading to a strengthening of US and Central American ties consolidated into a free trade agreement. In this case, the US government has invited or opened its door to national or ethnic minorities' participation in issues related to their homeland, hereby creating a political opportunity structure facilitating a process of diversity in the foreign policy establishment as well as of the representation of ethnic interests. In October 2004, the US Department of State initiated a historic event by bringing over 100 Central American community leaders to the US to have a dialogue with government officials. The event signified a recognition of a new perspective on, and a transnational approach to, Central America.

It is also possible that the efforts towards the ratification of a free trade agreement between the US and Central America may bring to attention the role of the Central American diaspora to strengthen its ties with their home countries. The Central American Free Trade Agreement (CAFTA) signals an end to Central America's turbulent history and perhaps a new page for the region's relations with the US. It opens up the possibility for the Central American diaspora to push for a trade agenda which considers nostalgic goods[5] from the home countries (Orozco, 2004b).

In addition to the four factors discussed above, there may be other additional variables that play an important role in the formation of diasporas. These include the political opportunity structure's openness, the level of cohesion in the ethnic or migrant community, and the length of time from the initial migration. The longer the separation in time between a migrant group's departure, the less likely a connection may exist. This trend is demonstrated in a direct proportional relationship between the length of time immigrants live in the US and the length of time they send remittances. Initially, as the length of time living in the US increases, remittance sending also increases. As the table below indicates, however, remittance sending decreases after longer periods abroad (around 10 years).

Table 1. MIGRANT REMITTANCES OVER TIME

Source: Orozco, Manuel. Survey carried out by the author.

Not all four variables (or their subsidiary ones) need to be present in order for a group to turn into a diaspora. Rather, diasporic development depends on the intensity of the interaction established by any one of those factors.

Finally it should be mentioned that such diasporic turns may not be permanent. As Chaliand and Rageau (1996) have pointed out, the identification of a diaspora requires time. And only time will show how long a diasporic connection will last.

DEGREE, FOCUS, INITIATION AND IMPACT OF DIASPORIC RELATIONS

Depending on which of the variables outlined above that play a role in determining a diasporic turn, four different dynamics will result. These are: (i) The degree or level of diaspora involvement, (ii) the focus or orientation the diasporic group takes, (iii) who initiates the diasporic relationship, and (iv) the impact of diaspora involvement on the host country. These dynamics are elaborated below.

Living Across Worlds: Diaspora, Development and Transnational Engagement

Degree and level of involvement

A diaspora may get involved in homeland issues to various degrees and at various levels. These can range from the exclusive maintenance of family ties in the homeland to establishing political connections that may lead to acquiring positions of power. In the following, involvement at the level of family and community is distinguished as is respectively social and political involvement.

In most cases, diasporas maintain family ties and some form of community and social connection to the homeland. Native-born diasporas, that is, those groups who are born outside the land of ancestry and who consider the "host" country as their first home, are the least likely to establish diasporic connections. When they do, the connection often occurs because of some family linkage or because their interests and values improve with the creation of linkages.

A typical example of this kind of connection is that of remittance sending. The current estimate for worldwide annual remittance flows is US$200 billion, with the Latin American and Caribbean region being the largest receiver (US$46 billion in 2004). Although varying by country, overall immigrants in the United States send US$250 12 times per year. Mexican immigrants are among those who send the largest amount by, on average, remitting 22 per cent of their income (US$400 monthly). Remittance receivers are most often immediate family members, primarily siblings and parents. These links demonstrate an obligation and commitment to family needs which result in distributing finances to households and sectors that tend to be economically disadvantaged (Orozco, 2004c).

Remittances are also part of a process in which nations are further integrated into the global economy through migrant's connections between the home and host countries. They also have multiplying effects through more varied and diffuse economic consequences which appreciate their impact on financial growth. These are the "Five T's" of global integration: tourism, (air) transportation, telecommunications, (remittance) transfers, and (nostalgic) trade. These dynamics, affecting both the home and host country's economies, incorporate the activities and practices in which diasporas remain connected with their homeland and people through visits, buying regional products, telephone calls, and sending money home. About 500,000 Dominican expatriates, for example, return annually to the Dominican Republic, spending an average of US$650 per visit. This represents about 20 per cent of total tourism to the country (Orozco, 2004d). In the region, between 50 to 80 per cent of earnings generated through telephone calls come from home to home calls made by immigrants. Additionally, nostalgic product export has come to reach some 10 percent of total exports for the Central American region (Orozco, 2004c).

Community connections mainly occur among small diasporic groups who establish links of various sorts with their community's hometown. For example, Mexican, Salvadoran and Guyanese migrant groups, to name some, correspond to this trend. Mexican and Guyanese hometown associations maintain active contact with their communities through liaisons in the

Conceptualizing Diasporas: Remarks About the Latino and Caribbean Experience

hometown which transmit needs and oversee the implementation of projects. Some Mexican HTAs communicate weekly with appointed representatives working in the hometown. The social connections that have been established between a diaspora with local homeland organizations are varied. Most of these connections are carried out with the purposes of helping to promote social causes, such as health care, education, or cultural connections.

Interestingly, however, the number of people that participate actively or have membership in these kinds of associations is relatively small compared to the total immigrant population.

Table 2: PEOPLE WHO BELONG TO A KIND OF HTA (% OF TOTAL WHO SEND REMITTANCES)

National origin	%
Colombia	5.6%
Ecuador	10.0%
El Salvador	1.5%
Guatemala	2.8%
Guyana	26.3%
Honduras	6.7%
Mexico	2.1%
Nicaragua	4.0%
Dom. Rep.	3.3%
Bolivia	1.4%
Average	5.5%

Source: Orozco, Manuel. "Transnationalism and Development: Trends and Opportunities in Latin America Survey of Transnational Communities", in *Remittances: Development Impact and Future Prospects*, editors, Samuel Munzele Maimbo and Dilip Ratha, Washington, DC: The World Bank, 2005.

Political links are less varied among non-exile diaspora groups and occur predominantly among migrants with political aspirations or who are interested in pursuing political careers in the homeland or in the destination country. Political exiles who struggle to return to their homeland and gain power are more eager to pursue political links. More recently, however, the political issue has been a struggle to affirm political rights of diasporas to vote and be elected in the home country.

Arguments towards the "vote from abroad" in homeland political elections include the bi-national nature of the migrant community and its relationships and social networks with various actors within the home country. With reference to the Mexican case, Miguel Moctezuma points out that migrants, especially through their participation in hometown associations, remain active and influential in their home communities. Therefore, their participation should be extended beyond the local level, and into national political issues. The Mexican government recognizes the value of migrant participation through pursuing partnerships with hometown associations, and through regular discourse between governors and migrant leaders in the United States. Furthermore, Moctezuma argues, Mexico seeks to gain a greater negotiating capacity with the US by granting the vote from abroad to Mexican immigrants (Moctezuma, 2003).

Focus

Focus refers to the orientation in which the diaspora puts or invests its energies in mobilizing politically. Milton Esman has conceptualized the triadic network between diaspora, homeland and host government. He further argues that the continuing links between diasporas and homelands can be politicized. In Esman's framework, seven classes of activity of either the home government, the host government or the diaspora – all observable in the context of international relations – are determined, namely:

a. diaspora attempts to influence home country events
b. diaspora attempts to influence host governments foreign policies towards home countries
c. home government outreach to the diaspora for self-interest
d. diaspora outreach to home government for protection from host government
e. host country outreach of diaspora to cultivate goals in home country
f. diaspora influence on international organizations on behalf of homeland, and
g. home government outreach to host government to influence diaspora (Estman, 1986: 340-343).

To the international activities mentioned by Esman, two more can be mentioned. One is international links among diasporic groups (particularly from the same source country, as in the case of linkages between Nicaraguans in the US and Costa Rica). The other is diaspora international mobilization to pursue non-homeland issues, such as environmental protection or democracy.

The international orientation of diasporic mobilization can have three different components. First, the diaspora may choose to mobilize to influence homeland domestic interests that benefit the homeland and the diaspora. This is the case of Esman's points b, e and g. The interest of Central American diasporas in supporting CAFTA is illustrative of this. Second, the diasporic group may mobilize on home country affairs in order to influence national politics or to keep links between sectors of society or a local community. This is the case of Estman's points a, c and d. The experience of hometown associations, for example, illustrates such practices. Third, and less likely, a diaspora may choose to mobilize on international issues per se. Point f and the additional two mentioned fall into this category. This is a less prominent practice and may be a function of resources and interests available to diasporas. Finally it must be noted that not all diasporas "implicate" themselves in all of these activities. Their involvement will depend on how institutionalized the diaspora is as well as on the influence of any of the four variables outlined in section three.

Sponsors

Who initiates diasporic communication also depends on which variables have a dominant influence on the ethnic or national group. Thus, sponsors of diasporic connections will usually originate from the ethnic or national group. This point is illustrated in the case of an organization like La Raza, the largest Hispanic civil rights organization in the United States. However, the host country as well as the home country can initiate or motivate diasporic contact depending on the value attached by the diaspora to pursue certain interests.

Luin Goldring draws a distinction between "migrant-led transnationalism" and "state-led transnationalism". Transmigrant organizations like HTAs preceded the Mexican government's efforts to reach out to its diaspora. Beginning in the 1980's, the subsequent state efforts embodied in the various matching grant schemes and the overt promotion of HTAs and their incorporation into federations, was a response by the state to the migrant-led transnationalism. These pursuits were motivated by a variety of factors, including legitimizing the PRIs political hold, responding to the legalization and reunification of Mexican families into the US due to IRCA, the creation of a "pro-NAFTA" lobby within the US, as well as encouraging remittance and donation sending by migrants and their assocations (Goldring, 2002).

Impact

Finally, diasporas can effect an impact on the host country policies. The impact of diasporic involvement on the foreign policy of the host country can have four implications. A diaspora may undermine the foreign policy of the host country when its mobilization runs contrary to the country's official foreign policy and thwarts its efforts. In other cases, the diaspora's international involvement may have no impact on the host country, as in the case of diasporic links with communities and social organizations where there are no issues at stake between the host country's foreign policy and the home community or social group. A recent experience is one in which a diaspora re-enforces a host country's foreign policy. Diaspora organization sponsoring development or community programmes compatible with those of the host country reinforce the host country position towards the diasporas' homeland. Finally, ethnic lobbying can help to expand a country's foreign policy by educating the establishment about important issues about which they were not aware.

CONCLUSION

The word "diaspora" has crept into the migration-development vocabulary in an under-theorized way. As the introductory discussion of the limitations in conventional definitions of what constitutes a "diaspora" has hopefully shown, there is scope for more theoretical reflection and conceptual work. In this regard the chapter pointed to the fact that not all diasporas are the result of migration. Some diasporas, like the Mexican, are the result of border redefinitions. Secondly, diasporas are not necessarily defined by dispersal. The act of migration, even to areas with high concentrations of migrants belonging to the same nationality or ethnic group, will not automatically nor necessarily lead to diasporic identifications. Finally, the maintenance of links to the homeland may, or may not, have a diasporic character.

That being said, however, the experience of Latino and Caribbean migrant collectivities in the United States – as well as the growing awareness of the potential benefits in sustaining diaspora links among home and host governments – points to new and interesting areas of development cooperation on a local, national and regional scale. Such links can be fruitfully explored by paying analytical attention to the factors enabling diaspora formation as well as to the different dynamics resulting from diasporic engagements.

Finally, it is important to consider the relationship between state and diasporas. How can states and other international players integrate diasporas as relevant players in the international and domestic context of their home countries? At least five elements are key to states effectively reaching out to their diasporas: recognition, communication, a mutual agenda, tangible diaspora involvement in the country of origin, and investment of resources. First, state outreach policy towards the diaspora must recognize and validate its communities living abroad. Second, states must establish a communication mechanism between themselves and organized diaspora groups. Third, both state and diasporic groups must develop a joint agenda that addresses issues of common concern. Fourth, the diasporic community must be allowed a substantial presence and possible influence in the nation state. Fifth, states must invest tangible resources, both material and human, to implement outreach efforts. These efforts should be regarded as minimum considerations for an effective process of cooperation in an increasingly intertwined world between states, the international community, and diasporas.

NOTES

1. Other definitions often used are those of Chaliand and Rageau (1996), Laguerre (1996), King (1997), Safran (1991), and Cohen (1996).
2. Direccion General de Atención a la Comunidad en el Exterior, Ministerio de Relaciones Exteriores, San Salvador, El Salvador. Available from World Wide Web: http://www.comunidades.gob.sv/Sitio/Img.nsf/vista/Documentos/$file/DGACE.pdf
3. Available from: http://www.comunidades.gob.sv/comunidades/comunidades.nsf/pages/revista
4. See http://www.laprensagrafica.com/dpt15/
5. I use the term "nostalgic goods" about homeland products such as food products, beverages and music. Diaspora demand of such products may have an important macro-economic impact on local economies.

REFERENCES

Alarcon, R.
    2000   *The Development of Hometown Associations in the United States and the Use of Social Remittances in Mexico*, The Inter-American Dialogue , Washington, September.

Andrade-Eeckoff, K.
    2003   *Mitos y realidades: Un análisis de la migración internacional de las zonas rurales de El Salvador*, San Salvador, FLACSO.

Chaliand, G., and J. Pierre Rageau
    1995   *The Penguin Atlas of Diasporas*, Viking, New York.

Cohen, R.
    1997   *Global Diasporas: An Introduction*, UCL Press, London.

de la Garza, R., and M. Orozco
    2000   "Family ties and ethnic lobbies", in R. de la Garza, and H. Pachon (Eds), *Latinos and US Foreign Policy: Representing the "Home-land"*, Rowman and Littlefield Publishers, New York.

Esman, M.J.
    1986   "Diasporas and international relations", in G. Sheffer (Ed.), *Modern Diasporas in International Politics*, Croom Helm, London.

Goldring, L.
    2002   "The Mexican state and transmigrant organizations: Negotiating the boundaries of membership and participation", in LARR, 37(3): 55-100.

    2003   *Re-Thinking Remittances: Social and Political Dimensions of Individual and Collective Remittances*, Centre for Research on Latin America and the Caribbean, Toronto, February.

King, C.
    1997   "Conceptualizing diaspora politics: Nationalism, transnationalism and post-communism, Paper presented at the American Political Science Association's Annual Meeting, Washington DC, 27-30 August.

Laguerre, M.
    1998   *Diasporic Citizenship*, Macmillan Press, Basingstoke.

Moctezuma, M.
    2003   "Justificación emperíca y conceptual del voto extraterritorial de los mexicanos con base en la experenica de zacatecas", *Migración y Desarrollo*, 1(1): 49-73.

Orozco, M.
    1998   "The Central American diaspora", *Hemisphere,* 8(3): 30-35.

    2000   "Latino hometown associations as agents of development in Latin America", Inter-American Dialogue and the Tomas Rivera Policy Institute, Washington, DC, January.

    2002   *International Norms and Mobilization for Democracy*, Ashgate Publishers, London.

    2003a   "Distant but close: Guyanese transnational communities and their remittances from the United States", Report commissioned by the US Agency for International Development, GEO project, 15 January.

Conceptualizing Diasporas: Remarks About the Latino and Caribbean Experience

2003b   *Hometown Associations and their Present and Future Partnerships: New Development Opportunities?,* Report commissioned by the US Agency for International Development, September.

2004a   *Family Remittances to Nicaragua: Opportunities to Increase the Economic Contributions of Nicaraguans Living Abroad,* Report commissioned by the US Department of Agriculture under a PASA for the US Agency for International Development Mission in Managua, 10 March.

2004b   *Rebuilding Central America and Free Trade,* Project Syndicate, Berkeley University, June.

2004c   *Remitttances to Latin America and the Caribbean: Issues and Perspectives on Development,* Report commissioned by the Office for the summit Process Organization of American States, Washington DC, September.

2004d   "Worker remittances, transnationalism and development", Paper presented at the Latin American Studies Association, 9 October.

2005   "Transnationalism and development: Trends and opportunities in Latin America survey of transnational communities", in *Remittances: Development Impact and Future Prospects,* S. Munzele Maimbo and D. Ratha, The World Bank, Washington, DC, 347-377.

Popkin, E.
2003   "Transnational migration and development in post-war peripheral States: An examination of Guatemalan and Salvadoran state linkages with their migrant populations in Los Angeles", *Current Sociology,* Winter/Spring.

Safran, W.
        "Diasporas in modern societies: myths of homeland and return", in *Diaspora: A Journal of Transnational Studies,* 1(1): 83-99.

Shain, Y.
1995   "Ethnic diasporas and US foreign policy", in *Political Studies Quarterly,* 109(5): 811-841.

Sheffer, G.
1993   "Ethnic diasporas: A threat to their hosts?", in M. Weiner (Ed.), *International Migration and Security,* Westview Press, Boulder, CO.

Zabin, C.L., and E. Rabadan
1998   "Mexican hometown associations and Mexican immigrant political empowerment in Los Angeles", The Aspen Institute, California Non-Profit Research Programme, Working Paper, Winter.

Mestizaje and Clothing:
Interpreting Mexican-US Transnational Social Space

Fiona Wilson

ABSTRACT

The focus of this chapter is on the early determinants of movement (1910s to 1940s) between western central Mexico and the US, seen not through the standard lens of labour migration but as producing a new, transnational, social space. In this social space, migrants could work with and negotiate greater self consciousness as mestizos and Mexicans. In particular, determinants and implications of movement are traced through the issue of clothing, and in relation to the question of when, why and how men and women in small town Mexico adopted "modern" styles of dress. In this, migration to the US opened up possibilities of dressing to cross social as well as national borders, such as men's adoption of jeans trousers which in the early days disrupted polarized social stratification between townsmen and peasants back home. Alongside migration, the spread of innovations of modernity in the countryside, the cinema and domestic sewing machine, allowed people at home to also visualize themselves as moving with the times. The increasing volume of migration in the 1920's was a subject of concern to both Mexican and US governments. As a result, social scientists were commissioned to report on the extent and implications of the movement. This body of contemporary material forms the basis of the chapter, in particular a pioneering study (made in 1931-2) of a representative migrant small town in the state of Jalisco where the author focuses attention on returned migrants' views on "race" and dress.

In the early 20th century, Mexicans from small towns and villages throughout the western-central region of the country became accustomed to move to and fro across the border with the US in search of work. Commentators on this history agreed it should be categorized as labour migration: an Hispanic country with surplus population but wracked by social and political conflict in the South supplied labour to a northern neighbour with a more advanced capitalist economy and higher rate of growth. The determinants were not so mysterious and three leading factors could be picked out. Wage levels were significantly higher in the US; information about opportunities were spread by labour contractors travelling in Mexico as well as local trading groups (especially the muleteers); and railways built during the Porfiriato (when Porfirio Diaz was President of Mexico, 1876-1910) linked towns of western central Mexico to the US border more than a thousand miles away. Country people, especially from the states of Jalisco, Michoacán and Guanajuato, went to work in the fields of Texas and California, the mines of Phoenix and the smelting works of Chicago. Temporary migration became a popular strategy through which to earn "migradollars", acquire modern goods and stock up on a fund of good stories to entertain unadventurous stay-at-homes (see Durand, 1991; Fonseca and Moreno, 1988). The outbreak of the Mexican Revolution in 1910 and counter-revolutionary Cristero wars of the 1920's increased the scale and scope of the movement north, while fluctuations in the US economy shaped demand for labour and employment opportunities for Mexicans, expanding them during First and Second World Wars and abruptly decreasing them at the onset of economic recession. In this paper, focus is put on this early phase of migration, from 1910's to early 1940's.

However, by labelling the early period of movement as labour migration, certain aspects were highlighted while others were obscured. Scholarly work focusing on the economic aspects of migration dealt with a limited number of "types". Less attention was given to cultural, social and political issues, how transnational mobility could "disrupt the stable isomorphism of identity and territory" (Bailey, 2001: 46), or long-term changes induced by an engagement in and formation of transnational social space. In general, according to Ong (1999: 8-9), predominant in the earlier framing of US-centred migration studies was "world system theory about exploitative relations between 'core' and 'periphery' countries or a neo-classical economic theory of diverse labor supplies flowing toward an advanced capital formation".

The aim of this paper is to go back (literally) to the early determinants of movement between western central Mexico and the US, and explore this field through a lens other than labour migration. This chapter opens up for more complex and plural understandings of social and national identities, more ambiguous modes of incorporating and resisting the "modernity" that was thrust upon Mexicans such as through the spread of the cinema, and more contested terrains in relations between migrants and those not moving far from the home community. Few Mexicans who moved back and forth across the border in the period up to the 1940s can now be interviewed and ethnographic material is sparse. However, one outstanding contemporary work exists. This is Paul Taylor's pioneering study made in 1931-2 on the repercussions that migration to the US was having on social relations in the *municipio* (district) of Arandas, a small town and surrounding rural area in the highlands of Jalisco (Taylor, 1933).[1] One theme underlined by Taylor was the extreme importance of dress for folk in Arandas, a finding confirmed by Luis Gonzalez (1974) in the history of his home town, San José de Gracia (Jalisco), and Fonseca and Moreno (1988) on early migration from Jaripo (Michoacán).

WHY DID RURAL MEXICANS CHANGE THEIR WAY OF DRESS?

During the early 20th century, country people in the densely populated region of western-central Mexico who saw themselves as mestizo rather than indigenous ceased to wear homemade clothing that denoted a specific locality and position in the socio/"racial" hierarchy and adopted a more uniform, more "Mexican", way of dress.[2] This reflects a widespread trend that Bauer (2001), in a recent history of consumption in Latin America, reports taking place throughout the continent after 1930. Clothing, he writes, "followed a tendency toward more variety in cloth and colour but within a broadly occidentalized pattern." Across social classes clothing was becoming "compressed into a kind of mestizo conformity" and this included native dress. Bauer goes on to suggest that it demonstrates how "(t)he ascendant mestizo population in general aimed to emulate the dress, and withstand the scorn, of their social betters while at the same time making sure to shed any association with their Indian or village past" (Bauer, 2001: 183). Change in way of dress has generally been explained as indicating urbanization, advancing modernity, integration into the wider society and national economy, and growing commoditization of garment production whereby a wider range of clothing items became industrially produced and available for purchase in the market.

If we take a finer-grained analysis, then the obviousness of broad-brush interpretations becomes more problematic. How was it that culture, custom and tradition with respect to clothing could be brushed aside and supplanted with such apparent ease? Were reasons for change everywhere the same? Furthermore, how does this finding mesh with a well-known counter argument that resistance to change is particularly strong in matters affecting the body, intimacy and identity? In Mexico, clearly not everybody was eager to change her/his way of dress. Changing patterns of consumption happened faster in some places than in others, were adopted by some social groups (identifying themselves as mestizo) not others (where indigenous peoples continued to oppose external pressures for change), and affected men before affecting women.

In the specific case of western central Mexico, what influences could have carried such weight as to promote a more uniform "national" way of dress? How had this come about? We know that change of dress was taking place as movement to and from the US was gathering momentum, but was it simply an "automatic" response to higher disposable incomes and greater availability of manufactured clothing in the US? This paper argues that re-envisaging the meaning of clothing was integral to Mexico's early transnational engagement with the US and was instrumental in demarcating a new transnational social space. As transnationals, Mexicans fought to overcome dislocation in their everyday life, but within transnational social space Mexicans came to view themselves as mestizo and modern – and this found expression in the attention they gave to how they looked and how they dressed. Before presenting case study material to illustrate this, the discussion will be framed by looking at two central concepts in play: production of transnational social space and processes of mestizaje.

PRODUCTION OF TRANSNATIONAL SOCIAL SPACE

Transnational space is seen to result from processes leading to "transnational communities" defined as a set of intense cross-border social relations that enable individuals to participate in the activities of daily life in two or more nations (Portes, 1996). Transnational movement and community building connect the space-time relations of daily life under capitalism with ruling ideas of belonging, nation and citizenship (Bailey, 2001; Portes, 1996; Smith and Guarnizo, 1998). The transnational perspective draws on post-structuralism and puts welcome emphasis on culture and agency, representation and translation. My fascination with transnationalism lies in the way it builds on interpretations of social space, though in many works this remains under-theorized. Like many geographers, I find inspiration in the way Lefebvre (1991) addresses the production of social space and the distinction he draws between space as practiced, conceived and perceived. To illustrate: studies of labour migration assume the first in the relatively straightforward spatial practice of migrancy. In contrast, a conception of space as national, abstract and homogeneous underlies the view of politicians and planners who pass and execute legislation affecting migration from one territory to another. But it is the third of Lefebvre's perspectives, the perception of social space, which is central to the argument here. The ways social space is perceived are both more intimate and less tangible. Distance and barriers to movement are no longer absolute but become elastic and negotiable. The implications of these three perspectives on social space in relation to Mexican movement to the US are commented below.

The social space produced by migration

From this perspective, social space is not an empty box waiting to be filled but is instead produced through the movement of people, things and ideas. One can start by thinking of patterns as thrown up in computer mappings, an imaging of differential configurations and densities of spatial movement at different scales and points in time. These could range from an overarching social space created through the total movement of Mexicans going to and from the US, to finer-grained maps depicting the flow of people between particular localities, to the wandering tracks made by individuals as they move around in transnational space (see Carling, 2003). In sum, social space can be seen as complex multi-tiered fields demarcated by movement and structured by flows.

What is known about Mexican-US migration within this spatial dimension? Knowledge of numbers and flows in the early migratory period owes a great debt to pioneering statistical studies undertaken by Manuel Gamio in 1930 (Gamio, 1991).[3] He estimated that in the period 1910 to 1928, around 1 million Mexicans had gone north as temporary workers. Remarkably, in the light of later trends, migrants included roughly the same number of women as men and a mixture of indigenous and mestizos. He found that in the period 1920 to 1928 while 600,000 had gone north, 700,000 had returned home to Mexico. More than half of all migrants hailed from just three states, Guanajuato, Michoacán and Jalisco, in western-central Mexico. The reason for the predominance of these states, Gamio thought, was not poverty per se but low wages, large numbers of independent small-holders, high population density and the disruption caused by the Cristero wars whose epicentre was this region.[4]

Space as conceived by governments

International labour migration is usually a matter of some concern to the governments of sending and receiving states. Authorities and officials take a "bird's eye view" and conceive of space as territory belonging to different nations. In the early period, the opinion of government and ruling elites on both sides of the Mexican-US border was divided on the question of migration. In Mexico, some judged the flood of workers going north to be detrimental to the country's economic and social well-being and damaging to national dignity, but others considered the movement beneficial in that it provided jobs to those without work and brought migradollars, goods and know-how back to Mexico. In the US, some put economic priorities first, and saw migration as a means to overcome labour shortage while others expressed concern at the influx of large numbers of foreigners of non-white race. The racial issue was highly salient in the first half of the 20th century. Up until 1942, Mexicans were officially classified as belonging to "the Mexican race", given an intermediary position between white and black people in this racially segregated society. However, this non-white population was considered preferable to Chinese/Asians whose arrival, many feared, was imminent along the Pacific seaboard (Bustamante, 1988).

During the 1920's the flow of Mexicans to the US had reached such great volume that it alarmed both governments respective. Each state appointed social scientists to come up with better information on volumes of migrants and remittances and the effects of migration at national and community levels. When some ten per cent of Mexico's labour force was thought to be in the US in 1930, Depression struck and US authorities deported half a million Mexicans. President Lazaro Cardenas tried to repatriate these workers on new rural co-operatives, set up under Mexico's agrarian reform (Fonseca and Moreno, 1988). The movement of Mexicans north resumed with a vengeance following the entry of the US into the Second World War, and was brought under state control. In 1942, the two governments signed an agreement setting up the Bracero Programme, a labour contracting programme that in its lifetime (up to 1964) issued temporary labour contracts to some 4.6 million Mexican men through official channels and prompted roughly an equal number of undocumented migrants to go north without holding official labour contracts at the outset (Durand and Massey, 1992).

Through this conception of social space, the US-Mexican border was treated as though it were a gigantic sluice-gate that could be opened or shut by US policy decision makers depending on the country's need for low-waged, temporary workers. Migrants were classified according to US racial categories; documentation was demanded and a distinction made between "legal" and "illegal" immigrants. Decrees were regularly passed to tighten up entry requirements: immigrants were barred on grounds of physical and mental ill-health, criminality, polygamy, illiteracy and membership of anarchist and subversive political parties. Migrants had to pay head taxes on entry and present an increasing number of papers to acquire visas at US consulates and at the border. Policing the border became a national issue for the US and in 1924 the Border Patrol was created by Congress to control movement more effectively. This bounded concept of space was in sharp conflict with the perception of space held by those who moved.

Space as perceived by those who move

Perceptions of social space adhere in particular signs, symbols and indicators, and these are constantly in flux over time. The argument here is that for historical reasons, in the early migration period clothing was closely interwoven with perceptions of social space. Being able to dress the part became a determinant as well as a consequence of transnational engagement. By engaging in migration and bringing into their lives experience of the rampantly capitalist US, Mexicans were plunged into a maelstrom of modernity that could be apprehended through its technological embodiments, felt in the mind and body and appropriated (and later countered) through consumption. Life in the US, however fleetingly encountered, could foster new aspirations of enjoying material success and well-being. But most migrants were brought up short on account of discrimination, exclusion, and uncertainty. Movement entailed new experiences as "bronzed" strangers, classified into an ambivalent, intermediary non-white position. Migrants would become more conscious of race in abstract terms and of themselves as belonging collectively to a Mexican nation.

Inherent in Mexico-US social space was the confrontation with and incorporation of images of modernity. One can suggest that this led to a shared consciousness along the lines expressed by de Souza Martins (2000: 249). "Modernity", he writes, "is only present when it can be both the modern and the critical consciousness of the modern – the situated modern, an object of consciousness and reflection... Modernity is a kind of demystifying mystification of the immense possibilities of human and social transformation which capitalism was able to create, but is not able to realise." In the early 20th century, Mexicans were learning fast about the duplicity of modernity. While there was nothing novel in labouring or exploitation per se, once framed in a transnational context and fused with capitalist relations and racism, this offered migrants a new vantage point from which to reflect on Mexico and mestizaje.

PROCESSES OF MESTIZAJE

In Latin America, it is not hard to discern how intellectual and political elites imagined the future of post-colonial society, and the place of the Indian in it. Though as Knight (1990: 71) reminds, "measuring the impact of ideas within society is notoriously difficult, especially when the ideas themselves (relating to racial inequality) are embedded deep in social relations, may rarely be overtly expressed, may be deliberately disguised or denied". Broadly one finds that reigning ideas about "race" held by elites veered between two poles hinging on the status given to mestizaje. Social Darwinist thinking uppermost in Mexico in the late 19th century denigrated hybrid degeneracy, but this view was challenged and changed in the process of national reconstruction after the Revolution. Indians were to be converted into citizens; a new mestizo nationalism was rampant; in *forjando patria* ('forging the Patria'), as one architect of the new nation called it, the mestizo was brought to the fore. Mestizos were neither Indian nor European, but a quintessential synthesis of the two (Knight, 1990: 84-85). They were celebrated as "men of the future", the "cosmic race", the "race of bronze".

As Knight (1990) points out, the pioneers of Mexico's nationalist mestizo project were intent on imposing their own racist view on the rest of society, albeit one that inverted previous hegemonic thinking. But theirs was not the only discourse of race around. Racial hierarchies and ways of thinking (reflected in skin colour, clothing, language, custom) affected how millions of Mexicans thought and acted. Even though most Mexicans could be considered mestizo, the borderlines of race/ethnic identifications were certainly not shared. Popular interpretations of and claims to new mestizo identities would have their own sources of inspiration and momentum. This would take place through what Gruzinski (2002) calls the constant creation and re-creation of intermediary spaces, in "strange zones" where exchanges and interactions between two worlds are brokered. Movement in the "strange zone" of Mexico-US social space could generate a capacity for invention and improvization, special receptiveness, flexibility in social practice and aptitude for combining highly diverse fragments into wholes. The next section explores the capacity of improvization, receptiveness and flexibility of mestizaje as demonstrated and performed through way of dress.

EXPLORING CLOTHING

When, why and how did people in western-central Mexico change their way of dress? The following section starts by giving a brief account of dress as "custom" and the gender, ethnic and class meanings attached to traditional attire, it then discusses two kinds of dislocation that interrupted the customary order. One was state intervention in the way country men dressed. The other was the way people used dress to negotiate new identities in transnational social space. The repercussions of movement are illustrated in a third section that takes up Taylor's case study of Arandas. Finally, the scope of transnationalism is broadened to take account of the ways mestizaje and modernity were visualized in the Mexican countryside.

Dress as custom

The dress of country people in western central Mexico in the late 19th century was described as austere and elemental. By virtue of the colour, design, and detail of their clothing, country people were linked to place both socially and geographically. It was a wife's role to sew the clothing needed by her family. With thread and *manta* (cotton cloth) acquired from traders or the hacienda stores, women made loose trousers (*calzones*) and shirts for their husbands and sons; and with lengths of cloth made skirts, blouses and aprons for themselves and their daughters. Some garments were adorned with embroidery and crochet work, skills and designs handed down from mothers to daughters. The feast of the village patron saint was the occasion when everybody expected to wear new clothes, after which they passed into everyday use and had to last the year out. If the luxury of new clothes was out of the question, then the poor made sure their clothes were clean.

But nostalgic remembrances of times past should not obscure the fact that this was the meagre and despised clothing of the poor. As González (1974: 44) in his history of San José de Gracia notes with respect to mestizo *ranchero* society of the 1880s:

> It is a cold region, and their garments were light. The sarape, which the men wore over a cotton shirt and trousers, was not warm enough. Women wore nothing under their cotton dresses. Pneumonia claimed more victims than any other disease: one out of every three deaths involved great pain in the chest. Both men and women had but one change of clothing: while they were wearing one, the other was in the wash. They protected themselves from the rain and sun with sombreros made of palm fibre and capes of palm leaves. Everyone but the wealthiest wore huaraches (leather-thong sandals). That they had not yet developed a taste for comfort could be seen in their dwellings too.

In small, isolated settlements, dress was not an important indicator of social standing since an individual's position derived from her/his family. But larger settlements, social differentiation was signalled by clothing and the way that people dressed was subject to scrutiny and comment. Way of dress in the small towns was linked to a rigid social distinction between rich (*los ricos*) and poor (*los pobres*), a duality that bore the marks of a post-colonial attribution of "race" whereby the rich were seen as more "white/Spanish" and the poor more "dark/indigenous". The division indicated enduring power relations. In country towns, the rich inhabited solidly built houses in well-ordered streets around the church and the central square, while the poor lived in straggling *barrios* and *ranchos* beyond. The rich owned land and livestock, were shop-keepers and traders, were in charge of local institutions and represented their towns in the outside world. The poor were day-labourers, hacienda *peones*, small or subsistence farmers and ranchers; they also worked as artisans and part-time muleteers. Generally they were enmeshed and subordinated in relations of dependence that were expressed particularly clearly in the sphere of exchange. Men demonstrated their status as *ricos* by possessing tailored suits (*trajes*) made by tailors in the towns and by wearing leather shoes. Such clothing was not necessarily worn every day, but brought out on Sundays, feast days and whenever men travelled beyond the confines of the district. *Los pobres* wore the ubiquitous dress of the poor – the white shirt, *calzones de manta* and *huaraches* (leather sandals).

Women in village and small town society were expected to act as markers of morality and decency on behalf of family and community; this was symbolized by the long fringed *rebozo* (shawl), bought from workshops in famous centres of production. Wrapped around and concealing the body, its use was said to protect the wearer against the inquisitive or malevolent gaze of others; and children concealed in its folds could be guarded against the evil eye. Above all, the *rebozo* was considered "an almost integral part of being a woman". Whether on the shoulders of the mistress or her maid, as one local author put it, it was "a covering, an ornament, a source of grace, a symbol of peace" (Tuñon, 1991: 220). In town and country alike, women were taught at an early age to cover themselves with their *rebozo* outside the house. However, in my conversations with countrywomen in the region (in the late 1990s), a less conformist story emerged. Many recalled their disdain for the *rebozo*, their refusal to use *rebozos* received as gifts from husbands and sons. Non-conformity might be resistance on a very small scale, but women still spoke about it with a smile of satisfaction. Despite the ubiquity of the *rebozo*, the social identity of the wearer could be read off from its material, refinement of decoration, and manner in which it was worn. Women from the small towns drew a distinction. Indian women, they said, used their *rebozo* to carry children about on their backs and bring goods to and from the market: "for the *indigena*, it was an instrument of work". In contrast, for mestizo women, it was an adornment.

The most dominating image of masculinity conveyed in the countryside coupled mestizaje with aggressive *machismo* and was expressed by the flamboyant, richly adorned riding clothes worn on festive occasions by *charros* (horsemen). In the *charreadas*, the riding sports so popular in the region during the late 19th century, men dressed in short jackets, waistcoats and trousers made of wool, cotton, deerskin or chamois leather heavily adorned with silver coins and chains. They wore huge sombreros and heavy spurred boots. The image of the *charro* was to fuse around the figures of Emiliano Zapata and other revolutionary leaders who stood out from their ill-clad followers and were transformed into icons of mestizo Mexico.

Disturbing custom: state intervention and migration

In the late 19th century, the Porfirian state sought to implant a capitalist economy, attract foreign investment and stimulate export growth. Mexico was expected to shift rapidly from backwardness to state-led modernity. In this connection, the dress of rural men became a matter of legislation. Peasant traditionalism was considered by ruling elites a grave hindrance to the process of modernization that the state was trying to engender. This led to a policy of cultural improvement through direct intervention. Notices were posted throughout the land that men had to wear proper trousers. According to one notice posted in Guadalajara on 7 June 1887, "for reasons of civilization and morality" men were prohibited from using *calzón blanco* and obliged to wear European-styled trousers when entering towns and public places. Notices were written in a language that equated the peasantry's use of *calzones de manta* with backwardness. A favourite term employed was *calzonudo*, a word that played on the image of a man being naked when dressed in *calzones*. Rural workers were reported to be "walking about like our father Adam", i.e., naked, by *El Monitor*, Guadalajara, 29 August 1892, while *calzonismo* was a derogatory term referring to the peasantry's obstinate adherence to tradition. *Calzonudos* were liable for fines, a week in gaol or a spell of "forced labour" on public works.

Rural families were forced to think in a different way about clothing and were preoccupied with the need to acquire European-style men's attire. Compulsion over dress was etched in social memory. In Jaltiche (Aguascalientes), for example, the elderly still recalled the time after the Revolution when men had to change from *calzones* into trousers when nearing the regional capital, Calvillo, otherwise they risked being fined and money was scarce. Elsewhere in the region, the old could remember when wearing *calzones* was transformed into a moral issue; such as when priest and townsfolk decided to prohibit their use at the towns' fiestas on the grounds of indecency.

This enforcement of modernity by state decree is one element that helps explain why men attached such importance to acquiring clothing in the US. Reminiscing on their experiences many decades later, migrants from the small town of Jaripo (Michoacán) who had gone north in the 1910s echoed the view of the elite towards the *calzonudos*. As they commented to local researchers Fonseca and Moreno (1984: 139-140):

Here we used to go around, as the saying goes, unclothed and unshod; you only wore your manta and leather huaraches.

As for clothes, here we used to go around naked. There, we bought trousers and shoes, hats, we bought hats for 10 dollars; not because we wanted to look like charros; I bought a suit for 50 dollars I'd earned, a tailored suit, we did not know this kind of clothing back home . (Ibid..: 152).

We brought back many things; we bought lengths of cloth for the girls, for the young ladies we had here, for my mother's sister, and clothes for ourselves; everybody brought their suits and watches of 50 dollars. We used to spend almost all the money on clothing and trinkets (chingaderas). (Ibid..: 151)

Young men were attracted to the possibility of adopting a more demonstrative masculinity:

At the start, I thought the men who came back from the north were very manly, and then as I say, this lad arrived with those boots, some boots with a heel that made a wonderful noise when he walked up and down, and then there was another, and an-

Mestizaje and Clothing: Interpreting Mexican-US Transnational Social Space

other, making such a noise on the paved street. Who was going to go north? I said to myself, why not me? (Ibid..: 162-163).

On arrival at the US border towns, Mexicans understood immediately the importance of paying attention to clothing. Styles of male dress known at home, the *calzones de manta*, tailored suits or *charro* dress, were inappropriate if men wanted to secure labour contracts. *Calzones* stereotyped the wearer as wet-backs or Indians, and by wearing suits or *charro* "costume" Mexicans ran the risk of ridicule and rejection by US labour contractors thronging the border towns on the grounds that they did not want work, only a free ride to other parts of the US. Negotiating the border led to unexpected expense for inexperienced migrants. As Santibañenz, appointed by the Mexican government in 1930 to study migration, observed in Texan border towns in the late 1920s, Mexican men arriving with their high, wide-brimmed sombreros accompanied by women wrapped up in their *rebozos* were soon made to feel out of place (Santibañez, 1991: 93). The production of transnational social space thus pressed those who moved to adopt modes of dress (almost a uniform) that allowed them to pass from one side of the border to the other with least hindrance.

Migrants saved hard in the US to acquire new clothing. Suits, hats, ties, boots and watches demonstrated men's success in the US, and many had photographs taken of themselves to send back to their families. The other clothing acquired was the jean overall, *pantalones de mezclilla*, the serviceable, hard wearing working-clothes of the working man. When men wore jean overalls or trousers, they were more likely to find employment and a measure of anonymity in the US. While still a rarity in the Mexican countryside, wearing jeans was a new way to attract the notice of village girls, and many migrants opted to get married in them.

The situation facing women migrants in the early period differed from the men. Some went to the US with their families but there were also large numbers of widows and abandoned wives, women whose menfolk had disappeared during revolutionary violence, who preferred to go to the north rather than live isolated lives in extreme poverty in the villages. For women with children, there was much less possibility of travelling back and forth and should they return, they faced greater opposition than men when they tried to negotiate a new social identity back home through their clothing. Thus for women, even though they constituted roughly half of the migration flow according to Gamio (1991), their transnationalism was more restricted in the early period than for men.

The migrants' change of dress, Santibañez (1991: 89) wished to assure his readers, was not because they had stopped loving their native land; they had been obliged to dress differently. Preoccupation with dress reflected a negotiation of racial identity in ways that Mexican men and women had not experienced before. Mexicans who could pass as "white" found themselves treated better. In Texas, they earned the label of "Spanish", thus reserving the derogatory label of "Mexican" for darker skinned compatriots. Some Mexicans risked being barred from semi-public places such as restaurants, and all suffered from the derogatory way Mexicans were being depicted (as killers, robbers, violators of women, gamblers and drunkards) in the films coming out of Hollywood. This prompted Santibañez, a strong nationalist and advocate of state-led mestizaje to observe: "In Mexico, fortunately we do not distinguish amongst ourselves on the basis of skin colour; all of us born under our flag are Mexicans and our differences derive from differential talents and aptitudes such as in commerce, not from our origins, for we are all equal before God and the law."

Contesting "race" and clothing in Arandas

Among the social scientists recruited by the US government to study migration was Paul Taylor, an agricultural economist from the US mid-West who together with his wife, the photographer Dorothea Lange, had made a study of Mexican migrants in California. He spent several months in 1931 and 1932 in Arandas, in the highlands of Jalisco, deliberately chosen as a place that represented conditions in western central Mexico as a whole. This is a unique eye-witness account written at a moment of crisis when Depression brought movement to the US to an abrupt stop. Given the inaccessibility of the English version, it is worth discussing in detail.

Arandas was a district populated by Mexicans who believed they came from Spanish stock and who cherished their Catholic faith. Many owned land, and most with "characteristic conservatism" had opposed the Revolution. Before the 1920's, there had been a history of movement, especially during warfare and unrest, when people from the district had left and formed *barrios* in larger urban centres in the region. "Going to the US", Taylor notes, "appears but a modern and expanded phase of a fairly continuous historical exodus from this populous district."

The people migrating to the US from the turn of the century had almost all returned home. Movement had been greatly facilitated by the railways, and once in the US many men worked laying rail tracks with Mexican gangs under Mexican foremen and had learnt little English. Some had gone further a field to find work in steel mills, automobile factories and in agriculture. The majority of migrants had been young, single men, but many women and families had also migrated. Migrants from Arandas were scattered in many different places; as yet there was little clustering and no "daughter settlements" had appeared. Differential wage levels were given by returned migrants as the most important reason for their movement and purchasing power in Arandas was seen to have increased notably thanks to cash remittances. While many early migrants had squandered their earnings, it had become possible in the 1920s even for poor families to buy land, and for the better-off to return home with investment goods: trucks, machinery and tools to set up new businesses. Out of a total population of 27,600 in the *municipio*, Taylor estimates that some 400 men had gone north in 1926, 600 in 1927 and 200 in 1928. Then Depression hit, and migration stopped.

While the majority of the population considered themselves of Spanish descent, Taylor reports, racial attitudes were by no means uniform. He talked to many who claimed a feeling of superiority due to "their clean blood and

Mestizaje and Clothing: Interpreting Mexican-US Transnational Social Space

old customs". One landowner told him proudly: "This is a white race, with a tendency to improve and economize. The people here are better dressed than in many other parts of the country. I attribute these things to the white blood in these people." Some Spanish-looking migrants had brought home a new racial terminology learnt in the US, insisting on their white-ness in contrast to Indian darkness. Yet he also encountered people who denied the existence of racist feeling and even claimed the superiority of an Indian ancestry. Coming from a racially segregated society, Taylor was struck by the variety of attitudes he encountered and concluded that in majority people exhibited moderation and tolerance. Unlike in the US, no public racial discrimination was in force. He was impressed by the words of one professional: "Although of the white race, the people do not regard with prejudice those who *are indigenas*. There is a more universal spirit here – more a spirit of social distinction and class than of race. There is no prejudice here. We are all Mexicans – but individuals."

Migrants were drawn from a wide spectrum of the population, but did not include the richest or the poorest people. The wealthiest men in the *municipio* (merchants, professionals, large landowners) had not migrated, but their children had. When Taylor probed migrants on discrimination in the US, some denied experiencing discrimination, some observed that while racial distinctions did affect Mexicans, those at greatest risk were poorer, darker or less clean than themselves. Others commented on the relative absence of racism in the north (around Chicago) compared to Texas. But in general, men who had never migrated tended to think of discrimination as a greater barrier than those who did. "They think we are all *prieto* (dark) and wear poor clothes", as one non-migrating merchant told him.

The weight migrants gave to clothing when talking to Taylor was indicative of its novelty and the social tensions still aroused. But it was no longer a simple picture. He notes that the daily dress of returned migrants had gone back to being roughly the same as that worn by non-migrants of the same occupational status. In the town of Arandas, one commonly saw men wearing US-style trousers or jean overalls, shirts, felt hat or cap, and factory-made shoes, even though not everybody wearing this clothing had been to the US. Many owned watches. To his surprise, he also found some returned migrants in the town wearing the despised *huaraches* of the peasantry. In rural parts of the district, former migrants still used palm *sombreros*, cotton shirts, *calzones de manta and huaraches* for everyday wear, but they stood out on Sundays and at fiestas when they put on their US suits, hats and shoes. Change in attire provoked barbed comments. "Look at that guy, he has good clothes but not a centavo in his pockets" or "they come back with clothes which last a year or two, then they dress the same as the rest of us. They think they are better than we, but they are not." However, as one man confided to Taylor: "They used to joke about migrants, and criticize their better clothing, but not now. Now they imitate them."

Talking to young women in Arandas who had lived in the US, Taylor found they were outspoken about the problems they had faced on their return. A young high school graduate told him: "Here the girls all dress alike, in black. But I'll never dress in black in all my life. Here it seems that when a girl is married, it's all over; then they don't care about clothes any more." In the early years, men had been none too keen that women accompany them to the US, and some confided to Taylor that they had been greatly shocked by the freedom of women in the US, finding American practices of divorce and birth control repellent and against the teachings of the Catholic Church.

At first Taylor concluded it was impossible to tell migrants and non-migrants apart simply by their clothing. Yet he also conceded that thanks to migration most wore better quality clothes than they would have otherwise done. However, with the onset of Depression, their savings used up, many migrants had been forced to sell the stock of US clothing they had brought back. Since movement was now impossible, US clothing had become a coveted good whose cash value was increasing. Taylor did not comment on the implications this had for the domestic economy. But clearly, when men bought clothes in the US women were relieved of the burden of making them but the family became more dependent on cash and on substituting goods bought in the market. Few items of new men's clothing could be copied at home. Given the toughness of jean cloth, trousers and overalls were garments impossible to handle on the domestic sewing machine. So the growing popularity of jeans led to a resurgence of workshop production in Mexico even before the onset of Depression. The temporary end of migration in 1930 gave a great impetus to import substitution and the production of US-style male clothing in Mexican workshops. Transnational engagement by fostering new patterns of consumption was in turn promoting an expansion in garment production in the migrant region (Wilson, 1999).

When migration to the US picked up again under the Bracero Programme in the early 1940s, it was a wholly male affair. While most migrants continued to adopt the style of dress of previous generations, for some young men clothing became disruptive in a different way. Young Mexicans going north came into contact with a counter culture that opposed the values and racism of white, Anglo-Saxon America. *Cholos* or *pachucos* performed their resistance to the values of family and society through clothing, language and life style. They adopted the zoot suit, a style first used by young blacks in Harlem: narrow-brimmed hats with a feather, jackets with huge lapels, flared trousers, narrow belts and enormous watch chains. Cosgrove (1989) describes how this clothing became engrained with social protest during the Zoot Suit Riots in 1943 on the west coast when black and chicano youth opposed the racist patriotism that surrounded US involvement in the Second World War. Young Mexicans now returned home with attitude: rebellious new clothing and a defiant way of looking at the world that brought a rude awakening to the small towns of the western-central region (López Castro, 1986).

Visualising modernity in western central Mexico

The spate of railway building in western central Mexico in the 1890s altered spatial relationships. Journey times were shortened and the region became increasingly accessible to Mexico City and the US border. Along with the railways came new kinds of traders, commercial travellers bringing manufactured goods from the US rarely seen before. One new good was to transform domestic clothing production: the sewing machine. "Singers" were spreading from the towns to the countryside in the 1920's thanks to "migradollars". Women developed new talents as machine sewers and repairers. Another innovation was reaching the small towns facilitated by the railways: the cinema (Lopez, 2000: 155). Film pioneers travelled the length and breadth of the country, showed films of spectacles (often infused with nationalist messages), and filmed local views, everyday activities and celebrations to entice new audiences. They filmed the Revolution and after the First World War continued to invent, adapt and experiment with film. In so doing, as Lopez (2000: 168) comments, they took active part in the problematization of the modernization process itself. This made the cinema "the principal interlocutor of Latin American modernity", where according to Carlos Monsiváis, "Latin Americans went not to dream but to learn to be modern".

The cinema was well entrenched in country towns by the time Taylor visited Jalisco. He attributed the growing interest in fashion amongst young women to its spread, as well as to the increased circulation of magazines, newspaper advertisements and mail order catalogues. Young women were beginning to bob their hair, shorten their skirts, and wear brighter coloured clothes and low-heeled shoes like *las americanas*. Their clothes, copied from films and pictures were made up on the now ubiquitous domestic sewing machine. But the observant Taylor thought that changes in women's dress were not being accompanied by any noticeable improvement in their social position. Young women were still kept under close supervision on their daily visit to church and walk in the plaza.

Stories collected for this study some 60 years later by older women from small towns in the region fill out Taylor's observations. *Doña* Felipe who lived in the small town of Concepción de Buenos Aires (Jalisco) after her marriage in 1932, remembered the arrival of two cinemas in the town. One, belonging to the priest's brother, showed films from Mexico and the US, and the other showed promotional films distributed by US firms, including Coca Cola, Pepsi Cola and Colgate. *Doña* Felipe claimed never to have set foot in a cinema, nevertheless she had a remarkable memory for the names of films and stars and still possessed free gifts handed out by US firms. Like most women of Concepción, she had used her sewing machine to make her own and her children's clothes. But only rarely had she left home; she never accompanied her husband on his trips to town, so it was he who bought her *rebozos* from the market in Guadalajara.

According to *Doña* Teré of La Piedad (Michoacán), a woman of humble origins who had married into a wealthy land-owning family, it had been the Mexican cinema that had overturned people's attitudes with respect to women's dress. The actress María Felix won enormous popularity in the countryside, and was remembered for the coquettish way she wore her *rebozo*. Young girls tried to emulate her, and by so doing paid more attention to their bodies and faces, to cultivating an elegant profile and putting shadow under their eyes. At home, women began to sew and wear more complicated clothing, full of tucks and pleats that showed off the body to advantage.

They had to convince the men of the family that this way of dressing was proper and modern so that they could discard the "old bags" they had worn previously. Although enjoying an interest in clothes, the women interviewed for this study were quick to point out they had never been *catrina*, a faintly derogatory term suggesting that well-turned out women could pay a bit too much attention to their appearance.

CONNECTING CLOTHING, MODERNITY, MESTIZAJE

What did the changes in dress that Taylor describes so conscientiously in the case of Arandas and the elderly now recall with nostalgia signify with respect to transnational engagement, perception of social space and meanings given to modernity and mestizaje? Without doubt, through their dress migrants were not only producing transnational space but also provoking upsets in social relations back home. By the 1920s, the visible polarity in social inequality as between *los ricos* and *los pobres* had been challenged and was apparently breaking down. One finds a parallel challenge of the younger generation against the old in the 1940s when angry sons returned as *pachucos* to the consternation of their families. These were revelatory phases of social contestation but they did not necessarily signify an enduring shift in patterns of privilege or class relations. Only when migrants returned home with investment goods and new knowledge could class/status be altered in a permanent way. Otherwise over time, as Taylor's observations suggest, after initial disruption old patterns of inequality began to reassert themselves, and clothing became re-aligned and incorporated into underlying social relations based on power, class and race, and were etched onto perceptions and values mapped out by transnational engagement. Women found less opportunity to openly challenge relations of gender outside the home. Nevertheless, changes were underway through which women were imagining their own modernity through national and transnational images of femininity relayed most powerfully by the cinema.

What happened to clothing in the 1920s can be seen as illustrating a "grassroots" process of *mestizaje*, but one given an ironic twist. The grounds for this had been prepared in previous decades when the state had associated the civilization and morality of male citizens with adoption of European-style dress. The introduction, widespread acceptance and later import substitution of American overalls and trousers made of jeans cloth seemed, on the face of it, a god-send in bringing both mestizaje and modernity. Here was an item of attire whose usage could materially and symbolically bring an end to the social polarity as between Spanish *traje* and indigenous *calzones*. The problem was that this clothing remained shot through with associations with the US. Thus although jeans in practice became a demonstrative aspect of Mexican *mestizaje*, filling the gap left after deconstructing the binary colonial world, this did not square with interpretations of Mexican nationalism engrained (at least in official rhetoric) in the idea of *mestizaje a lo mexicano* for this was transnational clothing par excellence.

Mestizaje and Clothing: Interpreting Mexican-US Transnational Social Space

In contrast to views put forward by elite and state, *mestizaje* for transnational Mexicans did not represent a neat shift from tradition to modernity, let alone a mystical fusion of races. It denoted a selective incorporation and appropriation of new ideas, cultural styles and models from the "strange zone" of US-Mexico. Pressure to take part in grassroots processes of mestizaje and to demonstrate this through clothing arguably had been the most important determinant of Mexico's transnational engagement in the early 20th century. In this emerging social space, new repertoires of social identity and meaning could be constructed that in time came to define a distinctive *mexicanidad* shared on both sides of the border.

POLICY IMPLICATIONS

Although the subject matter of this paper is historical, references have nevertheless been made to the field of policy issues and dilemmas and indications can be drawn out as to what might still be considered "policy relevant" half a century later. In the first place, the paper reminds us that "policy" has a long history and has been integrally connected with modernizing states and their espousal of "national interests"; so too has the practice of policymakers calling on academics to collect/process information and come up with answers. However, neither policymakers nor academics have sorted out, let alone solved, underlying political questions. When the political searchlight fell on Mexican migration in the 1920s, politicians on both sides of the border were deeply divided as to whether they should support it or prevent it; one could say that opinion would have remained in deadlock had there not been global Depression (1930s) and World War (1940s). Diverging views as to what was/is "in the national interest", in this case crystallized in the ideas of national dignity in Mexico and suitable national racial composition in the US, may scupper the possibilities for "policy" and block policy measures from being able to bring a "solution". Political interest and public interest more generally can always deflect, diminish and distract from what is proposed as logical and reasonable through an apparently a-political policy process.

A second point that can be drawn is that, then as now, labels matter. Designating movement as labour migration, as noted above, highlighted certain aspects but obscured others. Policy is formulated on the basis of the labels that stick; the two (policy and labels) may indeed be constitutive of each other. A label that sticks may be the one that is most suitable and amenable to intervention. Classifying migrants according to a simple typology and assuming that these identities and attendant spatial practices endure unchanged over time is an example of one such labelling device. But fixed labels, however convenient, are always reductionist and often seriously wrong. One of the great challenges for activists as for policymakers is how to give back the humanity and complexity of the social subjects for whom they plan.

A third, more specific, point concerns the "migradollars" earned in the US and brought back to improve people's lives in Mexico. The case study has illustrated how the usefulness of remittances, as well as the use to which remittances are put, are not constant but vary over time both in material and symbolic terms. The discussion has distinguished differences of use and use-fulness along two axes: from remittances used as "topping up" to indicating increasing dependence; and from remittances used tactically as a means of directly improving individual material or social position (in the short run) to being used strategically as a means to shift a family into a higher (i.e. pre-ferred) socio-economic or ethnic class (in the longer run). No linear rela-tionship should be assumed here, for one can expect switches and reversals depending on how individuals and families find themselves placed histori-cally and socially. This, of course, makes it difficult to understand or predict the more hidden quality of "usefulness", and more difficult to understand or predict the wisdom or effect of policy intervention.

Finally, the paper has discussed an issue that has received only partial documentation: policy aimed at the body. One of the arguments made was that in the early days, migration to the US was prompted in part by the policy adopted by the modernizing Mexican state, an intervention made with re-spect to the male body and the way poor men dressed. Proper citizens should wear trousers. Policy implementation was first of all put in the hands of "the authorities", rich, well-clothed men with political clout. Soon in western-cen-tral Mexico the policy could be claimed a "success", not because more force-ful intervention was forthcoming but because it had become internalized, a responsibility assumed by each man (and presumably his wife or mother) and for whom migration provided an answer. This historical example provokes questions that cannot be elaborated in this study. To what extent are bodies and the way bodies are presented and clothed still considered an appropriate or relevant policy matter; under what circumstances does this happen and in what places/societies is this most pronounced? This seems to be a live issue in national policy intervention (e.g. should Muslim girls be allowed to wear veils in classrooms of secular schools?) rather than a matter for development policy. However, one can go on to ask whether development policy in general and specific policy interventions carry indirect consequences with respect to the body and presentation of self and cultural identity: how else can one judge the "authenticity" of Indians or the indigence of the poor, if not by their clothing?

NOTES

1. My thanks to Jorge Durand for alerting me to Paul Taylor's work and presenting me with a copy of the original English text.
2. This section owes much to discussions with Patricia Arias and draws on our history of clothing production in the region (Arias and Wilson, 1997).
3. As Durand and Massey (1992) note, in his statistical work Gamio sought to rebut the view widely held in the United States that more than a million Mexicans were living there by 1929. His argument was that it was impossible to determine numbers due to the highly seasonal nature of the migration.
4. The Cristero wars were a violent backlash by ardent Catholics against the victors of the Mexican Revolution who were in the process of reconstructing the nation.

REFERENCES

Arias, P., and F. Wilson
　1997　*La aguja y el surco: Cambio regional, consumo y relaciones de género en la industria de la ropa en México*, University of Guadalajara, Guadalajara.

Bailey, A.
　2001　"Turning transnational: Notes on the theorisation of international migration", *International Journal of Population Geography*, 7(6): 413-428.

Bauer, A.
　2001　*Goods, Power, History: Latin America's Material Culture*, Cambridge University Press, Cambridge.

Bustamante, J.
　1988　"La política de inmigración de Estados Unidos: un análisis de sus contradicciones", in G. Lopez Castro and S. Pardo Galván (Eds), *Migración en el Occidente*, El Colegio de Michoacán, Zamora, Mexico, 19-40.

Carling, J.
　2003　"Cartographies of cape verdean transnationalism", *Global Networks*, 3(4): 335-340.

Cosgrove, S.
　1989　"The zoot suit and style warfare", in A. McRobbie (Ed.), *Zoot Suits and Second-hand Dresses: An Anthology of Fashion and Music*, Macmillans, Basingstoke, London.

de Souza Martins, J.
　2000　"The hesitations of the modern and contradictions of modernity in Brazil", in V. Schelling (Ed.), *Through the Kaleidoscope: The Experiences of Modernity in Latin America*, London, 248-274.

Durand, J. (Ed.)
　1991　*Migración México—Estados Unidos: Años veinte*, Concejo Nacional para la Cultura y las Artes, Mexico City.

Durand, J., and D. Massey
　1992　"Mexican migration to the United States: A critical review," *Latin American Research Review*, 27(2): 3-42.

Fonseca, O., and L. Moreno
　1984　*Jaripo, pueblo de migrantes*, Centro de Estudios de la Revolución Mexicana 'Lazaro Cardenas', Jiquilpan, Mexico.
　1988　"Consideraciones histórico-sociales de la migración de trabajadores michoacanos a los Estados Unidos de América: el caso de Jaripo", in G. Lopez Castro and S. Pardo Galvan (Eds), *Migración en el Occidente*, El Colegio de Michoacán, Zamora, Mexico, 65-84.

Gamio, M.
　1991　"Número, procedencia y distribución geográfica de los inmigrantes Mexicanos en Estados Unidos", in J. Durand (Ed.), *Migración México—Estados Unidos: Años veinte*, Concejo Nacional para la Cultura y las Artes, Mexico City, 19-33.

González, L.
1974   *San José de Gracia: A Mexican Village in Transition*, University of Texas Press, Austin.

Gruzinski, S.
2002   *The Mestizo Mind: The Intellectual Dynamics of Colonization and Globalization*, Routledge, New York/London.

Knight, A.
1990   "Racism, revolution and *indigenismo*: Mexico 1910-1914", in R. Graham (Ed.), *The Idea of Race in Latin America, 1870-1914*, University of Texas Press, Austin, 71-113.

Lefebvre, H.
1991   *The Production of Social Space*, Blackwells, Oxford.

Lopez, A.
2000   "A train of shadows: Early cinema and modernity in Latin America", in V. Schelling (Ed.), *Through the Kaleidoscope: The Experiences of Modernity in Latin America*, Verso, London/New York, 148-176.

López Castro, G.
1986   *La casa dividida: Un estudio de caso sobre la migración a Estados Unidos en un pueblo Michoacana*, El Colegio de Michoacán, Zamora, Mexico.

Ong, A.
1999   *Flexible Citizenship: The Cultural Logics of Transnationality*, Duke University Press, Durham and London.

Portes, A.
1996   "Global villagers: The rise of transnational communities", *The American Prospect*, 25: 74-77.

Santibañez, E.
1991   "Ensayo acerca de la inmigración mexicana en Estados Unidos", in J. Durand (Ed.), *Migración México—Estados Unidos, Años veinte*, Concejo Nacional para la Cultura y las Artes, Mexico City, 65-129.

Smith, M.P., and L. Guarnizo
1998   *Transnationalism from Below*, Transaction Publishers, New Brunswick.

Taylor, P.
1933   *A Spanish-Mexican Peasant Community: Arandas in Jalisco, Mexico*, University of California Press, Berkeley; Spanish version published in J. Durand (Ed.), 1991, *Migración México—Estados Unidos*, Concejo Nacional para la Cultura y las Artes, Mexico City, 131-221.

Tuñon, J.
1991   El albúm de la mujer, antología ilustrada de las Mexicanas, el Siglo XIX, Instituto Nacional de Antropología e Historia, Mexico City.

Wilson, F.
1999   "Gendered histories: Garment production and migration in Mexico", *Environment and Planning*, A, 31: 327-343.

Burundians in Belgium:
Constructing, Performing and Contesting Diaspora

Simon Turner

ABSTRACT

Taking its point of departure in ethnographic fieldwork among Burundians living in Belgium, this chapter explores the contradictory processes of making and unmaking transnational communities and diaspora identities. It explores the fault lines that appear to coincide with ethnicity and time of arrival but often are more complex, and argues that they are politically motivated. The chapter argues against theories that try to define diasporas through ever finer conceptual criteria and argues that we must move away from perceiving diasporas as ontological realities and instead perceive of diaspora as a process and an ideal. It follows the double movement of diasporic fragmentation and creation and argues that political manoeuvers of political entrepreneurs in the transnational political field shape diasporic networks and determine the discursive contents of transnational practices. In this manner, political struggles to define the role of the diaspora are shaping the field within which Burundians in Belgium may move and where they may seek belonging.

Beatrice: A Hutu from Brussels.

I am sitting in the home of an influential Burundian who has lived in Belgium since the late 1960s and has been a founding member of one of the first "Hutu" political parties. Today, I am interviewing his 21-year-old daughter, Beatrice, who has never been to Burundi, although she and her fiancé dream of settling there permanently one day. She never used to consider her foreign background as a child and has never met racism or discrimination. In her late teens, however, she became increasingly interested in her parents' natal country. She and some friends organized lessons in Kirundi, because she felt ashamed when meeting Burundians who were not much older than she and who arrived as political refugees in the late 1990s. Her older brother has organized an association for Burundian youth in Belgium, *Génération Afrique*, and is a very active contributor to various "Hutu" homepages. Asked whether she has any contact with Tutsi students, of whom there are plenty at her university, Louvain la Neuve, she admits somewhat ashamedly that she does not. "It is not that my parents have told me: Don't mix with Tutsi. Burundians are subtler. They say things indirectly," she explains. As her parents are Hutu refugees, she does not think it appropriate to mix with Tutsi.

Oscar: Fresh from Bujumbura's melting pot

Oscar is a Ph.D. student living on campus at Louvain La Neuve. He arrived in Belgium recently and is fed up with the fact that Hutu and Tutsi do not mix. "In Bujumbura, we are far beyond that stage," he says. "Now we get together and try to make things work, regardless of whether you are a Hutu or a Tutsi." Later, I bump into Oscar by accident several times, once at the IRAGI cultural group, another time at the commemoration of an important Hutu politician, and finally, in a café in Bujumbura. On both occasions in Belgium, he had been sucked into "Hutu" environments, one of them highly political and radical. However, he claims that he frequents *Chez Doudou* in Brussels' Matonge district – a bar that is run by a Burundian and frequented by a mixed – predominantly Tutsi – crowd of young Burundians who are either into business or music and try to stay out of politics. He also claims to mix with Tutsi when playing basketball and football on campus.

Belgian-born Beatrice, who has never experienced ethnic violence first hand has no contact with the Tutsi students at her university, while Oscar, who arrived in Belgium last year and has experienced all the violence of the past decade, mingles with both groups at bars and on campus to the degree that it is possible. However, Oscar is finding it increasingly hard to mix with the other ethnic group, as their acquaintances keep them in closed circuits.

This chapter explores some of these apparent contradictions and paradoxes, and the contradictory processes of making and unmaking of transnational communities and diaspora identities. It first explores why it is that Burundians who have little or no experience of ethnic conflict and violence in Burundi and who have been brought up in a liberal democracy where they have not necessarily experienced racism or marginalization from the host society can embrace such feelings of resentment and bitterness, while others are willing to compromise. The chapter then explores the fault lines that appear to coincide with ethnicity and time of arrival but are often more complex and it follows the double movement of diasporic fragmentation and creation, arguing that political manoeuvres of political entrepreneurs in the transnational political field shape diasporic networks and determine the discursive contents of transnational practices. In this manner, political struggles to define the role of the diaspora shape the field within which Burundians in Belgium may move and where they may seek belonging.

THE TRANSNATIONAL POLITICAL FIELD

Belgium does not have one but several diasporas, as my well-educated informants would often explain to me when I had presented my research project. For example, there are three cultural associations that all deal with traditional drumming and dancing: Hiba, Indanga and IRAGI. And although nobody mentions it and nobody likes to admit it, the organizers grudgingly and gradually explain that most of the dancers and drummers in Indanga are Hutu who arrived in the 1970s or earlier and their descendents, while IRAGI mostly attracts Hutu who arrived since 1990. Hiba is almost exclusively Tutsi, although this obviously is not mentioned anywhere in its official material (www.hibacultures.be), and its organizers express a wish to have Hutu members.

How do several diasporas emerge and how do they interact? Rather than assuming that diasporas exist because migrants and refugees are involved in similar transnational practices – thus characterizing them on the basis of objectively defined outside criteria – the aim of this study is to explore the creation of such communities "from the inside", so to speak. In other words, the study takes into account the internally generated discursive practices of constructing identities through difference. Diasporas are on-going political projects that are constantly disputed, contested and destabilized.

Obviously, we must avoid treating migrants and refugees as a homogeneous mass (Adamson, 2002; Østergaard-Nielsen, 2001). The question then is whether these differences in opinion are not merely the product of different times of arrival, different social backgrounds, different experiences of the war in Burundi, and different situations in the host society. On the one hand, the answer is yes, these factors certainly play a role in shaping the attitudes of Burundians in exile and in giving the groups their internal differentiation. But there is no simple link between these objective life conditions and the distinctions that Burundians in exile draw. They are pinned up on larger political struggles. Although at first glance there appears to be a correlation between ethnicity, time of arrival and group belonging, these standpoints and politics of difference are not simply born out of an objective position in the diaspora.

Some individuals act and take on opinions that apparently contradict their objective life experiences.

In order to grasp the transnational social field among Burundians in Belgium, where individuals are constantly positioning themselves and each other in relation to Burundi, I find it fruitful to introduce Bourdieu's concept of the political field (Bourdieu, 1991). The political field is like a game, he argues, where politicians gain a "practical sense" of the game and learn how to comply with the unwritten rules of the political field. By becoming competent players of the game, political entrepreneurs also reproduce it.

The positions that political representatives take are less determined by the interests that they claim to be promoting, and more by the structure of the field where they must position themselves *vis-à-vis* other players in a field that is constructed around polarities.

> [A]dopting a stance, a prise de position, is, as the phrase clearly suggests, an act which has meaning only relationally, in and through difference, the distinctive deviation (Bourdieu, 1991: 177).

In other words, the political entrepreneur positions himself vis-à-vis his opponents in an attempt to emerge as the true representative of "the people". And as the political field sets the limits for what is politically thinkable and what is politically unthinkable, the positions also create their constituencies. The field is created in the process of being contested.

In Fiona Adamson's words, the "transnational political field (…) is open to contestation, mobilization and/or capture by political entrepreneurs" (Adamson, 2002: 159). Hence, the transnational political field is created as a terrain upon which various political actors attempt to discredit each other and claim to be the true representatives of "the Burundian people". Here, the idea of a diasporic or transnational community is important. It is not enough simply to discard the concept, due to the stratified and fragmented character of the Burundian population in Belgium. As in other contexts, the idea of community remains a powerful imaginary construct. Ideologically, the community works as an "empty signifier" (Laclau and Mouffe, 1985) that promises to eliminate difference and antagonism. As much as we must not assume a "transnational community",[1] it is still a strong imaginary figure that many people strive for. It is a sense of community that political ideologies – and political entrepreneurs – promise their constituencies. Therefore, as much as we may deconstruct communities, transmigrant Burundians are constantly in the process of constructing them anew. This is an endless project, as Laclau would claim in relation to all ideological attempts at *suture* of society. And it is this endless project that becomes the driving force in the processes that can be witnessed in Belgium.

While people on the move are challenging the naturalized links between nation, state, territory and identity, the very same people are seeking to create clean-cut places of identity. There is a simultaneous process of flow and closure in a Deleuzean sense. The concept of "long-distance nationalism" (Anderson, 1994) illustrates this paradoxical and ambiguous nature of diaspora identities. As much as migrants challenge the nation-state – putting pressure on the hyphen between nation and state (Appadurai, 1996) – they can also strengthen nationalist movements in their country of origin. On this paradox, Anderson claims: "Nationalism's purities (and thus also cleansings) are set to emerge from exactly this hybridity" (Anderson, 1994: 316).[2] In the present era of globalization, this may be particularly evident. As Gupta and Ferguson have remarked: "The irony of our times is that as actual places and localities become ever more blurred and indeterminate, *ideas* of culturally and ethnically distinct places become perhaps even more salient" (Gupta and Ferguson, 1997: 39).

Although they are increasingly merging, diaspora studies and studies on transnationalism have distinct genealogies. To put it slightly crudely, transnational studies are mostly concerned with studying practices here and now that tie people together across boundaries, while diaspora studies are mostly about identity and history. This chapter links the transnational practices that tend to transgress and dissolve fixed assumptions of identity, place and community with diasporic identities that seek to "fix" and "close" identity and community. This tension takes place in – and creates – the transnational political field.

COMING TO BELGIUM

Being the former colonial power in Burundi, Belgium has received substantial numbers of Burundians over a long period of time. Some arrived shortly after independence on government scholarships to study everything from plumbing to psychology. Others came as political refugees, and finally, a small number have married Belgians. Burundians in Belgium talk about three main *waves* of Burundian (Hutu) arrival in Belgium. The first is *les anciens*; the Hutu refugees who arrived after the "selective genocide" in 1972 (Lemarchand and Martin, 1974). The second is the *boursiers*, students on Burundian government grants who are paid to do their *doctorat* in Belgium. With the political reforms and gradual democratization process that took place in the late 1980s in Burundi, increasing numbers of Hutu students were given such government grants to study in Belgium, which hitherto had been the privilege of the Tutsi elite. Finally, there was another big "wave" of refugees arriving after October 1993, when president Ndadaye was killed. While the first arrivals after 1993 were virtually all Hutu, an increasing number of asylum seekers are now Tutsi. According to the Belgian "Office of the Commissioner General for Refugees and Stateless Persons", 60 per cent of Burundian asylum seekers in the period 1988 to 2000 were Hutu, while 20 per cent were Tutsi and 20 per cent claimed to be of mixed heritage. Fieldwork in Belgium, Denmark and Burundi shows a tendency towards more Tutsi refugees in recent years.

As we saw in relation to the three cultural groups, these "cohorts" harbour a great deal of animosity and suspicion towards one another. But there are also overlaps between the categories. Let us look briefly at these overlaps and cracks in the dividing lines.

First, once one asks about individual life stories, one realizes that most people slip in and out of these categories. Many have been back and forth between Belgium and Burundi several times – for instance, first as students and later as refugees. They may also have lived in other African countries for a while – either as refugees or as students. Thus, most of the so-called 1972 refugees interviewed for this study had actually arrived as students before 1972 on government grants and had decided to stay on and seek asylum when news hit them about the massacres in Burundi. Burundians explained that those Hutu intellectuals who were in Burundi in 1972 were either killed or fled to neighbouring countries. They could not reach Europe. So the few who received asylum in Belgium were already in the country. Beatrice's father, whom we met in the opening scene, was thus studying in Belgium in 1972 when he decided to apply for political asylum.

Similar complexities emerge in relation to the larger group of Burundian refugees who have arrived after 1993. Isaac has a degree in geology from a Belgian university. He then received a grant for a Ph.D. in environmental planning in Belgium in 1996. However, it was difficult for the grant to come through due to the embargo imposed on Burundi in 1996, he claims. Also, his wife was having some problems that he is reluctant to elaborate on. In any case, he gave up his studies and applied for asylum.

Ali had been a student at Louvain La Neuve in 1993 and had been asked to join the government in Burundi in 1994, when most Hutu politicians were going in the opposite direction. He remained in government until 1996, when he fled to Belgium again. When I met him in April 2003, he was unemployed doing odd jobs at the University and contemplating returning to Burundi. He went to Burundi in July 2003 and is now employed at the national assembly as chief of the presidential cabinet. His wife has become a Belgian citizen and will join him once the situation in Burundi has stabilized.

Frederic is a Tutsi but was an outspoken journalist, not afraid of criticizing the government and the army. This finally became too much of a problem for him, and he came to Belgium to apply for asylum. As he explains, his case was quite straightforward, as he could document the threats that he had experienced, and he was given asylum without any problems. Now he has a Belgian passport that he uses whenever he goes to Burundi, which he tries to do at least once a year and preferably for a few months at a time. His Burundian wife, whom he met in Belgium, never applied for asylum. She was first a student in Italy and then in Belgium. She does not want the stigma of being a refugee.

The stories of Isaac, Ali and Frederic illustrate that the choice of becoming a refugee is complex and that the borderlines between immigrant, temporary migrant and refugee are fine and often blurred. Even Frederic and Ali, who both resemble the classical political refugee, a high-ranking politician and outspoken journalist, have made a number of other choices along the way.

However, in spite of these boundaries being blurred by individuals moving in and out of categories such as refugee, *boursier* and migrant, transnational identities have been constructed and solidified. These often depend on time of arrival and are shaped in part by the environment in the host society and in particular by the political climate in Burundi at the time. In the following, we examine some of these processes of positioning in the transnational political field.

LES ANCIENS – CONSTRUCTING A DIASPORIC OPPOSITION

Laurent is Palipehutu's (Parti pour la libération du peuple Hutu) representative in the Benelux. He belongs to the more moderate branch of the party, commonly known as *tendence Karatasi* because it follows the line of Etienne Karatasi, who is based in Denmark and has been the leader of the party since 1991. Laurent is a small, dusty man in his early sixties who welcomes me in his town house in a Turkish-dominated part of Brussels. His office is small and stuffy and jammed full of papers and dossiers on Burundi and some books on pedagogy and psychology. On the wall space that is not covered with bookshelves, hang pictures of his children's graduation ceremonies side by side with a poster-size photo of Rémy Gahutu, founding father of Palipehutu. Gahutu, who lived in a refugee camp in Tanzania and died in prison in Tanzania in 1990, is looking sternly across the office – the traditional stick of the *abashingantahe* (the elders) lying on the table in front of him. Next to him are the symbols of Palipehutu: a hoe, a hammer and a crossbow. Laurent explains that the picture was taken at a conference in Fribourg, Switzerland.

On Laurent's desk is a more discrete picture of Etienne Karatasi in a suit and tie and without the traditional symbols of power. The photo is obviously taken in a professional studio. When he had decided to create the party in 1980, Gahutu contacted Karatasi, who had lived in Denmark since the late 1960s, and asked him to be the party's vice president. He needed representatives in Europe.[3]

There is also a poster-size blow up of a newspaper picture from *Le Soir* of dead bodies being loaded on or off a truck. The enlargement makes it hard to discern the details. Apparently, it is from the genocide in 1972.[4] He is very proud of these pictures and explains in great detail what took place in 1972.

When questioning him about the birth of the party and his own involvement in it, it gradually emerged that Laurent never experienced the 1972 genocide. He left Burundi in 1968 to study psycho-pedagogy at Louvain La Neuve, followed by a course in development management at Antwerp. When he learned about the 1972 massacres, people advised him to apply for political asylum.

Laurent explains that a clandestine association for Hutu students, AS-SEBA (Associations des Etudiants Bahutu), was created in Belgium in 1965. This association was followed by MoLiBa (Mouvement pour la Libération des Barundi) in 1968 and MeProBa (Mouvement des Etudiants Progressistes Barundi), which was no longer clandestine but had an armed wing. Laurent was chairman of MeProBa but stepped down at the second party congress. This was because he was about to finish his studies, and the movement had decided to send him and others who had finished their studies to neighbouring countries (Rwanda and Tanzania) to prepare the revolution.

These plans were all disturbed by the events of 1972. Laurent explains that president Kayibanda in Rwanda (where a "Hutu revolution" had taken place in 1959 resulting in a Hutu elite taking political power) asked them to create a political party, so the exiled Hutu elite met in Kigali. The details around the attempts to create various movements and parties are rather complicated. Finally, however, Gahutu created Palipehutu in a refugee camp in Tanzania.

The point is that Laurent and his contemporaries had not experienced the kind of ethnic violence that many Burundians have today. One gets the impression of a small elitist group of very young students who were in Europe at a time when revolutionary liberation movements were "in vogue" at European universities. Just as Vietnamese, Algerian and Cambodian intellectuals were inspired by the revolutionary youth in Paris, Hutu intellectuals in Brussels seem to have been touched by the same spirit. In Africa, newly born independent states were run by youthful political elites who had been the spearhead in national liberation movements and keen on progress, development and modernity, and revolting against tradition and gerontocracy.[5] This was also the case in Burundi where a group of young, educated low-caste Tutsi had taken control in 1966 (the president, Colonel Micombero, was 26 years old at the time) and was ridding the country of traditional and colonial rule (Lemarchand, 1970; Turner, 2001). Laurent belongs to the same generation of revolutionary African youth. Furthermore, it is significant how transnational this movement appears to be. Laurent's long account is all about meetings and visits in Rwanda, Denmark, Switzerland and Tanzania.

How does this relate to the creation of transnational communities in Belgium? The fieldwork in Belgium shows that *les anciens* constitute a small group of exiles that have much the same background. Due to the fact that they were so few and that there were no other actors in the transnational political field, they quickly became a rather closely knitted group that dominated the field with their radical political opinions. This group did not limit itself to fellow Hutu in Belgium but was closely linked to the few Hutu who were in exile in other European countries, most notably Germany, Denmark and Switzerland. They would visit each other, phone and send letters.

In other words, the production of a diasporic community was centred on political issues and articulated very strongly in opposition to the homeland. None of these people visited Burundi, although they were very keen on gaining information on what was actually going on in Burundi. One of their main concerns has been to document political developments and human rights abuses in Burundi, as they were (rightly) convinced that the Burundian government was feeding the outside world with one-sided information. A central transnational political strategy of theirs has been to influence host society politics towards country of origin in a similar way to that Østergaard-Nielsen found among Kurds in Germany (Østergaard-Nielsen, 2001).

In spite of their strong transnational links to the Burundian Hutu diaspora elsewhere in Europe and East Africa, these Burundians were less transnational in other walks of life than more recent waves of Burundians in Belgium. As Beatrice explained, many of them spoke French at home, resulting in their children forgetting Kirundi. Likewise, being so few and far between (most Burundians take pride in the fact that they do not live in ghettos), it was more difficult to stick to only having Burundian friends then than now, they say. While there now are several bars owned by Burundians in Brussels and even one in Flemish-speaking Antwerp, there were none 10-15 years ago.

In sum, we have a group of people who are at once well-integrated into Belgian society (homeowners with respectable jobs as nurses and teachers and the like, and children at university), culturally delinked from Burundi, while making up the hard kernel of the political opposition in Burundi's transnational political field. And although politics can seem like a game when observing political meetings in Belgium, they are not innocent games without repercussions inside Burundi. Laurent has negotiated the future of Burundi with the Burundian government on several occasions, most notably in Arusha, Tanzania, under the chairmanship of first Julius Nyerere and later Nelson Mandela, resulting in Palipehutu (tendence Karatasi) becoming part of the present transitional government in Burundi.

LES BOURSIERS
– CONFRONTING THE DIASPORA

In the late 1980s, the Tutsi-dominated, one-party regime in Burundi gradually introduced democratic reforms and partially recognized for the first time that there was an ethnic problem in the country. This forced the Hutu opposition to take new positions in the political field (Turner, 1998). Obviously, it also had repercussions on the diaspora in Belgium.

The first concrete embodiment of this shift in government policy was the emergence of Hutu *boursiers* in Belgium around 1990. People who arrived at this point explained how they already had vivid images of the exiled politicians in Europe. "We thought they would have horns," one of them laughs, slightly embarrassed at his own naivety. "We all knew the names of Karatasi and Murengerantwari before we left Burundi." These names had achieved a mythical status, fascinating and frightening in the minds of many Burundians. In a more reconciling tone, Pierre, a young man who arrived in 1995, explains that *les anciens* had been diabolized in Burundi. "They are not more radical than others," he adds.

The suspicions were mutual. The old refugees were convinced that all students were pro-government, as they were on government grants and had "access to the embassy", which was a no-go area for refugees. They were therefore not to be trusted.

Most agree that when they actually met, the suspicion vanished together with the prejudices. But they also maintain that there are differences between *les anciens* and *les boursiers*. This difference is found in their political opinions: the former are more radical and less willing to trust the Tutsi. In this sense, there appears to be less difference between the *boursiers* and the 1993 refugees. The difference in political opinions is also reflected in other walks of transnational life, as when they join different cultural clubs. Here again, the students from the 1990s join the refugees from 1993 and onwards. As we saw in some of the life stories above, the difference between *boursier* and refugee can be hard to maintain at times. Nor does there seem to be much distinction between the two in their own constructions of competing diasporas.

1993 – COMPLEX DIASPORAS

The political reforms in Burundi in the late 1980s and early 1990s culminated in presidential elections and elections to the national assembly in 1993, when Frodebu and its charismatic leader, Melchior Ndadaye, won a landslide victory. Ndadaye was keen to collaborate with Buyoya's Uprona party and was careful to appoint Tutsi to important positions in the administration. However, his project of reconciliation was cut short, when Tutsi officers abducted and killed him and other top politicians on October 21, 1993 in what Reyntjens has called "the most successful 'failed coup' in history" (Reyntjens, 1993). Fearing that 1972 was going to repeat itself, Hutu all over the country put up roadblocks and started killing civilian Tutsi indiscriminately. The army clamped down with usual brutality, killing tens of thousands of Hutu and causing hundreds of thousands to flee. The political situation in the country after this was very complicated and obscure, resulting in a deadlock between Frodebu and a number of small Tutsi parties, while the army was engaged in a dirty war with various Hutu rebel groups.

This is when large numbers of Hutu and some Tutsi began entering Belgium and other European countries. Pierre explains that these refugees had "tasted liberty and democracy". Therefore, he claims, they were a lot more engaged and active than their predecessors had been. Many fled because they had been active in politics, in human rights movements or in the media in Burundi. They naturally continued this work in Burundi, where they have created a host of organizations and movements, some of which have the goal of "informing" the Belgian public about the situation in Burundi, while others have vague objectives of promoting peace in Burundi and the Great Lakes. Yet others are more focused on specific development objectives in Burundi, from women's groups supporting orphans in Bujumbura to a hometown association for Gitega that sends clothes or funds to the school there. Very few of these organizations are involved in what Østergaard-Nielsen calls "immigrant politics", i.e. the problems of immigrants in the host country. The majority are involved in what she terms "homeland politics" (Østergaard-Nielsen, 2001). Of course, this flourishing of organizations was not merely due to the fact that they had "tasted liberty and democracy". The mere fact that the size of the Burundian population in Belgium exploded allowed for all these activities to commence. Beatrice remembers how, as a child, there were so few Burundians to socialize with, despite the fact that both her parents were important figures in the political movement. It is only in recent years that there has been a critical mass able to arrange all-night parties for Burundians. It appears that individuals from older "cohorts" can benefit from the activities of the new organizations, as when Beatrice goes to the Burundian disco or takes Kirundi lessons. Likewise, there are plenty of occasions for them to meet: seminars, weddings and the commemoration of Ndadaye's death or the 1972 genocide. However, even on these occasions, conflicts occur over who has the right to organize the events, and who should give speeches.

PLAYING THE POLITICAL GAME

When attending political meetings in Belgium, it seems that everyone knows everyone in the room and that they know exactly what everyone is going to say. Still, they play the game of political dispute over and over again in grandiose seminars, commemorations, funerals and political meetings. That is to say, there are differences of opinion between the various factions, but they still interact in a rather small environment where "tout le monde se connait", playing the same political game far from the reality of Burundi. Although these "rencontres" provide a space to meet, they act as stages upon which various political actors can play their role vis-à-vis the others present, thus re-enacting symbolically their different positions in the political field.[6] During the breaks, they drink beer and chat before going back to arguing.

Such disputes usually concern the degree to which one should trust the present transition process in Burundi. Hardliners maintain that the Tutsi will never relax their hold on power and point to the fact that the army has not yet been reformed. They fear that the Tutsi have just negotiated a deal in order to appease the international community and trick the Hutu. Frodebu supporters and moderates in general claim that the negotiations have been a success and that the only option is to have faith in the transition process.

In private discussions, these debates are linked to questions of length of stay in exile and (lack of) contact with the population "back home". Thus, particularly newly arrived Burundians claim that *les anciens* live in the 1970s and have no idea about what has happened in their country since then. People like Frederic (the Tutsi journalist) and Oscar (the Hutu student), who frequently visit Burundi, say that *les anciens* get all their information from various internet sites created by their friends in Belgium, Denmark and Germany. "Whenever they hear of a rebel ambush in Burundi, they prefer to trust their own news channels that claim that it was the army who had staged the ambush".

The older generation is clearly in a defensive position on the issue of being in touch with the situation on the ground. They obviously have difficulties in arguing that they are more up to date than the others. However, as mentioned earlier, an important *raison d'être* for exiled Hutu in the 1970s and 1980s was to provide information that countered the official news from the Burundian government. Given the restrictions in Burundi and the logistic difficulties in Tanzania and Rwanda, party members in Europe played a vital coordinating role. This perception remains strong among some of *les anciens* today who still believe that people inside Burundi have less access to unbiased news than they do.

The issue of being "in touch" with what is going on in Burundi as opposed to living in a self-perpetuating isolated circle of like-minded exiles also follows Burundians who arrived later. Thus, there is an emerging division between those who arrived in the early 1990s and a younger generation who arrived during the last three-four years. Burundians who arrived in recent years as students or as refugees are fed up with what they see as a group of unemployed, middle-aged men with PhD degrees in useless subjects such as psychology or linguistics, who spend all their time talking about politics rather than getting a job and doing something useful for Belgium or Burundi or both. This new generation claims that in Burundi – or certainly in Bujumbura – people are no longer stuck in this ethnic mindset.

In sum, what we see here is a historical change in the political and social profile of the diaspora that have arrived since 1993. They appear to be more moderate, emphasizing democracy and human rights rather than Hutu liberation, as they are more in touch with the changes that have taken place in Burundi. This creates an antagonistic relationship to *les anciens*. This relationship is played out in various settings such as commemorations, where political actors position themselves vis-à-vis the others, all trying to claim to be the true defenders of Hutu interests. And the difference in attitude between *les anciens* and the new moderates is actively kept alive and used in political struggle. Thus, the new generation is actively using this difference as a political weapon to position themselves and to delegitimize their opponents. By claiming to defend democracy and human rights and to be against ethnic politics, they are also delegitimizing *les anciens* as being undemocratic ethnicists. The idea of being in touch with the latest developments in Burundi, of being educated, moderate, urban, active is used to disqualify others as out of touch, extremist, rural, and stagnant. When the yuppies conjure up the image of the unemployed PhDs talking politics, they are actively creating these divided diasporas more than describing a factual reality. In other words, if we were to compare the older and the younger generations in terms of unemployment, education and transnational practices – and political practices in particular – we may not find a clear difference between the two. Rather, the differences must be understood in terms of constructing difference in order to take a position in the political field. More broadly, such processes are connected to creating and stabilizing political identities.

THE TUTSI – A DIASPORA APART

Until recently, the only Tutsi to arrive were students or diplomats or people who had married Belgians. This meant that they did not have the same sense of being a "victim diaspora" (Cohen, 1997), arguably a defining characteristic of diaspora as discourse. They had not experienced the "exodus" experienced by Hutu refugees in 1972 and 1993, and which the Hutu could refer to regardless of whether they had actually taken part or not. However, with the shifting political field in Burundi, their position is changing and we are seeing more and more Tutsi movements articulating a victim discourse.

Once again, personal life stories do not always fit neatly into these categories. Some of the Tutsi who are most active in various movements, opposing the Arusha accords and the present transitional government, are in Belgium on regular work permits rather than as political refugees, whereas others who have received political asylum seem to have left their country due to lack of economic opportunities.

Sylvie came to Belgium in 1985 with her Belgian husband who died a few years later. She now lives with her two teenage children in a large well-kept flat full of Burundian souvenirs in a calm Brussels suburb. She feels that her European life is very lonely, and she misses Burundi. She visits the country as often as her economy allows. She also sends money home every now and then. She basically sticks to herself and does not get involved in politics, she says. However, it turns out that she is involved in a woman's group, supporting orphans in Burundi. And when discussing the problems in her country, she expresses typically "Tutsi" political opinions.

She tells me a long story about meeting a Burundian couple in her local church and falling into conversation with them after mass. However, their whole interpretation of events was so different to hers that she almost had a row with them. "They said that the army is shooting the population! How ridiculous. I told them that of course the army didn't just shoot at people. Obviously, the rebels must have attacked them. It takes two to fight. That's logical," she exclaims. The idea of the army killing civilians was completely absurd to her. Since then, the Burundian couple has avoided her, she says, going into a lot of detail about how they either leave church before or after her. This, she also finds strange. She would like to invite them for coffee. In other words, Sylvie is not involved in political networks, and she is outside the usual diasporic groups in Belgium. However, her friends are naturally Tutsi and her opinions so typically "Tutsi" that she finds it difficult to relate to Burundians who have different interpretations. Nor does she feel comfortable as a Belgian and misses the social life in Burundi.

Very few Tutsi have any relations with Hutu in Belgium and would rather socialize with Tutsi from Rwanda than Burundian Hutu. As opposed to the split between the Hutu groups that meet occasionally to mark their positions, the Tutsi have virtually no interaction with the Hutu. Although they refer back to the same country and the same conflict, they create versions of the truth that are so incompatible that Sylvie cannot even relate enough to her fellow churchgoers to have a cup of tea together. A former student at Louvain La Neuve tried to create a forum for Hutu and Tutsi students to debate the problems in Burundi, but the other Hutu blamed him for wanting to give away their secrets[8] and for letting himself be manipulated by the Tutsi. This would be acting like a traitor, he says, and adds that it is always the people who mix that are hit the hardest in ethnic conflicts – like mixed marriages in Burundi and Rwanda. Due to mutual suspicion, Hutu and Tutsi not only avoid dialogue but also make sure that nobody attempts to cross the line for fear that they will make the group vulnerable to the opponents' schemes.

The general mutual suspicion between Hutu and Tutsi takes on specific forms in exile. Both believe that they are the victims of a grand conspiracy (Turner, 2004) and that the other is well-connected with the host society, particularly churches, NGOs and government institutions. The Hutu refer to the colonial past to explain that the Tutsi have always experienced preferential treatment from the Belgian colonizers and can therefore still feed the Belgians with their version of events (as well as receive the majority of scholarships, jobs, NGO projects, etc.). The Tutsi on the other hand see a big conspiracy led by the Catholic Church. This narrative draws on the bad reputation that the church acquired during the genocide in Rwanda. Also, being heavily outnumbered in Belgium and usually having arrived later than the Hutu, the Tutsi feel that they are treading enemy territory.

OTHER OPTIONS
– INTER-ETHNIC MEETING PLACES

Agnes arrived in 2001 to join her husband in Brussels, only to discover that he had found a Belgian girlfriend. When I met her a year later, she lived with her four daughters in a tiny flat. She had no job and no money and was generally not very happy about being in Belgium. What seemed to keep her going was her Pentecostal church. Her face would beam and liven up when talk fell on the church. Twice a week she would attend the lively services of *l'Assemblé du Dieu Vivant* in a derelict storehouse, together with Angolans, Rwandans and Congolese. And every other Saturday, Burundian Protestants would borrow a small room from the Evangelical temple to pray together. Here, Hutu and Tutsi join forces in their common belief.

Another alternative to the politicized transnational space is created by transnational businessmen. Whereas Congolese immigrants are deeply involved in such business (MacGaffey and Bazenguissa-Ganga, 2000), very few Burundians seem to be engaged in business of any kind. Nevertheless, there is a small group of Muslim traders who allegedly do not consider themselves to be either Hutu or Tutsi. It is doubtful whether such a non-ethnic, Muslim business community actually exists. But the idea that it does is prevalent, and it could be a potential space of respite from the ethnicized and politicized space of the Burundian diaspora in Belgium. The perception originates in Burundi, where there are similar notions of a harmonious

Muslim community. Buyenzi and Bwiza districts in Bujumbura, which have a Muslim, Swahili population, have a reputation for being multicultural (the Swahili culture, itself a hybrid, came to Burundi with Tanzanian and Congolese traders), cosmopolitan (virtually all Muslims in Burundi live in urban areas) and "populaire" (as opposed the political elite who are believed to create all the problems). Here, people never killed each other during the bad times, they say with pride. They are not like the peasants who are easily manipulated to kill each other. They are too clever – in terms of being smart and streetwise rather than through formal schooling. They are also opposed to the urban elite that is so thirsty for power that it will commit genocide if need be. Muslim businessmen in Belgium can draw on these ideals if they wish to exit the ethnicized transnational political field.

However small these groups may be, it appears that religious identities may provide avenues to transcend the dichotomous space of the Burundian diaspora. Not any religious identity can replace a political identity, however. The Catholic Church, to which the vast majority of Burundians belong, is a powerful actor in Burundi and is accused by all sides of being politically biased.

DIASPORAS IN PLURAL

Many Burundians who took part to this study said that due to Belgium and Burundi's long common history, most Belgians try to categorize them as Hutu or Tutsi. They usually have an opinion about either the Hutu or the Tutsi. When a Burundian organization approaches a Belgian NGO or government office, applying for support to a development project in Burundi, they experience being categorized as either Hutu or Tutsi. They feel that they meet a suspicious attitude, as if they only support their own ethnic group. "Belgians prefer to pay Belgian NGOs. They don't trust us" they say. In Holland, it is not like that, Frederic says. There you are simply a "nègre", which in spite of its marginalizing and discriminating consequences can also be preferable to being categorized as Hutu or Tutsi. In other words, the transnational political field and hence transnational communities are shaped in part by the host society environment – in this case by Belgium's colonial legacy.

Burundians in Belgium and elsewhere are truly part of the political field in Burundi, which thus becomes deterritorialized. This affects the shape of the political field, first and foremost because it is dislocated in diaspora. It suffers from a kind of time lag, because certain actors refer to a Burundi that no longer exists. So although they are constantly referring back to the Burundian political field, they are doing so in different ways, due to time of departure. The older cohorts remember a different Burundi than the one that they are dealing with now. This affects their attitudes and political practices.

In Belgium, where individual rights are protected, one might expect a space to emerge for open dialogue between ethnic groups that in Burundi have fought each other for decades and ended up in a stranglehold. Such expectations rely on a Habermasian idea that people may sit together and find the rational solution to their mutual problems if only they are given the right conditions. This rationale underlies the many attempts by well-intentioned NGOs who organize seminars in Denmark, Holland, Canada, etc. to bring together all the political actors to the Burundian conflict in order to create dialogue. Such dialogues may even be stimulated by consultants from private firms with experience in "conflict resolution".

In her analysis of a Burundian internet newsgroup, Rose Kadende Kaiser claims that the internet provides such a power-free, destructured space for dialogue. She sees it as a kind of levelling field where people can communicate without the restrictions of class, ethnicity, age or gender (Kadende-Kaiser, 2000). My own findings on Burundian internet sites do not confirm this picture. On the contrary, there seem to be a number of parallel internet sites where like-minded Burundians in Burundi and most often abroad can create separate communities, dismissing the others as ethnic extremists. Although virtually all these sites introduce themselves as being non-political and non-ethnic, with the objective of promoting peace and reconciliation in Burundi, etc, Burundians in Belgium know exactly which sites are "Hutu" and "Tutsi".

Similarly, the transnational political field among Burundians in Belgium is far from resembling this ideal Habermasian space of exchange and is more in line with Anderson's vision of long-distance nationalists. He was worried that these long-distance nationalists were unaccountable, as they do not have to answer for the consequences of their actions. Being protected by their rights – often with citizenship in the host country – they cannot be imprisoned, tortured or killed in the home country. The danger, Anderson warns, lies in the fact that their political opinions have very real and material consequences for people "back home" who may pay with their lives. Thus, if Laurent and his comrades in Europe decide to withdraw from negotiations and continue fighting, there are real young men in flesh and blood who must continue to live in the mountains, ambushing army outposts and terrorizing civilians to support them.

My point is that it is not merely a question of being unaccountable, as Anderson suggests. It is also a question of how the political field works in diaspora. Whereas compromise is needed in political interaction in Burundi, such compromise is not necessary in exile. Here, there is no cost attached to remaining uncompromising. Burundians in Belgium can manage in their daily life without having to deal with and hence negotiate and compromise with the other ethnic group. That would be virtually impossible in Burundi.

This might give an impression that Burundians in Belgium always are more radical than in Burundi. This is not necessarily the case. In the various internal conflicts between factions in the rebel groups, questions of distance from the battlefield have played a central role. In some instances, the European-based leadership has been accused of being too "soft", as when Kabul Kosani split with Etienne Karatasi. However, whether the Burundians in Belgium are "softer" or "harder" than their compatriots at home and whether or not they contribute to exacerbating the conflict, they still live in a world

Burundians in Belgium: Constructing, Performing and Contesting Diaspora

where they can afford to be uncompromising. And this has consequences for the political field.

Just as this has consequences for the political field in Burundi, it also has consequences for how the diaspora is created. Thus, a main argument of this chapter has been that several Burundian diasporas exist in Belgium, and that they cannot be defined by objective criteria alone. What is interesting is to explore the processes that create and maintain them. Transnational communities do not just appear. They are constructed in a political game of creating difference, and among Burundians in Belgium this game of creating difference is uncompromising.

NOTES

1. See Schiller (1999) for a critique of the concept of transnational community.
2. Basch, Blanc and Schiller show similarly how nationalism often starts in exile (Schiller et al., 1995). Polish nationalism in the late 19th century.
3. After Gahutu's death, Karatasi took over as party president. However, not all party members found it appropriate for an opposition party with an armed wing to be led by a doctor living in Denmark. The leader of the youth wing, Kabul Kosani, based in refugee camps in Tanzania, broke with Karatasi, effectively creating a new party. Since then, the party has split several times – often on the issue of legitimacy and "distance to the masses."
4. I have seen the very same picture on several Hutu internet sites, such as www.burundi-sites.com.
5. For related debates on modernity and generations, see Barrett (2004), Ferguson (1999), MacGaffey and Bazenguissa-Ganga (2000).
6. Another stage for such political acting is the various internet sites.
7. E.g. Action Contre Génocide and Rassemblement pour la Démocratie des Communautés au Burundi (RADECO).
8. The issue of keeping one's secrets is central in Burundian political culture (Turner, 2004).

REFERENCES

Adamson, F.
  2002   "Mobilizing for the transformation of home: Politicized identities and transnational practices", in *New Approaches to Migration? Transnational Communities and the Transformation of Home*, Routledge, London and New York.

Anderson, B.
  1994   *Exodus,* Critical Inquiry (20).

Appadurai, A.
  1996   *Modernity at Large: Cultural Dimensions of Globalization*, University of Minnesota Press, Minneapolis, Minnesota.

Barrett, M.
  2004   "Paths to adulthood: Freedom, belonging and temporalities in Mbunda biographies from western Zambia", Acta Universitatis Upsaliensis, Uppsala Studies in Cultural Anthropology, (38).

Bourdieu, P., and J. Thompson
  1991   *Language and Symbolic Power*, Harvard University Press, Cambridge, Mass.

Cohen, R.
  1997   *Global Diasporas: An introduction*, University of Washington Press, Seattle.

Ferguson, J.
  1999   *Expectations of Modernity: Myths and Meanings of Urban Life on the Zambian Copperbelt*, University of California Press, Berkeley.

Gupta, A., and J. Ferguson
  1997   "Beyond 'culture': Space, idenity, and the politics of difference", in A. Gupta and J. Ferguson (Eds), *Culture, Power, Place: Explorations in Critical Anthropology*, Duke University Press, Durham.

Kadende-Kaiser, R.M.
  2000   "Interpreting language and cultural discourse: Internet communication among Burundians in the diaspora", *Africa Today,* 47(2): 121-148.

Laclau, E., and C. Mouffe
  1985   *Hegemony and Socialist Strategy: Towards a Radical Democratic Politics*, Verso, London.

Lemarchand, R.
  1970   *Rwanda and Burundi*, Pall Mall Press, London.

Lemarchand, R., and D. Martin
  1974   *Selective Genocide in Burundi*, Minority Rights Group, London.

MacGaffey, J., and R. Bazenguissa-Ganga
  2000   *Congo-Paris: Transnational Traders on the Margins of the Law*, International African Institute in association with James Currey Oxford, Indiana University Press, London Bloomington.

Østergaard-Nielsen, E.K.
  2001   "Transnational political practices and the receiving state: Turks and Kurds in Germany and the Netherlands", *Global Networks,* 1(3): 261-282.

Reyntjens, F.

1993   "The proof of the pudding is in the eating – the June 1993 elections in Burundi", *Journal of Modern African Studies,* 31(4): 563-583.

Schiller, N.G.

1999   "Transmigrants and nation-states: Something old and something new in the US immigrant experience", in C. Hirschman, P. Kasinitz, and J. DeWind (Eds), *The Handbook of International Migration: the American Experience*, Russell Sage Foundation, New York, 99-119.

Schiller, N.G., L. Basch, and C.S. Blanc

1995   "From immigrant to transmigrant – theorizing transnational migration", *Anthropological Quarterly,* 68(1): 48-63.

Turner, S.

1998   "Representing the past in exile: The politics of national history among Burundian refugees", *Refuge,* Canada's periodical on refugees 17(6).

2001   "The barriers of innocence – Humanitarian intervention and political imagination in a refugee camp for Burundians in Tanzania", PhD, Roskilde University.

2004   "Under the gaze of the 'big nations', refugees, rumours and the international community in Tanzania", *African Affairs,* 103: 227-247.

Spaces of Democratic Practice: Nicaraguans in San José, Costa Rica

Pia Steen

ABSTRACT

This chapter traces and examines the determinants of transnational engagements among Nicaraguan migrants in Costa Rica. It applies a class perspective in the discussion of the democratic potentials in these engagements. The analysis shows how both middle class and elite groups from the Nicaraguan diaspora have initiated activities directed towards their poor compatriots in the diaspora. Apparently, these activities are determined by a commitment that can be coined "political" in a broad definition of what *doing politics* means. These activities are taking place within alliances between church, diplomacy, academia, artists and business people on the one hand, and a larger group of poorer unskilled workers on the other. Hence, a network structure of *vertical ties* (top-down oriented) in addition to pre-existing *horizontal ties* among equals (top-top or bottom-bottom) is created. It is argued that this kind of micro-level activity can be interpreted as a manifestation of a new democratic political culture across former polarized class divides and contrasting political stands. It is further underscored that emerging democratic political cultures in the diaspora might feed into processes of democratization in both home country and host country. In the San José-Nicaraguan context, it is demonstrated how the Nicaraguan diaspora – with inspiration from the departed Sandinista participatory culture – establish a democratic platform from which struggles take off in two directions: one against the prevailing political culture in Nicaragua characterized by polarization and *caudillismo*, and another against the negative discourse about poor Nicaraguans that is being carried out in Costa Rica. Hence, these struggles articulate new stands towards the prevailing political culture in the home country as well as a competing counter-discourse of flight and migration in the host country. They provide evidence of a new *transnational* political field of action that has to be taken into account in the current political landscape.

Living as a transnational migrant, often originating from a more or less undemocratic home country and migrating to a country with more established democratic structures, might advocate for exceptional comparative experiences of how democracy, including political culture, functions and why not. These experiences do not only shape the migrants' individual doings and sayings in the host country, but also their kinds of relations to the home country and to each other within and across borders. This situation might urge migrants/diasporas to act collectively as new driving forces in democratization processes in what could be called a *transnational political field*. This field of action embraces both home and host countries in different ways.

The aim of this chapter is to explore such transnational political engagements and their determinants from a class perspective, drawing on empirical evidence from recent fieldwork among Nicaraguan migrants in San José, Costa Rica. The chapter shows how both middle and upper class groups (the elites) have initiated different micro-political activities directed towards their poorer lower class compatriots, with a view to promoting spaces of democratic practice across borders, class divides and different political stands.

A main argument is that a better understanding of the diversified spectrum of transnational political action is obtained by including *messier* types of informal political engagements. These engagements might not be identified within conventional definitions of what "doing politics" means, including what has been coined *broad political transnationality* by Itzigsohn et al. (1999). However, by stretching the domain of the political, these activities can be included within the realm of politics. In order to understand the determinants of such actions, the political culture in home and host countries should be explored as a concomitant factor. An assumption is that through the optic of political culture and political history, the more or less covert political agendas of such informal activities might be unfolded.

The chapter is structured as follows: First, in order to locate empirical data within a broader tissue, different approaches to political transnationalism are addressed. Second, the Nicaraguan case of flight and migration within a Central American context and in a historical and political perspective is presented. Third, some empirical examples of micro-political activities found among Nicaraguans in San José are introduced and analysed. In the context of a prevailing polarized political culture in Nicaragua on the one hand, and a more democratic culture in Costa Rica on the other hand, how these contexts determine and shape the transnational political engagement among people in the diaspora will be discussed.

POLITICAL TRANSNATIONALITY

Defining politics within the realm of migrants' and refugees' multiple transnational practices is a difficult task (Glick Schiller, 2004; Vertovec, 2003). Still, many studies have sought to establish a mapping of these engagements.

One way of approaching the issue is by defining the *kinds of actors* involved. This is mainly done from a class or scale perspective: from above, such as elitist agency; or from below, such as grass-roots political transnationalism (Smith and Guarnizo, 1998; Smith, 1994). Another approach is to look at *directions of practices* in terms of country of origin, country of destination, or both. This is often correlated to different *forms of practice*, like "electoral" or "non-electoral" political participation as proposed by Guarnizo, Portes and Haller (2003).[1] Østergaard-Nielsen (2001, 2003) underlines a further distinction regarding home country related activities in her distinctions between "diaspora politics" (often dealing with more sensitive political issues) and "trans-local politics" (directed towards a specific locality in the home country). These different forms of home country engagements, she argues, may take place directly in the home country or indirectly from abroad.

Itzigsohn et al. (1999) have developed a more specified mapping of transnational activities of different kinds, enveloped in four categories: economic, political, civil-societal and cultural practices. Each of these categories is positioned within an analytical scheme of "broad" and "narrow" transnational practices, seen as "opposite ends" (Østergaard-Nielsen, 2003) or "poles" in a continuum, defined by degrees of: institutionalization, involvement and movement (Itzigsohn et al., 1999). For example, doing transnational politics in the *narrow* sense refers to a rather institutionalized pattern of regular political participation with a high degree of movement involved, while *broad* transnational practices refer to less institutionalized activities on an occasional basis and without necessarily involving movement, or at least only sporadically. The pattern can be rather complex by creating parallel continua: a specific activity could be narrow in one dimension (for example: high level of institutionalization), and "broad" in another dimension (for example: only sporadic or no movement involved). In all cases along the continuum, both country of origin and destination are included as reference points.

Likewise, different attempts have been made to map the influence that home or host countries' political opportunity structures impose on transnational political activities, for example, the way outreaching or negative state policies shape these activities (Landolt, Autler and Baires, 1999; Østergaard-Nielsen, 2003; Levitt and Glick Schiller, 2003). Similar correlations are made with reference to, for example, migration and socio-economic status, length of stay, age, generation, gender and so on (Guarnizo, Portes and Haller, 2003). However, as underlined by the same authors, it seems that such functional modes of understanding the *why's and how's* in political transnationalism are confusing, not least because they often comprise opposite and contradictory claims. Or, at best, they do not cover the broader tissue of determining factors. Instead, such approaches seem to establish an aggregate of short-cut dichotomies. Thus, as proposed by Guarnizo, Portes and Haller (2003), greater sensitivity should be given to include a wider and more connected repertoire of changing contextual conditions and uneven distribution of diverse practices, in concert with an attention directed towards the social and spatial bounded-ness of transnational activities. Although these activities occur across borders, they are still played out in "specific territorial jurisdictions", in located settings. Thus, in other words, the transnational political field has

Living Across Worlds: Diaspora, Development and Transnational Engagement

to be diversified, contextualized and widened. This could be an urge towards including the "fuzzier dimensions" (Østergaard-Nielsen, 2000) of transnational political agency, and to include other kinds of determinants.

Along these lines, I suggest expanding the field of *broad political transnationality*. To illustrate this argument, some empirical data from my fieldwork among Nicaraguans in San José is presented. These data show a range of elite-driven activities, which could be coined "non-political" in the narrow sense, and partly political in the broad sense. However, from another analytical point of departure, these activities can be understood as important political driving forces in processes of democratization, such as the important links between different layers of the diaspora, as shown in my study. These links or ties can be explained and understood with reference to strong and weak ties, as defined by Granovetter (1973).

HORIZONTAL AND VERTICAL TIES

In his writings about strong and weak ties, Granovetter places special focus on the "strength" of weak ties (Granovetter, 1973). His basic idea is that weak ties among "unknown" persons are much more effective in terms of opening up to the world and broadening the life perspectives and opportunity structures than are strong ties among "known" persons. Weak ties can function as a bridge to wider networks and hitherto unexplored fields and strategies of action in terms of information, influence, innovation and mobility.

Converted into a migration context, migrants' ways and routes of manoeuvring in order to make their migration projects happen and succeed not only depend on strong ties between kin and friends. Also weak ties among unknown persons are at play (Borge, 2004). Weak ties are established as networks between groups, not within groups.

I use the logic here transferred to class. What I call vertical ties are weak ties among people from different classes, while horizontal ties are strong ties among people from the same class. The definition of ties as not only social ones, but also resting on symbolic functions, is an important insight in this context (Faist, 2000). The idea is to understand the strength of weak, vertical ties as bridges across class divisions in political processes related to polarized societies and polarized political cultures. The diversities between different types of ties are reflected in different forms of loyalties. The weak, vertical ties are established by the elites and based on differences between top and bottom. The ties express solidarity with the people in the form of empathy, and a more objective political form of commitment to "the cause", which is "bigger" than the people. The strong, horizontal ties among the people/the masses are based on equity expressed through reciprocity and solidarity. Reciprocity is here defined as mutual obligations related to individual causes, while solidarity comprises the intertwined commitment to politics as a "big issue" and politics as a "personal issue", closely connected to their own everyday situation as oppressed masses.[2]

What gives the weak ties strength, as used in this context, relates to the value of the ties as political tools aimed at creating new grounds for a democratic political culture. Enhancing tolerance, civic participation and the general claim of rights form part of what a broadening of political transnationality means in this context. In the following, I present and analyse the activities in question, with point of departure in the Nicaraguan history of flight and migration.

FLIGHT AND MIGRATION: THE NICARAGUAN CONTEXT

For decades, Central America has been a region of vast migratory flows, both intra-regional and outward migration, in particular to the United States. The root causes of these movements are a mixture of structural changes at the socio-economic level, poverty and the search for economic improvement, natural disasters, and violent political conflict. From the 1980s onwards, these regional and transcontinental migratory flows have been linked to the civil wars in Nicaragua, El Salvador and Guatemala, in all of which countries large-scale displacements took place, both as flows of internally displaced persons and as border-crossing flows of refugees to neighbouring countries and to USA. The fact that 90 per cent of the Central Americans living in the USA arrived *after* 1980, underlines the politicized context of these flows. By that time, the number of uprooted people in the region exceeded 2 million (Hamilton and Chinchilla, 1991). Though return thus became an option in the aftermath of conflict in Central America, major groups of former refugees decided to remain in their respective host countries (Stepputat, 1997), thus merging into a situation of transnational migrancy.

The Nicaraguan case of flight and migration provides a clear illustration of this blurred area between refugee-ness and migrancy. Furthermore, it shows how the changing political situation in post-conflict societies shapes the flows in and out of the country many years *after* the conflict has officially ended. Since the Sandinista revolution in 1979, there has been three waves of migration involving Nicaragua: political refugees fleeing the socialist revolution (1979-80); mixed flows as a consequences of the political reorganization of 1981-82 and the years that followed, and the last ongoing flow in response to the aftermath of civil war and the worsening economic situation from 1989/90 and onwards (Funkhauser, 1992). The spatial distribution is sharply divided into a transcontinental flow towards the North (USA) and a regional flow, mainly to Costa Rica.

The first ones who fled after the outbreak of revolution comprised a huge number of right-wing, upper-class groups, who had supported the ousted president Somoza. They went straight to the USA, where many of them received asylum as political refugees (CIREFCA, 1989; Torres and Jimenez, 1985). They settled mainly in Miami, and linked up with compatriot elite groups who already had established economic ties there. Through the 1980s and 1990s, other layers with different political views and socio-economic backgrounds added to the diversification of the pattern in the US. Among those who fled regionally during the first wave, the majority went either to Honduras or Costa Rica, mainly Miskitu Indians from the Atlantic Coast, but also "ladinos", including groups of contra recruits. In Costa Rica, the latter groups mainly belonged to the upper class layers, who little by little "rooted" into the Costa Rican society with great success. A wider range of professionals and middle-class people followed suite in the early 1980s and onwards, covering a broader political tissue and having mixed economic and political motives. Among them were many former Sandinistas who took the consequences of their political discontent and their professional marginalization, especially after the take over of government by Violetta Chamorro in 1990. These groups are well-educated and function as highly qualified professionals in business, trade, administration, investment and academia (Castro, 2002).

THE NICA-TICA CONNECTION

From the early and mid-1990s, Nicaraguan migration to Costa Rica changed dramatically. In addition to the relatively small group of better-off exiles and expatriates, huge masses of poor Nicas[3] boomed into Costa Rica in search for work and better living conditions. According to the latest official figures (INEC, 2001), 226,374 persons were registered in Costa Rica in the year 2000. This figure does not cover temporal migration, temporal return or undocumented migration. If such migrants are included, various estimates indicate the number of Nicaraguan migrants in Costa Rica to fluctuate between 400,000 and 500,000.[4]

This last group of migrants has a very different socio-economic profile than the already established groups, and consequently very different conditions for living their lives as migrants. They belong mainly to the working class with a predominance of people in productive ages (20-39) and with equal gender representation. The prime motive for migration is economic: poverty and lack of job opportunities at home. Certain working areas along gender lines are clear: most of the women work as *domésticas*, mainly in the urban San José area, but also in areas closer to the border zones, while the men work in construction and private security in the same urban settings, or in agriculture in rural areas. The living conditions are precarious for many, with wretched housing facilities and low wages and exploitative working conditions. In addition, they are confronted with a growing xenophobic and hostile Costa Rican society, including both civil society (*los Ticos*[5]) and the state. A tightening up of migration laws, regulations and control mechanisms literally criminalizes the migrant situation as such (*El Nuevo Diario*, 2003; Sandoval (Ed.), 2000; Ministerio de Salud, Flacso et al., 2003; Morales and Castro, 1999, 2002).

As demonstrated, the Nicaraguan migrants or diaspora consist of differentiated and partly separated groups of people. The middle- and upper-class layers are definitely not representative for the diaspora as a whole, neither in terms of profile nor numbers, but they are significant as representatives for the

Spaces of Democratic Practice: Nicaraguans in San José, Costa Rica

variety within the diaspora and because of their transnational engagement. These activities cover a wide range of areas along very different lines, such as economic investments, political infiltration, and socio-cultural trade and activities. Apart from these activities, some – mainly former Sandinistas, but also people from broader anti-Somoza groups – are involved in what I call *messier* forms of politics or *micro-politics*, within a stretched version of broad political transnationality. These activities have linked people together across class divides. My argument is that the forms and determinants of these engagements map a new political culture among Nicaraguans in the diaspora, reflecting the merging of experiences from Costa Rica and what they brought with them from Nicaragua. The experiences gained from these activities and the activities themselves might become valuable drivers in processes of democratization within and across borders. Formal politics and economy are other important drivers.[6]

MICRO-POLITICS IN SAN JOSÉ

Three kinds of activities have taken off in Costa Rica during recent years, mainly taking their point of departure in San José, the capital. First, the fast-growing interdisciplinary research interest in the issue of migration and diasporas, specifically with regard to the Nicaraguan case (Sandoval, 2002; Morales and Castro, 2002; Orozco, 2003; Borge, 2004). Secondly, a number of migrant-oriented activities initiated by individuals or networks of organizations and associations, all aiming at "helping the poor migrants". Finally, similar projects are seen within the media. Many of these are initiated and run by middle- and upper-class *Nicaraguans* staying in Costa Rica but with active transnational ties to their country of origin, not least through these activities, all of which have parallels in Nicaragua.

The school

Every single Sunday, a bunch of 100-150 Nicaraguan migrants pick up their pencils, papers and notebooks and take the bus (or walk if they cannot afford the bus ticket) to a borrowed public school in Central San José to learn English, from scratch. For most of them, it is their only day off. They have many day-to-day problems related to their lives as transnational migrants, and most of them have not had much schooling. But nevertheless, *they come* and join the project in spite of internal diversities in terms of age, sex, marital status, migrational circumstances and so on. Most of them have a plan: They want to improve their living conditions through better jobs, either in Costa Rica, USA, or preferably Nicaragua. First of all, they are willing to do something beyond day-to-day-survival strategies in order to become in charge of their own lives. As exemplified by José, the leader of the school, who himself is from Nicaragua though married to a *tica* for 15 years and working in a tourist agency specialized in Nicaragua tours. He came in the 1980s and stayed. Through his job and a personal, continuous commitment to Nicaragua and Nicaraguans, he started this Sunday school about two years ago. It is voluntary work, and he has engaged an American expatriate to help him run the classes from 9-12. He does this because of a social commitment directed towards the poor migrants from Nicaragua, a socio-ecclesiastical commitment connected to his religious upbringing, and a political commitment that is part of his Sandinista heritage and his own childhood experiences. He explains:

> Primarily because I am from Nicaragua. I come from a very poor family. When I was a child, we were eight brothers and sisters. My father died when I was nine years; my mother was alone taking care of eight children. In days like these, where it's rainy and the climate,… It's cold for us, not for you. We were very hungry with almost nothing to eat, so I understand what the people feel in this little "suburb". So, I think I'm lucky because I had this chance. Now I'm working in tourism, but I was a preacher. I wanted to preach to help people. But then I saw the preachers with good cars, beautiful houses, and then I said how come. I don't want to live from the money people are giving to the church. And the principal told me that I was a kind of revolutionary. I had in my mind the idea of helping the people. …When I moved to Costa Rica, I saw the situation of the migrants, and one day a man came to my house, knocking on the door – he was begging for something to eat. At that moment I just remembered my childhood. And I prepared him a bag. And I thought: what can I do for these people? And I started this English course. Normally, the jobs they can get are pretty hard jobs. They can have a better chance if they learn English…

All these commitments colour the set-up of his school and make it look like a kind of Paulo Freirian re-socializing project, where English is actually only the means to other greater projects: The migrants discuss politics, de-polarization, reconciliation, discrimination, ambitions, work and leisure. In complete contrast with their working conditions, this is a self-defined location in a rather equal environment with a democratic culture emerging as part of the project.

The restaurant

A portrait of Rubén Darío, the national poet above all others, hangs on the wall in the restaurant along with old photos of Managua dating back from colonial times before the earthquake in 1972, which practically destroyed the city. The flag is there and the front of the restaurant is painted in corresponding patterns in blue and white. The food is definitely *comidas típicas* and *típicas* are the employers and employed, too. Apparently pure nostalgia and patriotism!

Even though the Nicaraguans have been present in San José in large and visible numbers for many years now, this is a new thing. There are about 4 to 6 restaurants and a few more humble *sodas* in San José, and they have all been established recently. A positive attitude towards Nicaraguans and Nicaraguan culture has not been on anybody's agenda before. This restaurant was set up for exactly this purpose. The owner, Fernando, is a rich Nicaraguan who has been in Costa Rica since the decline of the Sandinista era, which he was a part of. He owns a big construction firm but is engaged in a range of activities aimed at helping and rendering visible the Nicaraguan migrants in Costa Rica. He is also a moneymaker, but he makes some of his money work for the poor migrants' cause. He has invested in reconstruction projects in one of the poorest and most wretched migrant settings in San José. He is also working for better consulate practices, for example, for voting from abroad in Nicaraguan elections. The conditions of employment for the Nicaraguans working in his restaurants are better than elsewhere (though still very poor). He explains:

> This restaurant and my idea with it is to "guide" and influence the Nicaraguan migrants, so that they are not against the Costa Ricans and vice versa. So that they integrate little by little, get accustomed to each other. I call it transculturation. I think the Nicaraguans should stop trying to hide their Nicaraguan-ness. But they should also learn from the Ticos. In Nicaragua, the national sport is *la política*, here it is *el fútbol*. In Nicaragua, the polarization is enormous. Here, I think it is different. I think the Nica who goes back to Nicaragua will not be the same Nica who left. The Ticos know something very important: to come to terms, … So I think there will be a very important influence from the Ticos to the Nicas here.

This restaurant is a meeting place across those polarizations: Everybody meets here, lower classes, middle and upper classes mainly, but not only Nicaraguans. They come because they love Nicaragua, the food and the atmosphere. The interesting part is that from time to time they meet each other across class divides and other divides. A new dialogue is obviously taking place, headed and personalized with Fernando's "initials".

Diplomacy and church

Diplomacy has always loved charity – and so has the Church. In San José, the Nicaraguans in both categories shake hands in different projects for the poor Nicaraguan migrants. *Las Damas Nicaraguenses* is a group of well-meaning diplomatic and other upper-class ladies who do a lot of charity work specifically directed toward their poorer compatriot migrants. They collect money and things to be distributed, and they arrange lotteries, make free meals and the like. But they are also engaged in more concrete projects for the betterment of life and housing conditions, workshops about childcare, health and cooking - especially in one of the poorest and most feared migrant areas in town (Herrera et al., 2001). In this environment, they sometimes participate in Mass held by the Nicaraguan *Padre*, who himself, like the ladies, is a Nicaraguan "migrant", even though they do not use the term with reference to themselves. This poor area belongs to the Padre's parish, and he is eagerly engaged in different social projects here, some of them with *las Damas*. The owner of the restaurant, Fernando, is a well-known and beloved figure in this environment where he has invested in rebuilding projects. Fernando sees it this way:

I'm a very good friend of this environment. I am their counsellor.
I have facilitated the water constructions. I got the school built.
When I knew this place about eight years ago, there were about
15,000 persons living there; now it's 35,000, 70% are Nicara-
guans. … Nobody is actually doing anything for them.. Anyway,
I try…

Along the same lines, different Catholic Church organizations, like
Caritas/Pastoral Social, are deeply involved in issues of human and civil rights
for migrants. They are organized in parallel in Nicaragua, and they work
closely together with people from all the other initiatives mentioned. Regarding the actual debate in Costa Rica about launching a new more restrictive
migration law, the church is actually one of the few public voices speaking
out for migrants' rights, apart from the network-organizations mentioned below. Thus, I argue that not *only* charity or social commitment is at play; so are
gestures of compatriotism across class divisions. This is a new socio-political
experience for all layers. The elites have a political agenda, although it is
informal and partly covert but with a clear democratic direction.

Networks, organizations and the media

In 2002, a Nicaraguan network of civil society organizations involved
in the migration issue was constituted in Managua with the participation of
22 organizations (Red Nicaraguense de la Sociedad Civil para las Migraciones, 2003). The participating organizations had different profiles before,
such as human and civil rights, refugees and development, women, professional rights, research and media, but now, through the constitution of the
network, they have joined under the migration umbrella with the explicit
goal of promoting fair conditions and dignity for (compatriot) migrants. In
terms of vision and mission, a clone of this network exists in San José. Here
a supplementary *foro* has monthly meetings for the exchange of information
and discussions of strategies and activities. In the near future, a bi-national
gathering of the two network structures is planned.

Two organizations in San José are specifically visible and well-known
for their work with Nicaraguan migrant women. One of them, ASTRADOMES
(Asociación de Trabajadores Domésticas de Costa Rica), is functioning as a
trade-union for domestic workers. They have fought for better working conditions and better wages, delivered free legal advice and have arranged workshops informing about rights and duties. A twin organization is about to be
established in Nicaragua, initiated by returned migrant women "trained" in
San José in the women's organization. The other organization, CENDEROS
(Centro Nicaraguense de Derechos Sociales de Inmigrante en Costa Rica),
works with psycho social counselling within a broadly defined framework
but mainly targeted at building self-esteem, cultural pride, socio-political
conscience and capability. They have recently established an associational
network of Nicaraguan migrant women in Costa Rica with the participation of hundreds of women from all over the country, and with the Church
organizations represented, too. In order to strengthen their efforts, these two
organizations plan to establish a more formal cooperation in the near future
and expand their bonds in Nicaragua.

Spaces of Democratic Practice: Nicaraguans in San José, Costa Rica

The leading team of CENDEROS are all professional Nicaraguan middle-class women with individual migration histories dating back to the mid-1980s and onwards. Maria explains:

> We have worked with more or less 6-700 women, Nicaraguan women from the lower classes. We have a psycho-social focus, and we include the recent history of Nicaragua. Nicaragua has been hit by many phenomena: natural disasters, hurricanes, earthquake, the war, unemployment. … For example, when the revolution failed, was lost, so was the life project of many Nicaraguans. Many were convinced that this project was good in order to develop the country and help the young ones. I thought so, as did thousands of Nicaraguans, maybe the majority, because it was the people's project with the Sandinista ideology. When it failed, so did the ideals, the dreams. … So the migration started as political, then it became economic.

> And we think we cannot return now. We can do more from here. Through my contribution here, I can strengthen the Nicaraguans. We try in CENDEROS to heal the wounds, to make people get new hopes and dreams. …

Along similar lines, different initiatives have taken off within the media, especially through different popular radio programmes, where a transnational voice directed towards Nicaraguan migrants in Costa Rica and their families back home has been heard in both countries during the last couple of years: *Radio CuCu*, *"Buscando la vida"* (In search for better life), *"Mujeres sin fronteras"* (Women without borders), *"Esta semana"* (This week). Some of the people involved are the same as those engaged in the above-mentioned initiatives. One of the radio programmes runs every day from 12 am to 2 pm, opening the air for music, information, interviews with key persons engaged in the migration issue, good advice, legal counsel, and above all, the opportunity for the listeners to send messages – without cost - to family members in Nicaragua and vice versa. Enrique, one of the involved journalists, says:

> It has been very interesting, because this programme was the first directed towards Nicaraguans, playing their music, singing their songs. People are so moved that they start crying. They also send messages to family members whom they haven't seen for years. It's like a social link…

All these activities give evidence of a growing and still more coherent *interaction* between different layers of the diaspora, headed by the elite groups. These are the main drivers in different democratic projects encapsulated in the activities: the questioning and reformulation of an old and "inherited" hierarchical and polarized political culture from Nicaragua; the revival of a Sandinista-inspired, non-hierarchical political culture of participation; the construction of ties between different layers of the diaspora, and the floating of a public counter-discourse about migration and specifically about poor *Nicaraguan* migrants. In the analytical scheme of Itzigsohn et al., some of these activities might be categorized within the narrow or broad field of "civil-societal" transnationality. But my argument here is that the more or less exposed political agenda of these activities make them "political", and that many similar activities with an important political "bite" might not be discovered at all, if the notion of transnational political action is too narrow.

In order to understand the wider determinants for such engagement, I suggest scrutinizing three parameters that have already been touched upon, and which seem to be significant: political culture, types of ties across class divides, and discourses on flight and migration.

DEMOCRATIZATION AND POLITICAL CULTURES

Diamond (2003) raises the question whether the whole world can become democratic. His answer is yes – no matter what preconditions may exist (poverty, religion, culture, etc.). A crucial point is that the nation's elite attempts to govern by democratic means and that a continuous pressure from below urges them to do so. In order to make these democratic processes happen, national, international and transnational drivers are at play, not least through the building of a culture of democracy. The building of a culture of democracy implies new norms of tolerance, trust, respect, civility and participation through civil society education in a broad sense and incentives to minimize economic and political polarizations. Thus, a definition of democratic political culture includes two main elements: One is the possibility for "extensive political participation", such as the right to organize civic groups, to work for political parties, to protest and to vote. The second is political tolerance or "inclusive political values", which refers to the willingness to "extend civil rights to proponents of unpopular causes" (Booth and Seligson, 1993).

Diamond gives a simple and minimal definition of democracy: "a system of government in which the people choose their leaders at regular intervals through free, fair and competitive elections". This definition of democracy frames an electoral democracy, which can contain violations of human rights, corruption and a generally weak rule of law. But one of his points here is that democracy in this minimal form can (and does) exist in all types of states in all regions of the world, even in very poor countries. In this sense, democracy can be said to have a kind of universal value. As referred to before, the political performance or the political culture of the elite groups at the top and the civil society at the bottom will be decisive elements in the further consolidation of democracy.

As is the case of many third world countries, Nicaragua is *lacking* a history of democratic rule from which experiences can be used towards creating the foundation for a new democratic political culture. The general picture in Nicaraguan history since the 19th century has been one of political polarization between conservatives and liberals, with the power shifting

Spaces of Democratic Practice: Nicaraguans in San José, Costa Rica

between the two, each of which has rather firmed positions. The intervention of the civil society in the form of democratic political institutions has been very limited (Anderson, 2003; Paguaga, 2002). In more recent history, three characteristics have effectively prevented processes of democratization from happening: One is the long duration of the Somoza dictatorship (1936-1979) that concentrated power among the elite groups, primarily within the Somoza family. Another is the high level of foreign interventions in domestic politics, which leads to the last point: the low level of domestic solutions to conflicts (see Paguaga, 2002 for this last argument).

With the overthrow of the dictator in 1979, the popular sectors of society became involved for the first time in political processes. Unfortunately, the Sandinistas later undermined this promising start through the exclusion and elimination of oppositional social and political forces. Thus, the official launching of the Nicaraguan democracy, or rather the fragile transition process towards an electoral democracy did not take place until Violetta Chamorro's victory in the 1990 elections. Likewise, this shift marked the elimination of explicit violence as a route to power in Nicaraguan politics (Seligson, 1995). However, during the following period of Arnoldo Alemán (1996-2001), former grounds for authoritarian rule were reinstalled. As argued by Close (2003), it seems that the political parties in Nicaragua have weakened democracy rather than strengthened it. Locations of a new course should preferably be found in changes in political culture, political institutions and the influence of citizen action.

Such steps *were* actually taken in the sixties, promoted through the Catholic Church and the political radicals and culminating in the ideological project of the Sandinista revolution, which led to the creation of what could be called "a participatory political culture" (Paguaga, 2002). However, the leadership performance of Daniel Ortega followed the well-known characteristics of "strong man's leadership", or *caudillismo*, along the same lines as the following presidents, Violetta Chamorro (though to a lesser extent) and Arnoldo Alemán. With the election in November 2001 of Enrique Bolaños, a person entered office who had much looser ties to the party, a cleaner (declared anti-corruptive) style of governance, and less inclination to "political bossism" or *caudillismo* (Close, 2003). In addition to the stabilizing fact that peace has apparently become permanent, this presidential choice might be an indication of a new course in the political culture going against "dispositions towards authority" (Diamond (Ed.), 1993). At least, this seems to be the route taken by major segments of Nicaraguan society. Nevertheless, a more *definite* change of the political culture is still in the making.

DISCOURSES ON FLIGHT AND MIGRATION

The micro-scale transnational activities discussed in this chapter can be understood as local reactions to discourses on flight and migration on a national/regional and international/global level. In the context of Central America, there is no reason to believe that the migration flows, whether intra-regional or towards the North, will decrease in the years ahead due to economic hardship in home countries and the existence of employment niches in the host countries, especially for less-skilled labour (Morales and Gaitán, 2000). But the agendas and attitudes of the involved governments are divided: Much evidence indicates that migration may induce strengthening of transnational ties and become an important regional factor promoting peace, democracy and development (*World Migration Report*, IOM, 2003). This tendency is reflected at government levels in the sense that some at these levels become transnational actors themselves by virtue of far-reaching initiatives aimed at migrant populations (Roberts et al., 1999; Glick Schiller and Fouron, 2001). Such initiatives cover, for example, directing and/or facilitating remittance transfers; the possibility of voting abroad; the granting of dual citizenship; the defence of migrants' human rights; proactive consular policies and different kinds of linkage programmes between nationals abroad and in the home country (*World Migration Report*, 2003). In the region, El Salvador provides an example of such a very proactive interrelationship between transnational migrants' activities and home country policy (Landolt et al., 1999), while the Nicaraguan case is an example of the opposite tendency: a policy of neglect and invisibilization on the part of the home country, hand in hand with a negative attitude on the part of the regional host country, Costa Rica (Cortés Ramos, 2003; Morales and Castro, 2002).

In Costa Rica, migration became a public issue, when the huge influx of poor Nicaraguans appeared throughout the 1990s. A master discourse of rejection and marginalization was launched, portraying the migrants as potential *threats* (Sandoval, 2002). This "threat" was partly related to the potential negative influence of Nicaraguan political and cultural views and practices on Costa Rican society, but mainly linked to the fear of *poverty*. As a relatively more prosperous third-world country, Costa Rica fears the possible negative impact on society due to an "uncontrollable and massive intrusion" of poor migrants. The master discourse on migrants in Costa Rica is thus a discourse on one specific *country*: Nicaragua, on certain *segments* of Nicaraguan migrants, and linked to one specific issue: poverty. All elements of fears of *poverty* are included: criminality, diseases, contamination, bad housing, bad manners, many children, low educational level, etc. This class-specific picture of the migrant population leaves out the other segments of Nicaraguan migrants, including those launching a counter-discourse that relates to compassion for the weak and persecuted co-citizen and compatriot.

A more globally installed discourse on migration is the one relating to issues of security and democracy. At a global level, a direct response to September 11 has been the reinforcement of the migration-security nexus: a "securitization of the migration issue" (Faist, 2002; Wæver et al., 1993) with increased control and exclusion strategies on the one hand, along with an urge for democracy-building in countries of origin on the other. As shown, the Nicaraguan case of flight and migration, and the way the diaspora responds to it, is part of these stories. In this case, poverty and Nicaraguan culture and politics are the threatening elements against which security and control mechanisms are activated.

This internationalized discourse on flight and migration as a matter of *security* and *control* has implicated some interesting paradoxes, which also relate to the Nicaraguan case and the way the diaspora takes action. For example, when trying to blame the victim ("the migrants") for breaking the laws in different ways, the national governments expose themselves to accusations of being lawbreakers in terms of limiting or jeopardizing established human, civil and political rights through their politics of criminalizing the migrant situation and constructing migrants as marginalized "others". The migrants' response to this can be manifold. As demonstrated, the Nicaraguan migrants, headed by the elite groups, become more proactive in claiming such rights in tandem with claiming and spreading these rights at a higher scale in relation to their more undemocratic country of origin.[7] Their own transnational engagement and the public discourses surrounding it thus raise issues of rights, democracy and political culture, issues that might not have been questioned or re-thought without the internationalization and securitization of the migration issue.

WHY ARE THE ELITES ENGAGED IN THEIR POOR COMPATRIOTS?

As shown, the political history of Nicaragua is marked by changes to excess: authoritarianism combined with a political culture of polarization, violence, and *caudillismo* on the one hand, and revolutionary upheaval including an intermezzo of a culture of participation on the other. The installation of an electoral democracy is until now the most convincing attempt towards the construction of a political project of democratization. This political landscape of past and present is an important backdrop for shaping political engagement in the Nicaraguan diaspora, together with what has been learned about democracy in Costa Rica.

It can be observed that in spite of the explicit class diversification in the diaspora population, as well as different migration histories, different opportunities in the host country and a criss-crossing of political stands, a joint venture of micro-political actions has emerged lately, as described above. When the upper- and middle-class groups, i.e. the elites, engage in making workshops for the "poor", collecting money for charity, or producing radio programmes for marginalized *Nicas*, it can be seen as an expanded field of "broad political activity". These activities are not really institutionalized; they happen on a very irregular basis, and there is not necessarily any movement involved, although there is an explicit reference to both home and host countries. Though situated at the margins of what could be called political, these activities certainly have a political agenda attached, the main goal being "more democracy" in transnational space.

When the elite groups take action to help their compatriots through newly established vertical, weak ties, this is a common legacy from the Sandinista period and the Sandinista participatory political culture. Thus, these actions are explicit marks of a political commitment as well as an act of solidarity with *el pueblo* and an attempt to educate *el pueblo*. At the same time, it is a way of promoting the rights-based agenda of democracy that has been learned and practiced in Costa Rica.

Furthermore, it is an act *of creating images*. First, we have the creation of an image of a professional who is involved in career-generating activities. I term this image *a professional, status-generating image*. Secondly, we have the creation of an image of the political activist, which I call *a solidarity image*, and in extension of this, we have the creation of an image of the political leader, which I term *an elite image*. Furthermore, an important determinant behind the activities is the urge to engage in giving the diaspora, or rather the poor segments of the diaspora, a "public face" of dignity and power, thus establishing a public counter-discourse. This feeds into the creation of an image of a *new diasporic public sphere*.

In spite of linking the elites with the poor and stigmatized *Nicas* through their engagements as described above, it seems that their hitherto unquestioned position as well-off and successful professional "Nicaraguans in Costa Rica" has not been challenged by these engagements, nor by the mere presence of a relatively recent influx of poor *Nicas*, who now comprise the absolute majority of Nicaraguans in Costa Rica. Hence, the elites are not being lumped with the *Nicas*. One explanation of this is that the problematization and stigmatization of Nicaraguan migrants in Costa Rica is first and foremost linked to class – followed by race, culture, politics and history.

Hence, the implications for the elites point in another direction. It seems that the very presence of the poor *Nicas* has given birth to a new and longed-for *political field* (Bourdieu, 1992). This political field is a site that has become transnational and enrolled in complex processes of subjectivation (the self) and objectivation (the political) related to the past, the present and the future. The elites have positioned themselves as political representatives located somewhere "between party and class". The relationship between party and class is according to Bourdieu a "symbolic relation between a signifier and a signified, or, better, between *representatives* providing a *representation* and the agents, actions and situations that are represented" (Bourdieu, 1992: 182). In this case, we are not facing political diversities or polarizations within the transnational political field we are talking about, but rather a merging of political objectives. The political project is a project of transformation: The hidden and almost forgotten "diaspora within" has transformed into a public self, which performs public acts in a public space. It is the creation of a political field through a political intention:

> Moving from the implicit to the explicit, from one's subjective impression to objective expression, to public manifestation in the form of a discourse or public act, constitutes in itself an act of institution and thereby represents a form of officialization and legitimation (Bourdieu, 1992: 173).

When the poor *Nicas* participate in these networks and activities to improve their conditions, or boost their self-esteem, it is a revival of a political memory from the early Sandinista heydays of the revolution, and an attempt to become pro-active in the shaping of a democratic political culture. The *Nicas* are not only enrolled in new vertical ties with the elites. Through these activities, they also revitalize their internal, horizontal, strong ties connected with migration experiences completely different from those of the elites. Basically, we have two different migration projects nurturing each other during the process of creating a third mutual project. Both groups have a shared knowledge and memory of politics and political culture from a Nicaragua that is lost and another one that is still in the making. This is an important ingredient in shaping the political platform created in the diaspora, where political discussions and everyday strategies for political actions are taking place. The non-formal character of the activities is a decisive legitimating element. The elites do not express any interest in either replicating a political landscape "from home", or creating new formal political party structures (not for the time being at least). As they make clear in word and action, their interest is rather the creation of a platform for democratic political cultures with "extensive political participation" through the organization of civic group education, and the furthering of political tolerance demonstrated through their own political performance.

So, what we can see from these examples is the creation of a joined diasporic political platform built on links between classes within the diaspora itself. Through the articulation of claims spanning national borders and internal oppositions (like class, political stands, economic situation and opportunity structures), a transnational political field is being constructed. What will be the long-term results of this new space for "doing politics" in a broad transnational way remains an open question.

DIASPORA AS PLATFORM FOR POLITICS

This chapter intended to paint a picture of a highly diversified diaspora. In spite of these diversifications, internal links across class divides have been established, and an ability to create a competing counter-discourse of flight and migration, mainly through the claim of rights, has been articulated. In the national and local context of Costa Rica and San José respectively, the disloyalty agenda[8] towards poor Nicaraguans has awoken a dormant middle-class solidarity with *el pueblo*, in itself an iconized, dormant reminiscence from the Sandinista period and the left-wing, politicized 1960s and 1970s. Hence, the transnational migration issue has put democracy and political culture on the agenda in both Nicaragua and Costa Rica.

The Nicaraguan diaspora in Costa Rica is not highly organized or organizing, as for example, the Salvadoran diaspora in the US. In the strict sense, they are not very active politically, neither in an electoral or a non-electoral way. Their home country government is not at all out-reaching. However, by including a broader definition of what *doing politics* in transnational space means, a huge range of activities become uncovered.

These activities were defined as incipient political expressions, and as expressions of a changing political culture that emphasizes the claiming and spreading of rights. From this point of view, the importance of looking at diasporas as *locations of change* is underlined, as is the socio-political commitment articulated across class divides. This commitment is seen as a possible platform for doing politics. This platform can of course be used in different ways. In this case, the political intentions for strengthening processes of *democratization*, both in home and host country, seem to be the master plan.

NOTES

1. "Electoral participation" includes: membership in a political party in the country of origin, monetary contributions to these parties, and active involvement in political campaigns. "Non-electoral participation" includes: membership in a hometown civic association, membership in a charity organization and monetary contributions to civic projects (Guarnizo, Portes and Haller, 2003: 1223).
2. For a detailed proposal for the analytical use of these terms: loyalty; reciprocity and solidarity in a migration context, see Faist (2000).
3. Nicas is a pejorative term used for the poorer segments of the Nicaraguan migrant population in Costa Rica. They also use it themselves, though, as slang.
4. This figure represents a good deal more than 10 per cent of the 3.8 million residents of Costa Rica, and a little more than 10 per cent of the native population in Nicaragua (4.8 million). Including those in USA, around 20 per cent of the Nicaraguan population resides outside their country of origin (Morales and Castro, 2002; *World Migration Report,* 2003).
5. Ticos is a neutral slang term for "Costa Ricans".
6. At the economic level, it is widely documented around the world that migrants have become the key source of income for their families back home and on a wider scale for their country, through enormous amounts of remittances. In the case of Nicaragua, the estimated amount from USA and Costa Rica is at least 500 million dollars per year, representing one-quarter of the GDP of Nicaragua (Orozco, 2003). These economic transfers are one type among other very concrete economic diaspora-home country ties, that are as diverse as tourism, telecommunication, transportation and nostalgic trade (the five T's as proposed by Orozco (2003).
7. The networks and groups of "activists" described in the chapter are quite active and still more successful in gaining access to dialogues with the Nicaraguan state. Their claims for voting rights from abroad and the possibility for obtaining a "cédula" (identification paper) through the consulate instead of having to travel to Nicaragua to get it, are still more "noisy" claims. They have recently opened a concrete dialogue with representatives from the government, together with the Nicaraguan diaspora in Miami, which held a First Congress in June 2004.
8. The "disloyalty agenda" refers to the negative master discourse against migrants, as described above (see Faist 2000 for the use of the term).

REFERENCES

Anderson, L.E.
2003   "Partidos en transición en nicaragua: La contribución de los partidos predemocráticos a una nueva democracia", Paper presented
at the I Congreso Centro Americano de Ciencias Políticas, UCA,
San José, 12-14 August.

Booth, J.A., and M.A. Seligson
1993   "Paths to democracy and the political culture of Costa Rica, Mexico and Nicaragua", in L. Diamond (Ed.), *Political Culture and Democracy in Developing Countries*, Lynne Rienner, Boulder.

Borge, D.
2004   "Migraciones de nicaraguenses hacia Costa Rica: Analisis de dos
redes sociales", UCA, San José.

Bourdieu, P.
1992   *Language and Symbolic Power*, Polity Press, Cambridge.

Castro, C.
2002   "Informe inserción laboral y remesas de los inmigrantes nicaragüenses en Costa Rica", in A. Morales and C. Castro, *Redes
Transfronterizas: Sociedad, Empleo y Migración entre Nicaragua
y Costa Rica*, FLACSO, San José.

CIREFCA
1989   Documento de la republica de Costa Rica, Guatemala C.

Close, D.
2003   *Political Parties and Democracy in Nicaragua: Not Yet, Maybe
Someday*, Memorial University of Newfoundland, St. John's, NL,
Canada.

Cortés Ramos, A.
2003   "Reflexiones sobre la dinámica migratoria entre Nicaragua y
Costa Rica en los 90s", Paper presented at the I Congreso Centro
Americano de Ciencias Políticas, San José, UCA, 12-14 August.

Diamond, L. (Ed.),
1993   *Political Culture and Democracy in Developing Countries*, Lynne
Rienner, Boulder.

Diamond, L.
2003   *Can the Whole World Become Democratic? Democracy, Development and International Policies*, Scolarship Repository, University of California.

El Nuevo Diario
2003   "Ley migratoria tica recrudecerá xenofobia", 18 July.

Faist, T.
2000   *The Volume and Dynamics of International Migration and Transnational Social Spaces*, Clarendon Press, Oxford.
2002   "Extension du domaine de la lutte", International Migration and
Security Before and After September 11, 2001, *International Migration Review,* 36(1): 7-14.

Funkhauser, E.
1992   "Migration from Nicaragua: Some recent evidence", *World Development,* 20(8): 1209-18.

Glick Schiller, N.
2004 "Transnationality", in D. Nugent and J. Vincent (Eds), *A Companion to the Anthropology of Politics*, Blackwell Publishing Ltd., London.

Glick Schiller, N., and G.E. Fouron
2001 "George woke up laughing", *Long Distance Nationalism and the Search for Home*, Duke University Press, Durham and London.

Granovetter, M.
1973 "The strength of weak ties", *American Journal of Sociology,* 78(6): 1360-80.

Guarnizo, L.E., A. Portes, and W. Haller
2003 "Assimilation and transnationalism: Determinants of transnational political action among contemporary migrants", *American Journal of Sociology,* 108(6): 1211-48.

Hamilton, N., and N.S. Chinchilla
1991 "Central American migration: A framework for analysis", *Latin American Research Review,* 26(1): 75-110.

Herrera, M.M., A.M. Cordero, and E.O. Ferrero
2001 "Tejedores de Sobrevivencia: Redes de solidaridad de familias Nicaragüenses en Costa Rica: El caso de 'La Carpio", *Cuaderno de Ciencias Sociales*, 118, FLACSO, San José.

INEC (Instituto Nacional de Estadística y Censos)
2001 *IX Censo de Población y Vivienda 2000, Resultados Generales*, INEC, San José.

IOM
2003 *World Migration Report*, IOM, Geneva.

Itzigsohn, J., D.C. Carlos, E.H. Medina, and O. Vasquez
1999 "Mapping dominican transnationalism: Narrow and broad transnational practices", *Ethnic and Racial Studies,* 22(2): 316-339.

Landolt, P., L. Autler, and S. Baires
1999 "From hermano lejano to hermano mayor: The dialectics of Salvadoran transnationalism", *Ethnic and Racial Studies,* 22(2): 290-315.

Levitt, P., and N. Glick Schiller
2003 "Transnational perspectives on migration: Conceptualizing simultaneity", CMD Working Papers #03-09j, Princeton University.

Ministerio de Salud, FLACSO (et al.)
2003 *Migración y salud en Costa Rica: Elementos para su análisis*, San José.

Morales, A., and C. Castro
1999 *Inmigración laboral Nicaragüense en Costa Rica*, FLACSO, San José.
2002 "Redes transfronterizas: Sociedad", *Empleo y Migración entre Nicaragua y Costa Rica*, FLACSO, San José.

Morales, N., and D.Z. Gaitán
2000 *Migración de Nicaragüenses a Costa Rica: Impacto territorial y respuestos locales*, Centro de Investigación y Promoción de Habitat-HABITAR, Managua.
2003 "Family remittances to Nicaragua: Opportunities to increase the economic contributions of Nicaraguans living abroad", Report

commissioned by the US Department of Agriculture under a PASA for the US, Washington, DC.

Østergaard-Nielsen, E.
2000   "Transnational political practices and the state", Paper presented at the conference on migration and development, Princeton University.
2001   "The politics of migrants' transnational political practices", Transnational Communities Programme, Working Paper Series WPTC: 01-22, Oxford.
2003   *Transnational Politics—Turks and Kurds in Germany*, Routledge, London.

Paguaga, C.
2002   "Enrique Bolaños Geyer- A step towards consolidating democracy in Nicaragua", Policy Paper, FOCAL (Canadian Foundation for The Americas), Ontario.

Red Nicaraguense de la Sociedad Civil para las Migraciones
2003   "Memoria del primer foro nacional "las migraciones en las políticas públicas de Nicaragua y Costa Rica", Editorial Ciencias Sociales, Managua.

Roberts, B.R., R. Frank, and F. Lozano-Ascencio
1999   "Transnational migrant communities and Mexican migration to the US", *Ethnic and Racial Studies*, 22(2): 238-265.

Sandoval, C.
2002   *Otros Amenazantes: Los Nicaragüenses y la formación de identidades nacionales en Costa Rica*, EUCR, San José.

Sandoval, C. (Ed.)
2000   *Como me siento en Costa Rica? Autobiografías de nicaragüenses*, Instituto de Investigaciones Sociales, UCA, San José.

Seligson, M.A.
1995   "Nicaragua 1991-1995: Una cultura política en transicion", in R. Córdoba and G. Maihold (Eds), *Cultura Política y Transición Democrática en Nicaragua*, Fundación F. Ebert Guillermo Ungo, Instituto de Estudios Nicaragüenses (IEN), Centro de Análisis Sociocultural, UCA, Managua.

Smith, M.P.,
1994   "Can you imagine? Transnational migration and the globalization of grassroots politics", *Social Text*, 39:15-33.

Smith, M.P., and L.E. Guarnizo
1998   *Transnationalism from Below*, Transaction Publishers, New Brunswick, NJ.

Stepputat, F.
1997   "National conflict and repatriation: An analysis of relief, power and reconciliation", Unpublished Report, CDR, Copenhagen.

Torres, E., and D. Jimenez
1985   "Informe sobre el estado de las migraciones en centroamérica", *Anuario de Estudios Centroamericanos,* 11(2): 25-66.

Vertovec, S.
2003   "Migrant transnationalism and modes of transformation", CMD Working Paper #03-09m, Geneva.

Wæver, O., B. Buzan, M. Kelstrup, and P. Lemaitre
1993   *Identity, Migration, and the New Security Agenda in Europe*, Pinter Publishers Ltd., London.

Spaces of Democratic Practice: Nicaraguans in San José, Costa Rica

Somali-Scandinavian A Dreaming When "the Diaspora" Returns to the Desert[1]

Nauja Kleist

ABSTRACT

Somscan & UK Cooperative Associations is a Somali-Scandinavian-British transnational umbrella organization, founded in 2000. The purpose of the organization is collective return through collective acquisition of land and establishment of a new neighbourhood just outside the town of Burao in central Somaliland. In 2003, altogether 330 Somali families from Sweden, Denmark, Norway and the UK had bought land on a collective basis, and the plans for the new neighbourhood were ambitious. Situated in the dry semi-desert outside war-scarred and poor Burao, the envisioned neighbourhood includes spacious houses with modern kitchens, playgrounds, parking lots, a mosque, a park, a market and other facilities.

This chapter is based on a visit to the Somscan area as well as on interviews with Somscan & UK members in Somaliland, Copenhagen and London and takes departure in theories of social space, transnationalism, and gendered aspects of home and return. It analyses the process of establishing a new neighbourhood and the handling of a conflict with local squatters, embedded in complicated relations of power and social space, especially the competing legacies of private property and clan territorialization. Likewise, the chapter argues that the dream of returning to the Somscan and UK neighbourhood is an expression of a gendered social order, where an ideal Somali-Scandinavian, Muslim family life can be realized.

Even in the early morning, it is very hot. The landscape is flat, with yellow-reddish sand and small bushes, a few trees. There are many goats, some camels far away, and a few people walking around in the distance. Nothing else. We drive on a dirt road just outside the town of Burao. The heart of Somaliland, as people say here. A tall Somali-Scandinavian man tells the driver to stop. "This is Danish land", he says.

In May 1999, a small group of Somalis in Sweden established an association in order to rebuild and return to Somaliland[2] through the collective acquisition of land and establishment of a new neighbourhood just outside the town of Burao (Ibrahim and Farah, 2001). The idea of collective return quickly spread to Denmark, Norway and later the UK, where similar organizations were soon established. In 2000, these organizations decided to work together, and they formed the umbrella organization, Somscan Cooperative Associations, which was extended to Somscan & UK Cooperative Associations when three British organizations joined in. The Danish land referred to above is one part of the area, as are the Swedish, Norwegian and British lands.

This chapter takes a closer look at the Somscan & UK project. The issues of power in relation to the establishment of a new neighbourhood are explored as well as how ideas of home and return relate to gender and status. Such an analysis touches upon power relations locally as well as transnationally. To start with, the analysis is located in time and space.

SOMALI MIGRATION

The majority of Somalis living outside Somalia or Somaliland has migrated due to the civil war, which started in 1988 when General Siyad Barre destroyed the main towns in the north-western part of Somalia, Hargeisa and Burao.[3] The civil war gradually spread to the rest of Somalia, and in the beginning of 1991, Siyad Barre was ousted from Mogadishu, while chaos, anarchy and hunger spread in the central and southern part of the country. The same year, the north-western part of Somalia, the former British Somaliland, declared itself independent as the Republic of Somaliland but has not been recognized by any country.

Somalis now live all over the world. The largest majority live in neighbouring countries, and a smaller but still significant number live in Western countries. Remittances from Somalis in the West and the Gulf form the backbone of the Somaliland economy. While big parts of the southern and central parts of Somalia are still considered highly insecure, Somaliland has enjoyed relative peace and stability since 1996. Growing numbers of Somalis from all over the world have returned for shorter or longer periods to visit, see the country and maybe buy land and build a house – especially in the capital of Hargeisa, while the process of urbanization is going a bit slower in Burao.

About 18,000 Somalis live in Denmark (Udlændingestyrelsen, 2003), about 11,300 in Norway (Assal, 2004: 31), 19,000 in Sweden (Johnsdottor, 2002: 35), and an estimated 75,000 in the UK[4] (Montclos, 2003: 44). Today many Somalis in Scandinavia state that they want to move, either to the UK (see Kleist, 2004; Nielsen, 2003) or "back home". One reason might be that Somalis in Scandinavia are generally portrayed and treated as very difficult to integrate by politicians, the media and public officials (Assal, 2004; Johns-dottor, 2002; Skak, 1998; Fangen, 2004; Halane, 2004). Furthermore, Soma-lis have been targets of several special efforts, such as repatriation efforts and DNA-profiling. A very low average employment rate also reflects a difficult social and economic position (www.inm.dk, 2003).

In this way, Somalis as a group have been constructed as "the difficult refugees" in a process similar to the stigmatization of strangers described by Bülent Diken (1998). One of the strategies the majority society uses to deal with the ambivalence of strangers, Bülent claims, is to freeze their culture and identities through processes of scapegoating and stigmatization (Diken, 1998: 133). In this way, the ambivalent stranger as "the person who comes today and stays tomorrow" (Simmel, 1950: 402) is turned into "an easily re-cognizable category, 'immigrant', which is then associated with what is prob-lematic, unwanted, alien" (Diken, 1998: 133). Furthermore, Diken claims, the "frozen" identity and culture of the stranger is related to the original territory to which the stranger is always said to belong, as for example when Somalis in Scandinavia are said to belong to Somalia and not Scandinavia. The question is if and how such experiences influence the engagement in Somscan & UK and the desire to return to Somaliland.

TRANSNATIONAL SOCIAL SPACES AND LOCATIONS

To answer such a question, it is necessary to shed light on issues of power, space, and social locations in a transnational perspective. Apart from the broad scholarship on transnationalism and diaspora, the theory of space by Lefebvre and feminist research on the politics of locations particularly inspired this study.

Sociologist Henri Lefebvre has proposed a three-dimensional model of social space in terms of spatial practices – or perceived space – the relation between embodied subjects and buildings, infrastructure etc.; representa-tions of space – "conceptualized space, the space of scientists, planners, ur-banists, technocratic subdividers and social engineers" (Lefebvre, 1991: 38, my emphasis); and finally representational space – "space as directly lived through its associated images and symbols" (Lefebvre, 1991: 39, emphasis in original). These dimensions make it possible to pose the following theoreti-cally informed questions to the Somscan & UK project (cf. Wilson, 1999):

- What are the spatial practices of the Somscan & UK area – before and after Somscan & UK bought the land?

- How is the neighbourhood conceived – i.e. how is it pictured and administrated?
- What representational space – symbols and images – does the Somscan & UK project draw on? What power relations and social orders does this relate to?

A further question relates to the dynamics between social locations and localities. I distinguish between localities and social locations, or the politics of location. The former refer to specific sites, for instance Burao, and the latter refer to the "the simultaneous situatedness within gendered spaces of class, racism, ethnicity, sexuality, age" (Brah, 1994: 204) that individuals and groups are located in or travelling through. This perspective is also reflected in the concept of gendered transnational spaces (Mahler & Pessar, 2001), which combines questions of spatiality, mobility and social location, i.e. the position of "persons" within power hierarchies created through historical, political, economic, geographic, kinship-based and other socially stratifying factors" (Mahler et al., 2001: 445-446).

A focus on social locations thus turns our attention to the hierarchical dynamics of positioning in which all social actors are imbedded. Furthermore, as transnational social spaces include different localities and thus different frames of reference, the social locations of transnational subjects are multi-local. They are never only local, but created and understood in relation to power relations and power hierarchies not only "here", but also "there".

This work on Somscan & UK, aims to capture this complexity through multi-sited fieldwork (Marcus, 1995) in Copenhagen, Somaliland, and London as part of a larger fieldwork on Somali-Danish transnational engagement. The chapter refers mainly to interviews with Somscan & UK members and government officials, as well as various reports. Ten Somscan & UK members in Somaliland, Denmark, and London – all men and almost all highly engaged in the organization were interviewed. While, as one interviewee observed, it is hard to realize anonymity under such circumstances, anonymity was maintained by changing names and not mentioning personal details such as country of residence.

SOMSCAN & UK

Today, Somscan & UK consists of eight organizations, each owning a piece of land next to each other. There are now one Swedish, two Danish, two Norwegian, and three British groups. The cost of purchasing the pieces of land was between 15,000 and 20,000 US$. Each Somscan & UK member family paid US$ 1,000 to cover the acquisition of land as well as other costs. Since then, the price of land in Burao has increased considerably. Altogether, 330 families are presently members of Somscan & UK, and the project is closed for new members. At the time of fieldwork, about 15 families were said to have returned to Somaliland and settled in Hargeisa, Burao or other Somaliland towns. Likewise, the Somscan & UK project has raised interest among local Burao families, who long to move out of the crowded town and own a bigger house.

In 2002, the Danish Refugee Council (DRC), a Danish NGO already active in Somaliland, submitted a proposal to the European Commission (EC), prepared in cooperation with Somscan & UK. The objective of the project was to avoid that the expected return of Somscan & UK members would drain scarce local resources and the insufficient infrastructure of Burao. The project kicked off in the summer of 2003, when the DRC received a positive response and large grant of 550,000 Euros for "Community-Based Assistance to Repatriation Project" by the EC High Level Working Group on Asylum and Migration (Jensen, 2004). The EC money was donated to upgrade the town's water supply and renovate a primary and secondary school. As the two schools are located close to the Somscan & UK area and a water pipeline will be led through this area as well, Somscan & UK is definitely also beneficiaries of the EC project. The organization is represented in the steering group of the EC project, and the DRC has employed two Somscan & UK members to coordinate the renovation in cooperation with other local and national partners. Furthermore, Somscan & UK is establishing electricity in the area with its own funds.

Somscan & UK constitutes a rather unusual hometown association, if it can be considered one at all. Somscan & UK members are not only compatriots from Burao who are raising funds to improve their hometown (cf. Landholt, Autler, & Baires, 1999), but originate from many different localities. Still, as pointed out by Landolt et al., hometown engagement is not only about reconstruction projects, but also about creating social networks among fellow compatriots abroad (ibid). While the latter seems to apply to Somscan & UK, the organization differs in many respects. The efforts to rebuild Burao are directed towards the establishment of a new neighbourhood with the ultimate aim of return, and they receive indirect EC-funding for this purpose. Rather, we could say that the "hometown" is in its making, and we are witnessing a new kind of transnational social formation.

Buying land

In 2000 and 2001, two delegations from Sweden and Denmark went to Somaliland to explore the possibilities of buying land and building a new neighbourhood on a collective basis. The delegations chose to buy land outside Burao for several reasons. First of all, Burao is situated in the middle of Somaliland; it is the heart, the very centre. If not all roads lead to Burao, then a good deal of them do, making it easy to access other Somaliland cities and not least Mogadishu, the Somali capital and commercial centre. Secondly, Burao was completely destroyed during the civil war and internal conflicts in 1995 and 1998, when heavy inter-clan fighting took place. It has only been modestly rebuilt, compared to other Somaliland cities. To rebuild Burao is crucial for making the whole Somaliland idea work, Somscan & UK members argued. Finally, the third reason is the availability of land in Burao, where it is much cheaper than the land surrounding Hargeisa.

These three reasons: centrality, nation building, and the availability of cheap land might however be extended with a fourth reason, clan relations. Clan refers to the patrilinear lineage system, along which Somalis identity themselves.[5] The importance of clan lineage has been reinforced during and after the civil war, and the question of *origin*, i.e. the area dominated by one's clan, seems to play a major role in present day Somaliland. The clan aspect has a double nature in the Somscan & UK case. On the one hand, it is a specific objective to overcome the logic of clan in creating a neighbourhood where people of different clans live together.

Since several of the initiators of Somscan & UK are not from the dominating clans in Burao, this is not an empty promise. On the other hand, a large share of Somscan & UK members is said to originate from Burao as members of one specific sub-clan.

At the time of fieldwork, Burao was divided into two areas, each inhabited mainly by two respective clan lineages. A third lineage lived between these two other clans. All three clans are *Isaaq*, the dominating clan family in Somaliland. As just mentioned, some Somscan & UK members are not *Isaag* and never lived in Burao, and they thus had to establish a local connectedness in the beginning of the project. Therefore, when the Swedish association wanted to buy land, they contacted *Dahabshiil*, the largest Somali money transfer company in East Africa and itself a transnational company. However, *Dahabshiil* is not only global in this context, it also local, insofar as the founder of *Dahabshiil* is from Burao. One man explained:

> The first group contacted *Dahabshiil*, because with the first group, we said, we have to contact someone we trust. Because we don't know what is happening there. (…) We contacted *Dahabshiil*, and he [the boss] was the one who arranged the contract about the land issue and ensured that the owner is the real one (…). But the rest [of the Somscan & UK groups], they found their relatives and some other guys in the city, so the process became easy afterwards.

Through the help of *Dahabshiil*, a piece of land was bought for a favourable price. The other Somscan & UK organizations, which were more locally connected, did not have to establish their position in the same way. Buying land requires local knowledge to ensure that the seller is the actual and only owner of the land, and that the deal is recognized and respected. People often just seize land, we were told, and local government officials might even sell government property. In other words: To buy land for a new neighbourhood is not something you just do, if you do not have the local connections, networks or contacts. This means that social capital[6] is essential in establishing oneself in a post-conflict locality like Burao.

Planning a Somali-Scandinavian neighbourhood

When we visited Burao in October 2003, the construction of three houses in the Swedish area had just begun, but the plans were ambitious. Changing the desert into a thriving neighbourhood worth living in for families returning from the West requires access to water, schools, electricity and new, spacious houses of a certain comfort. Indeed, the plan of the Somscan & UK residential house does have quite a Western middle class touch to it. The drawing shows a big house, a car, a man leaving the house in a suit, and two children accompanied by an adult next to the house. The plan of the furniture layout of the house includes a combined dining and living room with a dining table, a couch and a TV, a modern kitchen, a pantry, three toilets, a bathtub, three bedrooms, one master bedroom, and two verandas. Compared to more traditional Somali houses, where people sit on the floor and bathrooms and kitchen are built separately, this house is quite a comfortable and Western-style residence. Just as important, it is also a comfortable house compared to the often rather small apartments in social housing complexes that many Somalis in the West live in.

The Somscan & UK dream house. I thank Jama Yahin Ibrahim for his kind permission to reproduce the drawing

The drawing of the house – conceived space, to put it in Lefebvreian terms – also has symbolic or representational aspects. The drawing is not only a model *of* the Somscan & UK house, it can also be said to be a model *for* a certain kind of lifestyle, a dream house in more than one sense. Not only is it a dream house compared to the usual housing in the West and more traditional houses in Burao – though it is not more luxurious than other new houses built by returnees in Somaliland. It is also a dream house in the sense that it "sells" dreams of a middle class life that many might hope for, but fewer realize. As one man said, the drawing shows what you *could* do, what you might dream to do – not what Somscan & UK members actually *will* do.

The design and comfort of the Somscan & UK dream house, as well as the availability of unlimited electricity and water, also seems to have a *gendered* dimension, at least that was what the men told me. As in other cases of considered or actual return to Somaliland, men seem to be more eager to go than women (see Goldring, 2001 for parallels in the Mexican case; Fink-Nielsen, Hansen, & Kleist, 2002). One of the biggest problems, a man confided, is how to persuade the "ministers of the interior", i.e. the women, to settle in Burao. Another member expressed it like this, when I asked if women have any special considerations:

> Yes, they require the education and health system to be working. Also, when you build a house, you will have to make it easier to work in it. For instance, you will have to prepare a washing machine, a stove and a fridge and all what you are used to get here. You cannot go back to working with an old fashioned stove. (…) This is why it is so important that we get our own electricity to cover our needs. People use so many electric instruments.

This view was echoed in Somaliland. One man, however, not only related the question of gender to the comforts of Western welfare states in terms of good kitchens or proper health service, but also to issues of local power relations and notions of gender in general. Asked why the men seem to return first, this man said:

> I think the men return first, because men tolerate much more, and the women and the children, they don't have patience.... The women's first question is "where is the midwife?" and "the children need go to school". So they send the men to the hard times and the harsh areas, and they will try to figure something out.

Some women are different, this man explained, but he still doubted that women could resist the severe pressures from the local government as well as men. As illustrated by speaking of women as the ministers of interior, women are related to the domestic sphere, while men are the active negotiators in the public and political world. Such a depiction reflects a gendered political culture in which public and political life in Somaliland is highly dominated by men. At the same time, it is also an expression of a gendered social order, where men are seen to be the creators of an environment to which women and children can return and feel safe and comfortable. The socio-spatial dimensions of this social order relate to how space is perceived and lived – the appropriate places and spaces of gendered bodies. Likewise, teenagers have special needs that require special spaces, one man in the West explained:

> This is one of the things we consider *very* seriously to make sure that we do not ruin their lives and their future. We need to be prepared and therefore we are starting with the school. If they get home, they need a real school at a Western level. This wealth they have there – they go to day care; they go to school. … they have lots of things, lots of activities. If we just move them home without a school, without day care, that will be boring. Now, most of our children are born and raised here in this country, in Europe, in the Scandinavian countries, right? So if we just move, our children will have a hard time in Burao. … That is why we hope to do some things before we go home. We have to do something for them, like a football or baseball stadium or a playground or some libraries – places they can use in their spare time. (…) If we don't, we can be 100% sure that our children and teenagers will never be satisfied, because they grew up here.

To satisfy women, children and youth, special arrangements are needed. This is reflected in the overall arrangement of the Somscan & UK residential area, where about 15 per cent of all space is reserved for public facilities, such as local shops, a market, an elementary school, playgrounds, a mosque, parking lots, a medical clinic, a police station, and a park. If realized, the area will be much like a kind of "mini-Scandinavia", a small self-sufficient neighbourhood that would not need much contact with the rest of Burao. "Going home", then, would be less a question of returning to the local Somali lifestyle and more about realizing a Scandinavian middle class lifestyle situated in Somaliland surroundings.

The Somscan & UK neighbourhood, however, is not a total transfer of Scandinavian life. The possibility of practising Islam is a valued aspect of life in Somaliland, and several of the Somscan & UK members are very religious. Muslim life as well gender and family relations in the West are hotly debated among Somalis, and some Somali men have a rather critical stance towards these aspects of life in the West. Nor do Scandinavian ideals of gender equality seem to be part of the envisioned life in Burao, which rather seems to be a restoration of more conservative gender and family relations. The Scandinavian-like public facilities are thus to be embedded in a social order with more "traditional" gender ideals. In all cases, the visions of the Somscan & UK residential neighbourhood are the long-term goal, but the actual realization remains insecure. One man expressed it like this:

> We might not build all this stuff in the next ten years – it is open. We will see now. Reality now is that we are building houses and fixing water and rehabilitating the two schools in the area, and this is where our children will go with the local children. When a lot of families come back, then we must come up with the next plan.

However, this more realistic vision of the future might clash with the expectations of other Somscan & UK members, who require more facilities before they consider return. The tense clan composition in Burao is another issue that might make life in Burao risky. As one man said, "We don't know what is in the future here. We have some plans, but we don't know, if they are sustainable."

The squatter incident

The sensitivity of constructing a new neighbourhood in Burao became very visible when the "squatter incident" happened. Close to the Somscan & UK area is a big secondary school, the Sheikh Bashir Secondary School. As is the case for so many other public areas, squatters, about 700-800 people, lived in the school area since 1996. The squatters seemed to consist primarily of people originating from Burao, either former IDPs or poor townspeople with no other place to live. They were, in other words, not returning from the West to a comfortable house, but living in their *aqal*, huts made of old tarpaulins, clothes, sacks and other available materials. Together with returnees from Ethiopia, IDPs constitute one of the most vulnerable groups in Somaliland. There are an estimated 40,000 IDPs in Somaliland (Global IDP Project, 2004), and about 215,000 refugees have returned from Ethiopia from 1997 to 2003 through voluntary UNHCR-supported repatriation. The UNHCR provides the returnees with kerosene stoves, blankets, plastic sheets and a transportation allowance, while the World Food Programme offers food for nine months (UNHCR Briefing Notes, 2003). IDPs receive even less support than that. Returnees and IDPs have recently been characterized as "among the poorest of the poor", and returnee and IDP camps in Burao as having a desperate need for assistance (UNOCHA, 2004). The difference in living standard and life conditions for returnees from the West or the Gulf and returnees from Ethiopia or internally displaced persons is thus immense.

That such differences result in differing interests became clear when the Sheikh Bashir Secondary School was to be renovated, and the squatters therefore had to move out. First, they were told to move to a resettlement area for returnees from Ethiopia located a few kilometres outside Burao. The squatters turned down this proposal. Then, a piece of land was bought for the squatters with EC project money, next to the Somscan & UK area but still further away from the town. This, Somscan & UK members told us, had been expected to satisfy the squatters, as they would be the owners of the new land. However, on the big move-out day, the squatters resisted; a fight broke out, and one squatter was shot dead and two policemen were hurt. That night some of the squatters burnt down parts of the school, and the next day, students from the school were on the street ready to reciprocate, rumours said. Luckily, this did not happen. After some negotiations, the squatters agreed to move; the students were temporarily relocated to another school, and the rebuilding of the school began as well as the construction of three houses in the Swedish section, "to demonstrate that we are serious about it", as one man explained.

The squatter incident was interpreted in several ways. The official explanation was that the squatters had received incorrect information and were protesting against being evicted from the school to be sent out in the bush. This was the explanation Somscan & UK members in Copenhagen and Somaliland had received from a squatter leader as well as government officials in Burao. If only the squatters had been given the correct information, there would have been no problems, people said. Somscan & UK members in Copenhagen were quick to reassure me (at that time, on my way to Somaliland and pretty worried) that everything was under control. Even if the incident was tragic, it would not influence decisions of whether to return or not. Conflicts are to be expected, even if this conflict was unusual. It was all just a matter of communication.

Another interpretation was based on clan lineage. The majority of squatters were said to be from the clan living in between the two larger clan areas in Burao. The area of the school and the land that Somscan & UK bought were also said to be largely dominated by this clan. The hypothesis is that the squatters – or rather a warlord related to the squatters – wanted to maintain part of the Sheikh Bashir Secondary School as clan land. A clan territorialization process, in other words, interrupted by the EC renovation. The refusal of the squatters to move to the resettlement area first proposed can also be seen in this light, as the returnees from Ethiopia are mainly from the two other clans. As it were, the new squatter resettlement has been named the "Ali Hussein Resettlement". Ali Hussein was a hero in the Somaliland resistance movement, SNM, and the same clan lineage as the majority of the squatters. The clan interpretation points at a conflict between two kinds of legacies: claiming the right to land in the name of previous settlement backed by clan power, and claiming the right to land in the name of private property backed by state power. Furthermore, the name of the squatter resettlement makes it possible for the (former) squatters to draw on legacies, private property, and clan.

A third interpretation relates to the issue of social class. The Sheikh Bashir School is closer to town than the resettlement area the squatters were offered. The school has brick buildings and shade, and the squatters had been settled there for several years. Being poor, the squatters do not have the possibilities to actually buy their own land or make proposals to the EC. Thus, the squatter incident can be said to mirror the overall hierarchy of social class, mobility and destinations, since most people who had left for the West had been among the wealthier people. Due to the restrictive visa and asylum politics, travelling to the West as an asylum seeker is very expensive. This means that for poor people or people without connections to relatives in the West or the Gulf States, destinations are more limited (van Hear, 2002; Sørensen, 2004; Lisborg and Lisborg, 2003; Castles and Miller, 2003). Receiving asylum in the West, in contrast to staying in the region, circumscribes future opportunities as well – such as the conditions under which an eventual return can take place.

The Somscan & UK project can thus be seen to enlarge class divisions (see Sørensen and van Hear, 2003 for a discussion of this argument). Still, the squatters also had their say in the development of the course of action; they were not deprived of agency, even if they were in the hands of a "warlord with money and guns". However, while the squatters succeeded in getting a better deal than they were first offered, the local and national government of Somaliland acted in favour of Somscan & UK to promote the return of "the diaspora".

THE ROLE OF "THE DIASPORA"

Today the word "diaspora" has entered the Somali vocabulary. The "diaspora" refers to Somalis living in the West and the Gulf States, and not, it seems, to the hundred thousands of Somali refugees in neighbouring countries. There seems to be outspoken expectations connected to "the diaspora", especially in relation to the transfer of resources and skills. Both the mayor and governor in Burao expressed these expectations very clearly. The governor explained:

> If the diaspora returns with money and helps with their own accommodation, etc., it is good. We thank the countries that they are living in. If they cannot take care of themselves, they should not come back but send money. As the government, we cannot afford their accommodation as they demand more than the local people. They must come with their own materials and money. When we find oil and diamonds, then they can come back. We're happy that some come back, but as a government we cannot afford it....

Returning from the West with empty pockets is not welcome. "The diaspora" is expected to accept their responsibility in rebuilding Somaliland by supporting people economically and initiating projects that will benefit the local people as well. The economic support of family members is *not* expected to stop, even in the case of return. "If you have left without money, you cannot come back without money, resources or land", as the mayor said. The people who do return without these resources are scorned and called *nafo*, handicapped. The logic seems to be that unsuccessful returnees from the West should not strain the fragile and very poor Somaliland economy; if you cannot contribute, you better stay where you are.

The reality of such expectations was also emphasized by returned Somalis from the West whom I talked to. To return not only requires the ability to take care of oneself, but also to support other family members, even quite remote ones. One man supported his parents with US$ 200 every month and spent about US$ 100 on people who came by, asking him for money. The economic support from the West is a crucial livelihood strategy, since remittances are the main source of hard currency in Somaliland and the sole economic income for many households (UNDP, 2001; Horst, 2003; Horst, 2004; Gundel, 2002). This "economy of sharing", in which the wealthier provide for the less fortunate, is explained both as an accepted cultural expectation and as a burden that makes it difficult to return (Horst, 2003; see also Horst, 2004).

The expectations to continue economic support of relatives *and* be in the vanguard of the rebuilding of the country indicate that people from the West are expected to maintain their class position. Or in other words, the moral economy of repatriation as "the ideal solution of refugee situations", where refugees return from exile to rebuild their homeland and live like the locals without exacerbating class divisions (cf. Fink-Nielsen & Kleist, 2000), is a far cry from the realities of returning Somalilanders. Rather, they are expected to make a difference if they can.

Making a difference, being different

Several Somscan & UK members in the West also mentioned "making a difference" as one of the prime reasons for returning to Somaliland. One man expressed it like this:

> It is mostly that we should participate in the rebuilding, and the only way to do that is to contribute yourself and come and do something about it. (…) In a war, you know, all the educated people, all the people who are important to the country are the first ones to move. And when they move here, even if you are a doctor or an engineer or a professional secretary, they don't use you. But if you go back, you are a person who is respected; you are a doctor. But here you are nothing. So the people living in Somaliland or the people living abroad, they say, okay, we want our trained people, (…) so when they come back, they can do something; they can participate in the reconstruction.

Returning to Somaliland is thus a possibility for upward social mobility in terms of recognition and respect. Coming to Denmark or anywhere else as an asylum seeker, having to start one's education all over again or be on public welfare, can be seen as an immense decline in status that makes especially the men "very angry and sad" (Kleist, 2002). The majority of the prominent Somscan & UK members, however, seem to have "made it". One example is Omar, who was trained and able to work as an engineer in Somalia before the civil war. After his flight to Scandinavia, Omar started in secondary school, graduated again as an engineer and got a regular job. Still, living in Scandinavia, he was just "one of the other engineers, one of the black guys", while he feels more useful working in Burao. Asked if he feels different from the other Somalis living in Burao, Omar said:

> Yeah, I am different. Firstly, they met difficulties here, shootings. For me, it was just history. They met the problems. (…) I've seen another world. I gained experience. You see how other people developed it. And I studied. I met Swedes, Danes and got some ideas. I learned how to work together more effectively and systematically.

Several government officials and other returnees repeated the idea of a positive exposure from the West in terms of work experience, efficiency and political procedures. Likewise Somscan & UK members see themselves as future actors in Somaliland – as promoters of democracy and collectivity, or as politicians. As one man explained, "The people in the country don't have the resources; they don't have the mentality we inherited from Europe. Therefore, we need to share our experiences with them". The social locations of the involved men turn upside down, so to speak, in Somaliland, where their contributions, status and qualifications are valued and respected. Or in other words, contributions from Somalis in the West are not only about economic remittances. They are also about new spaces of identification and the consciousness of being different. It is about transfers of skills and a "Scandinavian" mentality, or what Peggy Levitt has called social remittances (Levitt, 1998).

SOMALI-SCANDINAVIAN DREAMING

As shown above, the Somscan & UK project, with its focus on transferring Scandinavian or Western ideas to a new neighbourhood in Burao, has both transnational and local perspectives. The very name Somscan & UK is a striking indication of the transnational orientation of the project. Hyphenated identities were also expressed, when I asked Somscan & UK members in Copenhagen and Somaliland the rather awkward question: "Do you consider yourself Somali, Danish, Somali-Danish or something else". One man in Copenhagen explained that he perceives himself as Somali-Danish – and that he realized he had this hyphenated identity, when he visited Somaliland for the first time after his flight to Denmark and found himself as a stranger. Staying abroad seems to intensify the feeling of being "Somali" (cf. Anderson, 1995; Kleist, 2002), but visiting the "homeland" equally emphasizes the sense of belonging to the country of exile. While such a sense of belonging might be about a "double strangeness" or "double distance", it might also be about having two homes. As one man said, he is at home both in Scandinavia and in Somaliland and tries to "maintain two legs".

"Maintaining two legs" means that relations to the Scandinavian country of residence as well as Somaliland are kept up. Such a bifocal frame of reference is not only about hybrid identity. It also is about maintaining *access* to the West by holding a Western passport. A Western passport as a security mechanism is considered important because of the unstable situation in Somaliland, which still has not been recognized by any country. Somscan & UK members share this anxiety – and the strategy to overcome it; about 90 per cent of the Danish members are estimated to hold Danish passports. Also in this way, Somscan & UK is a "dream project"; it requires an optimistic belief in the future and the stability of Somaliland to invest in, not to mention return to, Somaliland. Furthermore, should decision and policymakers think that all the 330 Somscan & UK member families will actually return, immediately and once and for all, if only water is supplied and schools are renovated, they might be dreaming as well. As expressed in a recent presentation of the organization:

> The vision of a "fully equipped" neighbourhood with playgrounds, schools, police station, health clinic, etc. remains far in the distance, but the members are equipped with patience and willing to progress step by step, not following a set time frame. Some are ready to repatriate shortly, whereas others will await more facilities to be in place before they will give up their lives in Scandinavia/UK and return their families. Even, some might end up not returning at all (Jama and Jensen, 2004).

In other words, the Somscan & UK operates within a long and flexible time frame. Also, it is my guess that return is dependent on holding a Western passport. As I and others have pointed out, voluntary repatriation to Somaliland is more likely to happen with the acquisition of a Western passport than the repatriation support offered by European governments (2001; Fink-Nielsen et al., 2002). Furthermore, return often seems to be of a more circular and temporary character than the permanent movement envisioned in mainstream ideas of repatriation (see Hansen, this volume).

Discourses of return

This chapter raised the question how the status and standing of Somalis in Scandinavia and the UK relate to their transnational engagement in Somscan & UK. Given the often rather hostile environment in Scandinavia, a straightforward answer could be that return to the Somscan & UK neighbourhood – once there are sufficient facilities – simply would offer the best of two worlds: Scandinavian comfort in a Somaliland environment. While this might be the case for some members, the answer is more complicated than that.

First of all, one of the stated aims of Somscan & UK is to rebuild Somaliland; it is not to get out of Scandinavia or the UK. None of the leading members of Somscan & UK expressed any *personal* encounters of racism, though all the interviewees agreed that the situation is difficult for Somalis in Scandinavia. This "absence" of racist encounters coincided in almost all cases with success in terms of getting a job or education. The positions of "being a successful man" and "victimized Somali refugee in a racist host society" do not seem to be compatible. And, indeed, the men who make a difference in Somscan & UK also seem to have made it in their Western countries of residence: They have practical and organizational skills. They hold jobs, but work extra hours for Somscan & UK, and might even be engaged in other kinds of community work as well. They are organizational nodal points with lots of social capital by virtue of their engagement in a range of activities and relations. While they – with the exception of the two employees in Burao – do not earn a salary, they do gain experience, respect and status in the Somali communities in the West and in Somaliland. In this way, their status seems to be related to positions *within* the "Somaliland diaspora" and *in* Somaliland (Schiller and Fouron, 2001; Goldring, 1998; Goldring, 2001), rather than in relation to the Western host societies, where transnational engagement is much less appreciated.

Another group of transnational actors, however, are Somalis who state that they have returned or plan to do so because they feel unwanted in Scandinavia, where the environment is getting more and more discriminatory, and where they encounter successive experiences of racism. These men are often unemployed and have not made it to the same degree as the prominent members. For this group, the engagement in Somscan & UK seems to be less framed in the rather abstract development and nation-building discourse and more about emphasizing the opportunity to buy cheap land, probably one of the best investments in Somaliland. However, there is no contradiction between these two sets of articulations; rather, they reflect two tendencies that are articulated differently by the two groups of members.

The return of "the diaspora"?

So, finally, will "the diaspora" return to transform the desert? I hope it is now clear that the question cannot be phrased that simply. Somscan & UK is about more than building new comfortable houses. It is also about recognition, power relations, opportunities, nation-building, and gender.

So far this chapter has shown that the process of "getting local", i.e. the development and transfer of social capital has played an essential part in the establishment of Somscan & UK. Burao, as a post-conflict locality situated in the dry semi-desert, visibly scarred from the civil war in terms of poor and damaged infrastructure, high unemployment and a complicated and tense clan structure, is not an easy place to return to. Somscan & UK as a collective actor from "the diaspora" is both locally and transnationally connected through the two employed coordinators, the "local" clan lineage of many members, and the relations to DRC. Also, the value of the EC grant probably cannot be underestimated; the ability to attract development projects must no doubt contribute to the accumulation of social capital and prestige.

The concept of social capital, however, is not sufficient to explore all dimensions of transnational spaces. By drawing on the multi-faceted understanding of space offered by Lefebvre and the concept of social locations, this chapter shows how the local conflict of the squatter incident is embedded in complicated relations between power and space – such as the competing legacies of private property and clan territorialization. Furthermore, I have proposed that the vision of a Scandinavian-like neighbourhood can be seen as the dream of a gendered social order, where an appropriate Somali-Scandinavian and Muslim family life can be played out. Apart from comfortable houses, this place of dreams offers the opportunities for maintaining valued aspects of Scandinavian welfare states, such as public facilities, recreational areas and – in a broader context – democracy, efficiency, and orderliness. At the same time, "the diaspora" is met with recognition and respect insofar as they live up to the expectations of making a difference and continue supporting family members.

Finally, it is essential to remember that the future and realization of a fully equipped Somscan & UK residential neighbourhood remains unsure. Nobody actually knows if a large-scale return is going to take place. Still, houses are being built, plans are made, and dreams are dreamt. One thing is for sure: It could be extremely interesting to visit "the Danish land" in ten years time and see what it looks like.

Somali-Scandinavian A Dreaming When "the Diaspora" Returns to the Desert

NOTES

1. This chapter is a revised version of a paper presented at the workshop: "Determinants of Transnational Engagement", Santa Domingo, 27-29 November 2003, at the Sussex Migration Seminar Serial, Brighton, February 2004, and at the ASA conference "Locating the field", Durham, 29 March – 1 April 2004. I wish to thank for all comments and suggestions. I also thank Peter Hansen for good company during fieldwork in Somaliland, 5-17 October 2003; the DRC and Lone Hvid Jensen for precious help; Richard Black, Cindy Horst, Fiona Wilson and Ninna Nyberg Sørensen for useful comments. Most of all, I thank Somscan & UK members for their time, help and confidence.
2. I refer to Somaliland to indicate the geographical region claimed by the Republic of Somaliland.
3. See Kleist (2004) for a more detailed historical account of Somali migration.
4. The exact number of Somalis in the UK is unknown; some observers estimate up to 200,000 people.
5. For different discussions about clan, see Lewis (1994), Griffiths (2002) and Farah (2000).
6. For a discussion of the importance of social capital in transnational migration, see Levitt (1998) and Faist (2000).
7. Such a political culture is not, of course, unique to Somaliland. Though the context is different, there are parallels to the gendered engagement in Mexican hometown associations, described by Goldring, where "men [are cast] as active and prominent in the "public" realm of politics and women in supporting, passive roles" (Goldring, 2001: 503).

REFERENCES

Anderson, B.
   1995   Exodus, *Grus*, 16:12-22.
Assal, M.A.M.
   2004   "Sticky labels or rich ambiguities?", *Diaspora and Challenges of Homemaking for Somalis and Sudanese in Norway*, University of Bergen, BRIC, Oslo.
Brah, A.
   1994   "Cartographies of diaspora", *Contesting Identities*, Routledge, London & New York.
Castles, S., and M.J. Miller
   2003   "The age of migration", *International Population Movements in the Modern World*, 3rd Ed., Palgrave, Houndmiles & New York.
Diken, B.
   1998   *Strangers, Ambivalence and Social Theory*, Ashgate Publishing Company, Aldershot.
Faist, T.
   2000   *The Volume and Dynamics of International Migration and Transnational Social Spaces,* Clarendon Press, Oxford.
Fangen, K.
   2004   "Identity and symbolic ethnicity among Somali immigrants in Norway", paper presented at the 9th International Congress of Somali Studies, 3-5 September, Aalborg.
Farah, N.
   2000   "Yesterday, tomorrow", *Voices from the Somali Diaspora*, Cassell, London & New York.
Fink-Nielsen, M., P. Hansen, and N. Kleist
   2001   "Roots, rights and responsibilities, Place-making and repatriation among Somalis in Denmark and Somaliland", paper presented at the workshop "Living at the Edge, Migration, Conflict and State in the Backyards of Globalisation".
   2002   Repatriering – afsluttet eller fortsat mobilitet? *Den Ny Verden*, 35: 52-65.
Fink-Nielsen, M., and N. Kleist
   2000   Tilhørsforholdets politikker, En analyse af hvorfor så få somaliere repatrierer fra Danmark, MA thesis, Institute of International Development & Institute of History, Roskilde University Centre.
Goldring, L.
   1998   "The power of status in transnational social fields", in M.P. Smith and L. E. Guarnizo (Eds), *Transnationalism from Below*, Transaction Publishers, New Brunswick, New Jersey, 165-195.
   2001   "The gender and geography of citizenship in Mexico-US transnational spaces", *Identities: Global Studies in Culture and Power*, 7: 501-538.
Griffiths, D.
   2002   "Somali and Kurdish refugees in London", *New Identities in the Diaspora*, Ashgate, Aldershut.
Gundel, J.
   2002   "The migration-development nexus: Somalia case study", Centre for Development Research, Copenhagen.

Halane, F.W.

2004   "Otherness, A challenge or an obstacle for Somali-Swedish Women in Sweden", paper presented at the 9th International Congress of Somali Studies, 3-5 September, Aalborg.

Horst, C.

2003   "Transnational nomads: How Somalis cope with refugee life in the Dadaab camps of Kenya", PhD, University of Amsterdam.

2004   "Money and mobility: Transnational livelihood strategies of the Somali diaspora", *Global Migration Perspectives*, 1-19.

Ibrahim, J.Y., and A.J. Farah

2001   Frivilligt återvandringsprojekt, Al-hijra Informationscenter & Somscan Cooperative Associations, Örebro & Copenhagen.

Jama, A.F., and L.H. Jensen

2004   "Somscan and UK - Diaspora joining forces to better the chances of return to the homeland", paper presented at the 9th International Congress of Somali Studies, 3-5 September, Aalborg.

Jensen, L.H.

2004   "Debriefing note", Danish Refugee Council, Copenhagen.

Johnsdottor, S.

2002   "Created By God: How Somalis in Swedish exile reassess the practice of female circumcision", Lund Monographs in Social Anthropology 10, Lund.

Kleist, N.

2002   Når hjemme er mere end et sted, Møder med Danmark blandt somaliere i diaspora, *Kvinder, Køn & Forskning*, 11:31-40.

2004   Nomads, Sailors and Refugees, A brief history of Somali migration, Sussex Migration Working Papers, 1-14.

Landholt, P., L. Autler, and S. Baires

1999   "From hermano lejano to hermano mayor: The dialectics of Salvadoran transnationalism", *Ethnic and Racial Studies*, 22: 90-315.

Lefebvre, H.

1991   *The Production of Space*, Malden, Blackwell Publishing, Oxford and Carlton.

Levitt, P.

1998   "Social remittances: Migration driven local-level forms of cultural diffusion, *International Migration Review*, 32: 926-948.

Lewis, I.M.

1994   "Blood and bone", *The Call of Kinship in Somali Society*, Lawrenceville, The Red Sea Press, New Jersey.

Lisborg, A., and M. Lisborg

2003   "Destination Denmark - Om asylmigration, menneskesmugling and mobilitetsstrategier", MA thesis, Institute of International Development Studies and Geography, Roskilde University Centre.

Mahler, S.J., and P.R. Pessar

2001   "Gendered geographies of power: Analyzing gender across transnational spaces", *Identities – Global Studies in Culture and Power*, 7: 441-459.

Marcus, G.E.

1995   "Ethnography in/of the world system: The emergence of multi-sited ethnography", *Annual Review of Anthropology*, 24:95-117.

Montclos, M.A.P.
2003　"A refugee diaspora': When the Somali go West", in K. Koser (Ed.), *New African Diasporas*, Routledge, London & New York, 37-55.

Nielsen, K.B.
2003　"Next stop Britain: The influence of transnational networks on the secondary movement of Danish Somalis", MA Migration Studies, University of Sussex.

Schiller, G.N., and G. Fouron
2001　"Georges woke up laughing", *Long-distance Nationalism and the Search for Home*, Duke University Press, Durham & London.

Simmel, G.
1950　"The stranger", in K. H. Wolff (Ed), *The Sociology of Georg Simmel*, The Free Press, New York, 402-408.

Skak, T.
1998　De er så svære at integrere, in A.-B. P. Steen (Ed.), *Kan vi leve sammen? Integration mellem politik og praksis*, Munksgaard, Copenhagen.

Sørensen, N.N.
2004　"The development dimension of migrant transfers", Final Report, Danish Institute for Development Studies, Copenhagen.

Sørensen, N.N., and N. van Hear
2003　"Study on livelihood and reintegration dynamics in Somaliland, IIS-research component to DRC's community based integrated rehabilitation programme in Somaliland", Draft Report Copenhagen.

Udlændingestyrelsen
2003　*Udlændingestyrelsens Årsrapport*, Udlændingestyrelsen, Copenhagen.

UNDP
2001　*Human Development Report Somalia*, Nairobi, United Nations Development Programme, Kenya.

UNHCR Briefing Notes
2003　North-West Somalia: over 9,000 have returned since July, www.unchr.ch.

UNOCHA
2004　SOMALIA: IDPs, returnees desperate for assistance in Somaliland - UN www.irinnews.org: UN Office for the Coordination of Humanitarian Affairs.

van Hear, N.
2002　"From 'durable solutions' to 'transnational relations': Home and exile among refugee diasporas", CDR Working Paper, Copenhagen, (02)9 :1-18.

Wilson, F.
1999　"Introducing violence and social space", in F. Wilson (Ed.), *Violencia y Especio Social: Estudios sobre conflicto y recuperación*, National University of the Centre of Peru, Roskilde University Centre & Centre for Development Research, Huancayo & Copenhagen.

www.inm.dk
2003　Homepage of the Ministry of Refugee, Immigration and Integration Affairs.

Revolving Returnees in Somaliland

Peter Hansen

Living Across Worlds: Diaspora, Development and Transnational Engagement

ABSTRACT

Based on ethnographic fieldwork in Somaliland, this chapter explores and challenges the notion of "return" as a migratory practice. Following the declaration of the independence of Somaliland and the establishment of relative peace and governance, Somalilanders from Western countries are coming to Somaliland to invest in small businesses, build houses, marry, visit friends and family, work, and have a curious look at the place they have observed at a distance for several years. Almost all of these "returnees" are not staying in Somaliland permanently, however. This chapter argues that "return" and "repatriation" are sedentary concepts reflecting an understanding of identity that does not capture the mobile practices of today's world of transnational flows. The chapter develops the concept of "revolving returnees" to capture the dynamics between an ideology of return and final homecomings on the one side, and mobile migratory practices on the other. The chapter characterizes the different kinds of "revolving returnees" and analyses the nature of transnational engagements in Somaliland. The chapter also explains why "revolving returnees" maintain continued forms of mobility between Somaliland and the West, and concludes that people need networks, knowledge, money and documents to be able to "circulate" between Somaliland and the West. Many "revolving returnees" come to Somaliland because they believe they have better "opportunities" here than in the West. These "opportunities" relate to a variety of economic, social and cultural factors. In exploring the diversity of these "opportunities", the chapter cautions us not to see transnational practices as mere adaptation to global socio-economic circumstances.

Many external observers and policymakers often understand migration as a single event that changes a person's place of residence permanently. Within this dominant narrative of migration and identity, the practice of migration from a country of residence to a country of origin is seen as a single event, as a one-way and permanent change of place. Within the past decades, "return migration" and "repatriation" as special migratory practices have emerged as important elements in many Western governments' migration policy (IOM, 2004: 7). "Return migrants" can be defined as "refugees or migrants" who have obtained (Western) citizenship and who "return" to their country of origin. "Repatriating refugees" can be defined as "refugees" who return to a country of origin where they also hold citizenship. Within the "refugee regime", the return or repatriation of refugees is seen as the ideal solution to "the world's refugee crisis" (UNHCR, 1980, 1985, 1993, 1994, 1997; Allen & Morsink, 1994; Aleinikoff, 1995).

As has been noted by many observers, the idealization of return rests to a large extent on the supposed existence of a natural relationship between person and place that roots people in particular cultural and national spaces (Hansen, 1998; Stepputat, 1994; Warner, 1994; Malkki, 1995; Rogge, 1994; Fink-Nielsen & Kleist, 2000). In this chapter, "return migration" is examined not as a policy but as a migratory practice. However, there is a fundamental problem in applying theories on "return migration" (see for example Bascom, 1994; Ghosh, 2000; Gmelch, 1980, 1992; King, 2000) and "repatriation" (see for example Bakewell, 1996, 1999), since this scholarship does not reflect or theorize the empirical phenomenon of migrants' continuous movements – even after "return" or "repatriation". As Hammond (1999) rightly argues in her scrutiny of the discourse of repatriation, the terminology we use to describe processes of return does not do justice to the empirical world of movement. The point is that "return" and "repatriation" are concepts originating from a sedentary understanding of identity, and they do not capture the mobile practices and contexts characteristic of today's world of transnational flows of people, ideas, goods, technology and capital (Appadurai, 1990).

Based on ethnographic fieldwork in Somaliland, this chapter explores and challenges the notion of "return" as a migratory practice. Instead of talking about and analysing "return migration", this chapter explores the empirical phenomena of "circular migration" (Duany, 2002) between Western countries and the Republic of Somaliland. These migrants are referred to as "revolving returnees", as they engage in a discourse on final homecomings while maintaining mobile practices that run contrary to how they describe their coming to Somaliland. In this sense, "revolving returnees" are "circular migrants" who apply a discourse on final and permanent return to the homeland, but who for a number of reasons do not return for good. Following decades of civil war, the declaration of the independence of the Republic of Somaliland, and the establishment of relative peace and governance, Somalilanders from North America and Europe are coming to Somaliland to invest in small businesses, build houses, marry, visit friends and family, work, and have a curious look at the place they have followed at a distance for several years. Most of the Somalilanders coming to Somaliland from the West are not staying in Somaliland permanently (Hansen, 2001). This chapter characterises the different kinds of revolving returnees and analyses the nature of their engagements in Somaliland. Finally, this study analyses why they tend to uphold continued forms of mobility between Somaliland and the West.

DISPERSAL AND DIASPORA

Migration is often said to be at the heart of Somali nomadic culture. Lewis (1961, 1994) describes the livelihoods of Somali pastoralists as being characterized by strategies of mobility and dispersal that make survival possible in an extremely harsh climate. In this sense, practices of mobility and dispersal have been crucial to nomadic Somalis for centuries. The migration of households and their livestock has been attuned to the seasonal rhythm of the rain. For the past century or more, migration among Somalis has been defined, not only by the falling rains and filling wells, but also by opportunities for employment and education and lately for finding safe havens. In other words, both voluntary and involuntary migration has scattered the Somalis around the world.

The Somali diaspora grows out of a long tradition of labour migration. Some of the first Somalis to leave the Horn of Africa to work abroad were seamen, who since the early twentieth century went to Europe, America, Russia or Arab countries to work in the maritime trade (Cassanelli, 1982: 260). Today, after sailing the world's oceans for almost a century, several retired seamen have settled in cities like Cardiff and Copenhagen, while others have returned to live in the Somali-inhabited area of the Horn of Africa. A second wave began at the start of the 1960s, when a large number of Somalis migrated to the Middle East and the Gulf states to work in the booming oil-driven economies. Today, the many Somalis who remained in the Gulf and in Arab countries are facing difficulties. Employment opportunities have declined dramatically and most migrants (Somalis as well as other foreign nationals) are either faced with poor legal status or have been forced to leave. A third wave consists of Somalis who migrated for the purpose of education. During the 1970s, young Somalis went to North America, Europe and Russia to work towards university degrees. Today, in part owing to the difficulties of travelling to any Western country on a Somali passport, and partly because of problems of access to and the cost of education, a large number of resourceful Somalis are turning to India and Pakistan for university degrees.

Lastly, a fourth wave consists of the large number of Somalis who have left the Horn of Africa because of civil war and political unrest. In the 1980s, many Somalis left the country and applied for political asylum in the West, while others, the majority, fled to neighbouring countries. In 1988, the civil war broke out on a larger scale than ever before in the history of Somalia. Hundreds of thousands of refugees fled across the borders to Ethiopia, Djibouti and Yemen, and further afield to Europe and North America. Following the defeat of the Somali government forces and the declaration of the independence of Somaliland in May 1991, large numbers of refugees left the camps in Ethiopia and Djibouti and went back to what was left of the homes and possessions from which they had fled so abruptly three years earlier. But while the war was coming to an end in the northern part of Somalia at the beginning of 1991, it broke out on a large scale in the south, again causing people to flee their homes. Somalis from the south fled to neighbouring countries like Kenya and Ethiopia, further afield to Europe and North America, or to the Republic of Somaliland.

Due to the difficulties of identifying who is a refugee and who is not, as well as double counting on the part of governments and international organizations, statistics on refugees and migrants in the Somali context are highly dubious. Out of a total Somali refugee population of 425,455 (at the end of 2002), UNHCR estimates that approximately 155,000 were living in Kenya, 38,000 in Ethiopia, 20,000 in Djibouti, 81,000 in Yemen, 34,000 in North America, 33,000 in Great Britain and 10,000 in Denmark (UNHCR, 2003). In relation to Somaliland, it is often said that half the population lives outside its borders. For people in Somaliland, the past 15 years and more have meant numerous displacements across borders, leaving the entire population (estimated at around 3.5 million) as either repatriating refugees or internally displaced persons.

MOBILE MARKERS

As indicated in the above mentioned short history of the dispersal of Somalis, there are many different migratory histories and practices in Somaliland today. Not only by observing the different migrants, but also by physically moving around Hargeisa, the capital of the Republic of Somaliland, one senses how this place and its people, small and provincial as it might be in certain ways, clearly has been part of a larger world for many years.

Coming from the airport heading towards the centre of Hargeisa, the newly built Ambassador Hotel is one of the first buildings one notices. Like almost all new buildings in Somaliland, the hotel has been constructed by a Somalilander who partly lives outside the country. Today, the hotel is one of the biggest and most impressive buildings in the country. To many people in Hargeisa, the hotel symbolises the peace and progress that Somaliland has achieved since its self-declared independence in 1991, and the positive role the Somaliland diaspora has played in the private sector in Somaliland. The millions of dollars invested in the hotel is a tangible manifestation of the confidence many Somalilanders feel towards the future of their country. The hotel has even attracted Somalilanders from North America and Saudi Arabia to come and work at the hotel. They have been impressed by the building and the project of setting up a fine hotel in a place that is not exactly known for its thriving tourism. Not only the name of the hotel, but also its garden, of which the hotel management is especially proud since it is probably the only one of its kind in Somaliland, is associated with travel and distant horizons. Like so many families in Hargeisa with transnational links to more lush and prosperous pastures in the West, the garden is truly a global configuration. The grass has been imported from Canada, the flowers from Holland, the grapes from Germany, and the banana trees from Kenya. As it has also become one of the favourite places for the Hargeisa upper class to dine at night, the garden shows the value people today associate with foreign countries and being well situated within transnational flows.

Moving towards the centre of Hargeisa, one also notices the many new houses that have been built or are under construction. This ongoing physical construction gives Hargeisa an atmosphere of a place very visibly in the making. Most of these houses are constructed by Somalilanders with histories and links to Europe, North America or the Middle East. These days, new parts of Hargeisa are mushrooming and given names like "Half London", "Norway Corner", "New York" and "Berlin", signalling the links that the houses' owners and residents have to these distant places. Previously, the neighbourhoods of Hargeisa were given names like "Little Jigjiga", "Sheik Madar", "Soweto", "Civilian Area", "The Eye of Borama", "Lion's Place", "Red Sea", "Camel Place", "Radio Station", "Drinking", "Falling Water", "26 June", "Region Five", "Clouds", "Sinai", "Indian Place", "Paradise Place", "Fucking Area" and "Shit". Whereas the old neighbourhoods of Hargeisa refer to local and regional geographies, the colonial history and daily practices, the new neighbourhoods point not only towards different experiences and more distant horizons, but also towards the importance of diasporic identities in Hargeisa. Today, some Somalilanders even suggest that their diasporic identities are replacing their clan identities. They argue that their diasporic identity of for example having a British or Canadian passport is replacing their clan identity as being the most significant social marker to them in Somaliland. Whether diasporic identities are in fact replacing clan identities as the most important aspect in social interaction in Somaliland today is of course highly questionable. However, it expresses the high status many people in Somaliland ascribe to a life in the West, to Somalilanders with Western passports, and to diasporic histories and transnational connections.

Other elements of daily life in Hargeisa point towards global and regional flows. One of the finest medical clinics in Hargeisa has two doctors from India and one from Pakistan. Before coming to Somaliland, they worked as doctors in Iran, the US and England for several years. The lab technician is from Rwanda, the secretary from Djibouti, and the nurses are young Somali women from Canada and Kenya. The money supporting the clinic comes from a Somali investor that has lived most of his life in Saudi Arabia. The medical clinic shows not only the confidence that many Somalilanders have in the possibility of investing in the country but also the work opportunities that other nationals are finding in Somaliland these days. Also in the same building as the medical clinic, several shops have been opened by Somali businessmen who have lived in Saudi Arabia for several years. Due to increased unemployment in Arab countries, the Somalis and Somalilanders living there have been thrown out of the country. Even if they have lived there for decades, they have no legal right to stay in the country if the authorities terminate their work permit. Therefore, there are quite a substantial number of families that have come to Somaliland after living a lifetime in Arab countries.

The weekly local newspapers in English also testify to the dispersal of the Somalilanders and the continued links between the diaspora and Somaliland. Every week there are several stories about the Somaliland community in Europe or North America. According to the editor of one of the biggest English language newspapers in Somaliland, they give priority to stories about Somalilanders in Western countries, because they are very important for what goes on in Somaliland. Stories about Somalilanders in the diaspora can roughly be divided into two categories. The first kind of story describes the "successful Somalilander in diaspora" who has graduated from university, works in a well-known company making lots of money or in other ways projects "the successful migrant". The second kind describes the activities of Somalilanders in the diaspora who work for the recognition of Somaliland. According to the editor, these kinds of stories are "good stories", because they relate directly to what goes on economically and politically in Somaliland. As has been documented elsewhere (Hansen, 2004), a large proportion of the inhabitants in Somaliland depends on remittances sent from family members living in the West. The portrayal of the successful migrants sustains the notion that Somalilanders living in the West have the responsibility to remit money to their poorer relatives. In reality, however, most often the remitters living in the West are not outright success stories, and they often have to remit money out of a meagre budget based on social welfare. Also the story of the "successful migrant" sustains the notion that a big proportion of the intelligentsia and hence future of Somaliland resides in the West.

Besides stories written *about* members of the Somaliland diaspora, stories are also written *by* Somalilanders living in the West. The stories and articles in the newspapers say something very characteristic about the Somaliland community. First of all, they show that although the Somaliland community is spread out over the world, it is still partly held together by the flow of information. People in Hargeisa read about how family members and friends or other Somalilanders in general are doing in far away places. Also Somalilanders living in the diaspora appear to have a great interest in discussing politics that relate directly to the administration of Somaliland and sometimes also to portray their own diasporic lives to an audience in Somaliland. The Somaliland community may be spread throughout the world, but still, events that take place in Western countries are part of the local news in the newspapers in Somaliland. And the Somaliland diaspora may live their lives thousands of miles away from Hargeisa, but they still have an interest in engaging in and staging themselves in a local political context in Somaliland.

Other clear indications of the dispersal of the Somaliland community and the interaction of ideas, goods and people between Hargeisa and Europe and North America are not difficult to find. A special kind of shop is "Coffers" or "Salons", which thrive on the increased number of weddings being held in Hargeisa. They provide the bride and female guests for the wedding with the proper dresses, makeup, hairstyles, henna decoration and wedding cakes. The names and history of these shops indicate not only the flow of people but also how Western names are good for business – especially when it comes to dressing up women. The coffers have names like "Washington", "New York",

"Paris", "London" and "Copenhagen", pointing to the fact that many of the shops are started by Somaliland women from Western countries. Among the more obvious indicators of transnational flows are the more than 20 money transfer companies, the many travel agents, the second-hand clothes from Scandinavia, the thousands of second-hand cars from Japan and Europe, the 50 or so internet cafes and the hundreds of telephone "substations" that have clocks on display showing the time in places like London, Sydney, Ottawa, Dubai and Hargeisa.

SCALE AND ENGAGEMENTS

As illustrated above, the Somalis are a prime example of what Roger Rouse has called a "transnational migrant circuit" that is maintained through the circulation of people, money, goods and information (Rouse, 1991: 15). Airport statistics from Hargeisa Airport show that approximately 16,000 passengers entered and 12,000 passengers left Somaliland in the first half of 2003. From these figures, one could conclude that there were around 4,000 "return migrants" in Somaliland during the first half of 2003. However, to make an accurate estimation of the scale of "return migration" to Somaliland, one would need to accumulate more statistical information spanning several years. What the airport statistics do indicate is that there are many Somalilanders, especially during the summer holidays, who come to Somaliland for shorter or longer periods of time. According to Ethiopian Airlines, which operates a daily flight to Hargeisa from Addis Ababa, most overseas passengers come from London and Copenhagen, but by far the largest share of passengers is regional coming from Addis Ababa and Nairobi.

One way of characterizing the "revolving returnees" in Somaliland is to look at their engagements in Somaliland today. Before doing so in any detail, it is important to stress that the Somali diaspora has been engaged locally in present day Somaliland since Somalis started migrating out of Somalia more than one hundred years ago. For example, the establishment of an armed resistance movement against the former Somali dictator, Siad Barre, was organized by Somalis living primarily in Saudi Arabia and the United Kingdom (Lewis, 1994). During the civil war, Somalis in the diaspora sent money, blankets, medicine and other supplies to Ethiopia to help the fighting militias. Since the toppling of Siad Barre in 1991, Somalilanders in the diaspora have become involved in conflict resolution and development projects. Today, the Somaliland diaspora is heavily involved in political, economic and judicial processes.

One large group of Somalilanders from the Western diaspora is employed within the "development industry". Since the collapse of the government and public services in Somalia, there has been a rapid growth in the number of local and international NGOs. In Somaliland, NGOs have played vital roles in processes of rehabilitation and reconciliation. "Revolving returnees" within the "development industry" have been very important in transferring ideas and knowledge from the West to a country that has suffered from a severe brain drain over the past 25 years. They have been crucial in establishing a civil society and raising issues relating to human rights, minority rights, good governance, the environment and the position and role of women in the society. Besides being well-educated, these people can be said to have been relatively "successful" in the West. As explained to me by a male Somalilander from Sweden:

> I think that those who are successful in Sweden will also be successful here. One way of being successful is to get a Swedish or Danish passport or whatever passport. Then they are secure enough and then they can come back… They can go back and experiment…but until they get this naturalization, they don't come back… All those who are successful in Sweden, who become employed in Sweden and who are able to collect some money, send some money, build a house while they are away, those are the people who are coming here… The losers will never think about coming back, because they are not anything there in Sweden; they are not involved there, and they cannot be involved here either…

The group of revolving returnees employed within the "development industry" in Somaliland can be seen as members of an elite, similar to the "cosmopolitans" analysed by Hannerz (1996) who have easily portable credentials and specialized skills. As explained above, it is necessary to be "involved" in the West to be "involved" in Somaliland also. The revolving returnees are part of a mobile elite that has access to international jobs, that are well connected within the donor community, that have Western passports and hence access to travel and the protection and help from the foreign departments of Western countries. As noted above, revolving returnees are privileged in the sense of having the opportunity to "experiment" by coming to Somaliland. Several of the migrants that are employed within the "development industry" live in Somaliland without their spouses and children. Often the "experiment" falls out "unsuccessfully", and they will only stay in Somaliland for the duration of their contract or until their NGO runs out of money. Then they will return to the West and try to find a new job or to lobby for money among Western donors to start a new project in Somaliland. Still others have returned to Somaliland with their spouses and children, or they have established families in Somaliland upon return.

A second group of revolving returnees have become involved in Somaliland in the context of its political and bureaucratic circles (ministers, director-generals, political spokespersons and people from the diaspora wishing to become involved in politics). A minister in Somaliland is paid only approximately US$300 a month; therefore, these revolving returnees often rely on their own savings, profits from investments in private businesses or remittances sent from the West. To come to Somaliland and engage in politics, one needs to be very well connected to the local realities. This, of course, poses a challenge to people who often have lived in the West for more than ten years.

Revolving Returnees in Somaliland

A third important form of revolving returnees concerns the private business sector. Somalilanders from the diaspora are currently engaged in opening small-scale businesses, such as restaurants, beauty salons, transport companies, supermarkets and vending kiosks. Compared to starting a private business abroad, the capital needed to start a restaurant or open a small shop in Somaliland is relatively modest. Partly because of the absence of a functioning state with its financial, economic and social institutions, the private business sector has grown tremendously in Somaliland. Even though Somaliland has the most stable administration in the former Republic of Somalia, traditional government services such as the provision of education, health services and electricity have largely been taken over by private companies. Somaliland may not officially be a state that provides these services, but, in fact, Somaliland is a free trade zone, where it is possible to import and export goods almost without taxation. Many Somalilanders from the West come to invest in the supposedly booming and unregulated economy. The group of revolving returnees in the private business sector tends to consist of young and old, men and women. The number of jobs available in Somaliland is very limited, and there is no social welfare as in Western countries. A good private business will provide for a person and his/her family, and it can provide insurance against unemployment. Many of the revolving returnees that are employed in the "development industry" also invest in private business in order to secure themselves and their families in case of unemployment. The business potentials in Hargeisa and Somaliland are often exaggerated. As explained by a Somalilander from Toronto:

> I'm a returnee and many of my friends have returned as well. The problem is that there was a lot of optimism around 1998. Before that time, it was almost impossible to return; there was the civil war and it simply was not safe, but in 1998 people started believing that it was possible to return to Somaliland, that there was peace and that there was some kind of system, and a lot of opportunities…but a lot of people didn't do their homework. They just came…and just because there is no Thai restaurant in Hargeisa, it doesn't mean that if you open one there will be a market for one.… So the ones that didn't stay here didn't plan it well.…

The revolving returnees in the private business sector may live half their lives in Somaliland and half their lives in the West. Many of them are split between spouses and children living in the West and the larger extended family residing in Somaliland.

A fourth group of revolving returnees relates to securing ownership or buying plots of land in Somaliland's major cities. Following the rapid urbanization, people are now fighting (and killing each other) for land. Before the war and among the nomadic Somalilanders, camels, wells and grazing rights used to be the only assets worth fighting and killing for. Today, one of the most common reasons for conflict between families relates to arguments over who owns a plot of land. These plots represent one of the few tangible assets in Somaliland. With people coming from all over the world, the market price for a plot of land in a city like Hargeisa has increased many times in just ten years. Many Somalilanders have come to Somaliland ten years ago, bought plots of land in Hargeisa for a few hundred dollars a piece, and are now selling each plot of land for five thousand dollars. Whereas Somali seamen used to invest in camels, the contemporary diasporic Somalilanders are investing in plots of land and houses in Hargeisa. Buying or owning land in Hargeisa is not easy, however. Today, there are many diasporic Somalilanders in Hargeisa who spend months sorting out disputes over land. They may have bought a piece of land ten years ago but in the meantime other owners have appeared to claim the same piece of land. People have no guarantee that the authorities have not issued several ownership papers on the same plot of land. In practice, the same plot of land may be owned by several owners, all holding papers to certify that they are the rightful owners. Without a well-functioning and trustworthy legal system, people often end up settling the dispute through their clan elders and customary law or with guns. Reasons for securing or buying plots of land in the major cities are not only related to making a profit but often to the future return of the family as well. As one woman from England explained about her plot of land in Hargeisa:

> I'm here in Hargeisa to settle a land dispute. I bought the plot in 1981 and it was part of the city plan for Hargeisa. I have a document from that time that says that I'm the rightful owner… and I also have a document from the Somaliland authorities that states me as the rightful owner…but every time I visit my plot there seems to be someone that shows up and claims the land also…. I pay them a few hundred dollars and then they go away again…. But now there is a family that claims to have papers on the same plot of land also and they won't accept a few hundred dollars…. Now I have contacted the leader of my clan and he will meet with the leader of the other clan…. Then they will sort it out… Maybe I will never build a house on this piece of land but I want to make sure that my daughter has the possibility of coming to Hargeisa. I want to make sure that she can come here in the future….

A fifth group of revolving returnees relates to people visiting Somaliland during their holidays. Some of these visitors may come to visit their spouses and children living in Somaliland with the aim of planning a future family reunion in the West. Others may come to look for future spouses, to meet friends and family members they have not seen for several years or out of "curiosity" or to chew *chat*.

The last group of revolving returnees to be mentioned here consists of young Somalilanders. They have either come to Somaliland voluntarily to learn something about Somali culture and history, or they may have been forcibly sent back to Somaliland by their parents to learn how to behave in a way that is acceptable according to their parents' interpretation of Somali culture. The number of young Somalilanders who are sent back to Somaliland for corrective education is difficult to estimate, but several cases for this purpose have been reported for Denmark alone.

RISK MANAGEMENT
AND TRANSNATIONALISM

As shown in this chapter, a large part of the population of Hargeisa, and life in Somaliland more generally, needs to be seen as being heavily entwined in a global world of dispersal, travel, remittances, communication and trade. Looking historically at how Somalis have survived in the Horn of Africa for centuries, it appears that they have been practicing forms of trans-nationalism long before the term was introduced into migration research and defined as the processes by which migrants forge and sustain multi-stranded social fields that cross geographic, cultural, and political borders (Basch et al., 1994: 7).

As pointed out by Horst (2004: 2) in her study of livelihood strategies among Somalis in a Kenyan refugee camp, Somalis have been accustomed to dealing with insecurity even before the war and flight. Therefore, when the war broke out, Somalis employed an already elaborate mobile strategy in their attempt to manage insecurity. According to Horst (ibid), this mobile strategy or "nomadic heritage" consists of three elements: a mentality of looking for greener pastures, a strong social network that entails the obligation to assist each other in surviving, and risk-reduction through strategically dispersing investments in family members and activities. Horst points out that these three "nomadic" characteristics, developed from local circumstances of life in Somalia, have now acquired a transnational character and are still supporting Somali refugees in the Kenyan camp in their daily survival (ibid). In other words, many Somalis, both as refugees living in camps in Kenya, as asylum seekers in Western countries or as revolving returnees in Somaliland, employ transnational livelihood strategies: They travel between different socio-economic settings to take advantage of more than just one place; they operate within strongly dispersed social networks; and they invest in different socio-economic settings and activities. In this sense, travelling within a transnational family that spans both Europe and Somaliland, investing both in pursuing ones professional career in Somaliland and Europe, or building a house in Somaliland and at the same time applying for better housing in London are all part of the same "nomadic cultural pattern".

However, in order to understand revolving returnees in Somaliland today we need to reflect on what a "transnational livelihood strategy" is and question whether it is mere adaptation to global socio-economic circumstances. In a study of circular migration between Puerto Rico and the United States, Duany (2002) concludes that subsistence strategies among migrants have broadened geographically to include several markets, multiple home bases, extended kinship networks and bilingual and bicultural practices. Of course, circular migration and other forms of transnational practices are expressions of some form of "subsistence strategy" emerging from an adaptation to more than one socio-economic locality. Even so, we need to be careful not to reduce mobility and transnational practices to mere global adaptation to emerging political, social and economic circumstances. Reflecting on a life-long engagement with nomadism, Salzman (1995: 160) points out that migration patterns cannot be seen as an empirical index of socio-economic variables. In other words, patterns of mobility, dispersal and diverse investments should be seen as cultural constructions brought to an environment rather than behaviour patterns generated by the environment. Paraphrasing Salzman's conclusion on how to understand pastoralism and "nomadism proper" (ibid: 163), we need to see "transnational adaptation" or "transnational nomadism" (Horst, 2004) as a complex and plural process including the interaction of cognitive, affective, technological, demographic and organizational factors that generate patterns of human custom and action. In other words, we need to stress that people relate to their surroundings with much more than a rational calculation of economic opportunities in mind.

With regard to revolving returnees in Somaliland, we need to stress that they engage in transnational activities, not only or even primarily out of a strategy of "risk management", but for a variety of reasons. Looking economically at migrating to Somaliland, it often makes no sense to come to Somaliland after having spent many years in the West. To many, it resembles more "risk taking" or "experimenting" than "risk management". In the remaining part of this chapter, some of the most apparent reasons why revolving returnees engage themselves in Somaliland are underlined and reasons why they tend to maintain mobility between Somaliland and the West are analysed.

OPPORTUNITIES AND INDIVIDUALITY IN A VIRGIN COUNTRY

There is a widespread conception among revolving returnees that they have "great opportunities" in Somaliland. Whether they are in Somaliland to do business, pursue their professional careers, get in contact with "their culture" or buy land they believe they have "better opportunities" to do so in Somaliland. This "opportunity talk" corresponds well with the "nomadic heritage" of always looking for greener pastures. It appears that the newness of Somaliland presents the possibility of a new beginning and gives the country an aura of "virginity". As explained by a revolving returnee from Norway:

> Here I can be involved in making decisions. I can be somebody. I can become a minister. I can become whatever I like. There I was a home teacher, teaching Somali…and it will continue like this forever…, but here I can make my career and might be able to go up with the luck and the contacts. I think here it is virgin. Things are not mature like in Norway, where things have already been done. Everything…here everything is undone, up to now… and then you can start things. You can start with other people. You can do whatever you like…. It is a bit like going to America in the old days….Somaliland is like the new found land….

The image of "virginity" reflects the impression that Somaliland was destroyed during the civil war and now faces a process of rebuilding and revival. In this sense, revolving returnees see themselves as persons who will play an important role in the future of Somaliland. Besides filling empty chairs in ministries and opening up shops in the main streets of Hargeisa, many revolving returnees also take up part-time farming and thereby physically engage themselves in "cultivating the virgin country". The image of "virginity" presents Somaliland as a new and emerging entity that, with the proper care and attention, will bear fruit and become a well-functioning country in the future. The above-mentioned Somalilander from Norway returned to Norway after spending half a year in Somaliland, however. He was unable to realize his dream of finding a job in politics and therefore decided to return to Norway to work as a teacher. His wife had come to Somaliland several years earlier to work for a local organization funded by several international donors, and she stayed in Somaliland. He returned to Norway very disillusioned at not having been able to find a job and knowing that he would now have to live alone in Oslo.

To many revolving returnees the notion of "virginity" corresponds to a feeling of being "reborn"; of once again being able to reclaim individualized identities lost in diaspora. Revolving returnees in Somaliland stress how they have been subjected to stigmatization and racism in the West. They explain that very few in the West care about or recognize their individual characteristics, and instead see only "a black refugee from Somalia". Revolving returnees explain that in Hargeisa, they enter another social sphere where the anonymity and stigmatization of being a Somali refugee burdening the West is replaced by the recognition and appreciation of individual identities and merits. Hargeisa is a city where a lot of time is spent talking about "who is who" and socializing. In this way, revolving returnees are positioned within a known social world of friends, family, rumours and gossip, where people know who they are. As explained by a male Somalilander from Canada:

> I got tired of living in other places. I have worked in Canada for a long time and I thought that it was about time to go back.... Otherwise, I would stay in Canada, and my intention had never been to stay there.... Some people will make home wherever they go, but some will never fit in; they will remain outsiders... ...Also, you want people to know who you are... ...One time, I was walking in France with a friend, and after two hours we realized that we had not met anyone that knew us.... This can be nice...but when you come here everybody knows you.... When you arrive in the airport, even the porter knows who you are.... This gives you status, and it makes you feel part of society....

The relationship between "returnees" and "stayees" varies of course for the different empirical cases. Both "stayees" and "returnees" may be welcoming, tolerating, accepting, rejecting, antagonistic or even violent towards each other (cf. Van Hear, 1998: 56). In Somaliland, the relationship between revolving returnees and those who live more permanently in Somaliland seems to be neither outright positive or welcoming, as identified by Kibreab

(2002) in the case of Eritrea, nor especially conflictual, as identified by Stefansson (2003) in the case of Bosnia. Contrary to both the Eritrean and Bosnian cases, almost everyone fled Somaliland. In other words, there are only few "stayees" to claim the moral high ground in relation to revolving returnees. The general picture is one of acceptance and high expectations towards revolving returnees or "Somalilanders from the diaspora". Many people in Somaliland look upon revolving returnees as having a special responsibility for their personal and national well being. However, if revolving returnees from the West are not able to meet the financial demands made by a vast number of relatives, friends and acquaintances, they may face social exclusion, harassment or even threats (see Farah, 2004). The above-mentioned Somalilander from Canada works for an organization in Somaliland and lives partly in Somaliland and partly in Canada. At the end of 2003, he went back to Canada to celebrate Christmas with his family and to lobby for more money for the organization he works for in Somaliland.

LOCAL AND DIASPORIC CAPITAL

As pointed out above, revolving returnees travel between Somaliland and Western countries for a variety of reasons. Revolving returnees only engage themselves in Somaliland when and if they have the possibility to do so. This section, does not primarily analyse *why* revolving returnees engage themselves in Somaliland, but rather *how* they do so.

To a large extent, revolving returnees use their skills, networks and money from the West to position themselves within society in Somaliland. They are not just individuals whom people recognize as having this or that very local and specific personal background; they are also people with a distinct "diasporic capital". The notion of "diasporic capital" points to a combination of economic, cultural and social capital forms accumulated in or referring to the diaspora. Lamont and Lareau (1988:156) define cultural capital as "institutionalized, i.e., widely shared, high status cultural signals…used for social and cultural exclusion." Revolving returnees in Somaliland use their "cultural capital" in a variety of conscious and unconscious ways. For example in relation to the "development industry", they have language skills and Western education that enables them to find employment within development institutions. Moreover, they build relatively impressive houses, drive big cars, wear "Western" clothes, and listen to Western music, and with these cultural signals, they stage themselves as diasporic Somalilanders in Somaliland. Social capital has been defined as "the aggregation of the actual or potential resources that are linked to possession of a durable network or more or less institutionalized relationships of mutual acquaintance or recognition" (Bourdieu, 1985: 248). Social capital is a useful notion in understanding revolving returnees in Somaliland because it focuses our attention on the positive sides of sociability, and highlights how non-monetary forms of capital can be important sources of power and influence. Revolving returnees in Somaliland use their transnational networks to find employment in Somaliland. For example, many revolving returnees are well connected to British or Danish development institutions with running projects or funding

Revolving Returnees in Somaliland

capabilities in Somaliland. In this way, social capital needs to be thought of in relation to a theory of transnational and very local networks.

An important point, however, is that their "diasporic capital" will not secure their success or well being in Somaliland. In order to "be somebody" as a businessman, development worker, politician, or just to live and function socially in Hargeisa, you will need to be well connected to the local context and to know your way around the social fabric of society. Most things in Somaliland work through personalized networks and only very seldom through bureaucratic structures or formalized systems. For people without friends, family or social skills, Hargeisa presents a tremendous challenge. People use their connections, ties, friendships and family relations whenever they want to achieve or obtain something, and a lot of time is spent on socializing simply because you want to expand your network for potential future use (cf. Simons, 1995). If a diasporic Somalilander is not well connected in Somaliland, he or she will only rarely be able to convert any form of "diasporic capital" into a successful private business or political career. You may have the opportunity to invest hundreds of thousands of dollars in Somaliland, but without the right local connections to important business partners, the government, clan elders and other important persons and institutions, such an investment will be close to impossible. Therefore, revolving returnees all have personal histories and ties to Hargeisa and the Somaliland society. It is precisely the fact of being "locals", having a family history and a good knowledge of how the society works that enables them to also "become somebody". In this sense, revolving returnees present an interesting combination of having both accumulated economic, cultural and social capital in the West, and of being well embedded in local realities and agendas.

An example that illustrates this point well is a Somalilander from England who has started a transport company in Somaliland. At present, the European Community is importing food aid to Ethiopia through Somaliland. This has created quite a lucrative business for Somaliland transport companies that are paid more than five times the local rates for transporting European surplus food from the port of Berbera to eastern Ethiopia. This man has bought two trucks in England and sent them to Somaliland via Holland and Djibouti. He lives in Hargeisa together with his grandfather, father, mother, sisters, brothers and cousins in a house that has been with the family for many years. He was born in Hargeisa, and his family has a long history in Hargeisa. According to him, his grandfather was quite famous, and if he mentions his nickname, everybody knows who he is. Half the year he lives and works in Hargeisa, and half the year he lives with his wife and two children in London. The money for buying the trucks and setting up a transport company in Somaliland has been accumulated in London by working at two cleaning jobs. He is planning to bring his wife and children to Hargeisa, and he is building a big house with its own playground that will hopefully persuade them to join him in Somaliland. He wishes to settle more permanently in Hargeisa. First of all, this is where he grew up and where most of his family lives. Secondly, he has the possibility of starting his own transport company in Hargeisa, something he would never be able to do in England.

Many factors enable him to start and run a successful transport company: He speaks the Somali language; he has a family name that many people know and trust; he knows his way around the city and the country; he knows how to approach the people that need goods to be transported; and he knows what to do in case he has an accident or if someone damages his truck. If he should have an accident and kills someone, members of his extended family will help him pay the compensation to the family of the deceased – this system, based on clan identities and loyalties, is quite important, since there are no functioning insurance companies in Somaliland. Also, if for some reason he should be arrested by the police or "get into trouble" in other way, his extended family will secure his release or help him in whatever way they can. The point is that in doing business, he relies on his family and friendship ties to Hargeisa and Somaliland, and he also has a good understanding of cultural values and practices. The fact that people trust him because they know his family is very important. Without a well known and trusted family in Hargeisa, it would be very difficult for him to do business. In this sense, "being somebody" also enables him "to do something".

The point about social capital is that it highlights the fact that participation in groups and deliberate construction of sociability can be instrumental in accumulating economic capital. Of course, networks and social relations are not given but need to be created through interaction and often in Somaliland also by economic investments in friends, family and potential network members. Compared to cultural capital that is "inside people's heads", and economic capital that is in people's banks or money transfer accounts, social capital has a more intangible character (Portes, 1998). Through social capital, actors in Somaliland may gain access to economic capital such as loans, information about the market, investment opportunities or contracts with the European Commission. Through networks, revolving returnees are also be able to accumulate cultural capital, in the sense that they come in contact with people that know more about doing business or driving a truck. In short, it is the interplay of economic, cultural and social capital that enables people to engage in Somaliland.

THE CONTINUATION
OF TRANSNATIONAL PRACTICES

In this chapter, I have analysed migration between Somaliland and Western countries as a specific form of transnational practice. One of the most basic conclusions to be drawn is that people engage in transnational activities only when they can. As I have described, they need networks, knowledge, money and documents to be able to "circulate" between Somaliland and the West. Revolving returnees in Somaliland have many reasons for engaging in transnational activities, as they relate to their surroundings in a variety of ways. Whatever their motives for migrating may be, they believe that they have better opportunities in Somaliland than in the West. These "opportunities" and the wish to "do something" and "be somebody" may relate to making money, pursuing personal careers, living with family and friends, living in a society that is known and appreciated, and in general becoming who they want to be. In this sense, transnational practices are not mere adaptation to global socio-economic circumstances and opportunities. Migration to Somaliland more resembles "risk taking", "experimenting" or "gold digging" in a virgin country than actual "risk management".

As has been pointed out, many migrate between Somaliland and the West because they are not able to find a permanent job in Somaliland or provide a stable and high income for themselves and their families. The unemployment rate is very high and the well-paid jobs within the "development industry" and the private business sector are very limited. Wannabe politicians may fail in talking too much about women's rights and democracy, and restaurant owners in not reading the signs and opening up a Thai restaurant. People may not be adequately skilled in socializing, in creating and sustaining ties, connections and alliances, or they may simply not have the patience and stamina needed to settle more permanently in Somaliland. They will return to the West, because they become annoyed, irritated and tired of always having to mobilize and negotiate networks whenever they need or want something. They will return to the West, when they become weary of the often unrealistic expectations of family and friends that they pay for everything every day. They will return when they run out of money, get sick, need to have their teeth fixed, or when their children have to start school. In Somaliland, quite a few of them are tired of the "chaotic system", "clan politics" and "corruption". They miss the security and comfort of living in a Western country that provides health services, social security and education. Often, they are almost nostalgic about the "Western system" with its "laws and regulations", "governance", "order", "punctuality" and "effectiveness". In short, it is the interplay of economic, material, social and cultural aspects that determines their engagements in transnational activities.

REFERENCES

Aleinikoff, T.A.
  1995   "State-centered refugee law: From resettlement to containment",
          in D.E. Valentine and J.C. Knudsen (Eds), *Mistrusting Refugees,
          California*, University of California Press.

Allen, T., and H. Morsink
  1994   "Introduction: When refugees go home", in T. Allen and
          H. Morsink (Eds), *When Refugees Go Home*, United Nations Re-
          search Institute for Social Development (UNRISD), Geneva, 1-13

Appadurai, A.
  1990   "Disjuncture and difference in the global cultural economy", in
          M. Featherstone (Ed.), *Global Culture*, Nationalism, Globalization
          and Modernity, SAGE Publications, London, 295-310.

Bakewell, O.
  1996   *Refugee Repatriation in Africa: Towards a Theoretical Framework?*,
          University of Bath.
  1999   "Returning refugees or migrating villagers? Voluntary repatriation
          programmes in Africa reconsidered", *New Issues in Refugee Re-
          search*, UNHCR, no.15.

Basch, L., N. Glick Schiller, and C. Szanton Blanc
  1994   "Nations unbound: Transnational projects, postcolonial predica-
          ments and deterritorialized nation states", Gordon and Breach,
          USA.

Bascom, J.
  1994   "The dynamics of refugee repatriation: The case of Eritreans in
          eastern Sudan", in Gould, W. T. S., A. M. Findlay (Ed.), *Population
          Migration and the Changing World Order*, John Wiley & Sons,
          New York, 225-248.

Bourdieu, P.
  1985   "The forms of capital", in J.G. Richardson (Ed.), *Handbook of
          Theory and Research for the Sociology of Education*, Greenwood,
          New York, 241-58.

Cassanelli, L.
  1982   "The shaping of Somali society: Restructuring the history of a pas-
          toral people 1600 – 1900", University of Pennsylvania Press.

Duany, J.
  2002   "Mobile livelihoods: The sociocultural practices of circular mi-
          grants between Puerto Rico and the United States", *International
          Migration Review*, 36(2): 355-388.

Farah, N.
  2004   *Links*, Picador, London.

Fink-Nielsen, M. and N. Kleist
  2000   Tilhørsforholdets politikker. En analyse af hvorfor så få somaliere
          repatrierer fra Danmark, Kanditatspeciale ved Internationale
          Udviklingsstudier og Historie.

Ghosh, B.
  2000   "Introduction", in B. Ghosh (Ed.), *Return Migration: Journey of
          Hope or Despair?*, International Organization for Migration and
          the United Nations, 1-5.

Gmelch, G.

1980   "Return migration", *Annual Review of Anthropology*, 9: 135-159.

1992   "Double passage", *The Lives of Caribbean Migrants Abroad and Back Home*, The University of Michigan Press, Ann Arbor.

Hammond, L.

1999   "Examining the discourse of repatriation: Towards a more proactive theory of return migration", in R. Black and K. Khalid (Eds), *The End of the Refugee Cycle? Refugee Repatriation and Reconstruction*, Berghahn Books, New York and Oxford, 211-227.

Hannerz, U.

1996   *Transnational Connections: Culture, People, Places*, Columbia University Press, New York.

Hansen, P.

1998   "Frivillig repatriering – en beskrivelse og kritik af et ideal", *Dansk Sociologi*, 1(9): 23-39.

2001   *Afsted – en analyse af betydninger af sted blandt tilbagevendte flygtninge I Somaliland*, Specialerække nr. 187, Institut for Antropologi, København.

2004   "Migrant remittances as a development tool: The case of Somaliland", IOM Working Papers Series No. 3 June, Department of Migration Policy, Research and Communications.

Horst, C.

2004   "Transnational nomads: How Somalis cope with refugee life in the Dadaab camps of Kenya", PhD-dissertation, University of Amsterdam.

IOM

2004   *Return Migration, Policies and Practices in Europe*, International Organization for Migration, Geneva.

Kibreab, G.

2002   "When refugees come home: The relationship between stayees and returnees in post-conflict Eritrea", *Journal of Contemporary African Studies*, 20(1): 53-80.

King, R.

2000   "Generalizations from history of return migration", in B. Ghosh (Ed.), *Return Migration*, International Organization for Migration, Geneva, 57-100.

Lamont, M., and A. Lareau

1988   "Cultural capital: Allusions, gaps and glissandos in recent theoretical developments", *Sociological Theory*, 6: 153-68.

Lewis, I.M.

1961   *A Pastoral Democracy*, A study of pastoralism and politics among the Northern Somali of the Horn of Africa, James Currey, Oxford.

1994   "Blood and Bone", *The Call of Kinship in Somali Society*, The Red Sea Press, Lawrenceville.

Malkki, L.H.

1995   "Refugees and exile: From 'refugee studies' to the national order of things", *Annual Review of Anthropology*, 24: 495-523.

Portes, A.

1998   "Social capital: Its origin and application in modern sociology", *Annual Review of Sociology*, 24(1): 1-26.

Rogge, J.
1994 "Repatriatrion of refugees. A not so simple 'optimum' solution", in T. Allen and H. Morsink (Eds), *When Refugees Go Home*, United Nations for Social Development, Geneva, 14-49.

Rouse, R.
1991 "Mexican migration and the social space of postmodernism", *Diaspora* 1(1): 8-23.

Salzman, P.C.
1995 "Studying nomads: An autobiographical reflection", *Nomadic Peoples*, 36(37): 157-166.

Stefansson, A.
2003 "Under my own sky? The cultural dynamics of refugee return and re(integration)", in Post-War Sarajevo, PhD Thesis, Institute of Anthropology, University of Copenhagen.

Stepputat, F.
1994 "Repatriation and the politics of space: The case of the Mayan diaspora and return movement", *Journal of Refugee Studies*, 7(2): 175-185.

Simons, A.
1995 *Networks of Dissolution*, Somalia Undone, Westview Press, Colorado.

UNHCR
1980 Note on Voluntary Repatriation, Submitted by the High Commissioner, Executive Committee of the High Commissioner's Programme, Sub-committee of the whole on International Protection, UNHCR REFWORLD CD-ROM. 7, *edition: January 1999*, Genève, 27 August.
1985 Conclusion no. 40, Voluntary repatriation, *UNHCR REF WORLD CD-ROM. 7, edition: January 1999.* Genève, 36.
1993 Information note on the development of UNHCR's guidelines on the protection aspects of voluntary repatriation, Executive Committee of the High Commissioner's Programme, Sub-committee of the whole on International Protection, *UNHCR REFWORLD CD-ROM. 7, edition, January 1999.* Genève, 23rd meeting, 3 August.
1994 General conclusion on International Protection. No. 74 (XLV), *UNHCR REFWORLD CD-ROM. 7, edition: January 1999*, Genève.
1997 Annual Theme: Repatriation Challenges. Executive Committee of the High Commissioner's Programme, UNHCR REFWORLD CD-ROM. 7, *edition: January 1999*, Genève, 48 session, 9 September.
2003 *2002 Annual Statistical Report: Somalia*, UNHCR, Genève.

Van Hear, N.
1998 "Migration crises and the making of diasporas", in *New Diasporas: The Mass Exodus, Dispersal and Regrouping of Migrant communities*, UCK Press, London, 13-62.

Warner, D.
1994 "Voluntary repatriation and the meaning of return to home: A critique of liberal mathematics", *Journal of Refugee Studies*, 7(2): 161-174.

Revolving Returnees in Somaliland

Transnational Family Life Across the Atlantic:

The Experience of Colombian and Dominican Migrants in Europe

Ninna Nyberg Sørensen

Luís E. Guarnizo

ABSTRACT

I t is generally accepted that migration motivation and decision making is embedded in larger family concerns. However, assessments of the role that migrants play in promoting development in the source countries still take their point of departure in issues such as remittances, return and diaspora support *without* considering who migrates and who stays behind, under what circumstances, for what purposes, and with which consequences. In analyses of the feminization of particular migration streams, the developmental impact is moreover often assessed in negative terms and as leading to spatially fractured family relations and even family breakdown.

This chapter aims at critically supplementing this debate through an analysis of transnational family life among Latin American migrants in Europe by addressing two crucial issues. The first concerns the question of whether and how the feminization of migration translates into new and distinct transnational family relationships. The second issue concerns the consequences of spatially fractured husband-wife / parent-child relations. It is concluded that fractured family relations tend to precede rather than result from female migration. Moreover, state regulation in destination countries, as well as sending states' attitudes towards incorporating transnational migrants into the nation, seem to be related to the more implicit, micro-political forms of exclusion and inclusion in the everyday lives that shape the standing and status of differently situated and hierarchically ordered family members.

Living Across Worlds: Diaspora, Development and Transnational Engagement

153

In his latest book, Göran Therborn (2004) describes changes in the family institution throughout the 20th century. Therborn applies a global historical and sociological perspective on the family and uses this to show how the development of different, territorially delimited geo-cultural family systems has been far from evolutionary. He concludes that despite the fact that the family institution has undergone profound changes, there is no empirical evidence for declaring the post-family society. Therborn's global perspective refers to the interconnectedness of social phenomena, variation and inter-communication, which he then juxtaposes with more universalistic and uni-linear understandings of socio-cultural development. His analysis incorporates the influence of international migration on historical changes in the family and is primarily concerned with hybrid/creole family forms that took shape after large-scale migrations, for example, from Africa to America. However, Therborn's analysis mostly focuses on territorially bounded family structures and only to a limited extent encompasses family life in which relations and functions are carried out *across* rather than *within* specific and well delimited geo-cultural spaces.

This chapter aims at supplementing the family-theoretical discussions within sociology and demography by drawing on the recent theoretical literature on gendered cultural politics, migration and transnational processes. The transnational turn in international migration research has sparked vigorous debates among migration scholars. From the early 1990s to the present, the study of transnational migration – or more broadly transnational social practices – has expanded its terrain from anthropology and sociology into geography, political science and international development studies, where it has led to new conceptualizations of mobility's (and to a lesser extent immobility's) transformative effects on the relationship between the social and spatial. Throughout the chapter, we attempt to contribute to this project through an analysis of transnational family life, which according to Vertovec (2004) is the "everyday provenance of most migrant transnationalism".

Early transnational theorizing established that "family processes and relations between people defined as kin constitute the initial foundation for all other types of transnational social relations" (Basch et al., 1994: 238). Although based on a rather conventional construction of "family" – i.e. father-mother-child bonds and heterosexual normativity – such studies maintained that a focus on transnational family life is crucial to the analysis of what makes people engage in transnational activities in the first place. Challenging the notion that the motivation behind migration is mainly economic, Hondagneu-Sotelo (1994) found that in the case of Mexican migration to the US, several women embarked on migratory projects in order to change their relationships with spouses or other relatives that oppressed them back home. Their migration often involved leaving behind a set of limiting family relations and finding in the US opportunities to question their more traditional roles as mothers and housewives.

Drawing on such insights, the specific aim of the chapter is to introduce a more nuanced analysis of the relationships established between different family members' transnational family formations and the power relations served and sustained through transnational family ties. This slight expansion in focus is helpful in accounting for continuity and change in family structures caused by international migration. The following analysis addresses two issues. The first concerns the question of whether the feminization of particular migration streams translates into new and distinct transnational family relationships. The second issue concerns the consequences of spatially fractured husband-wife / parent-child relations. Then follows a discussion on how transnational family life generally is understood and applied in contemporary analyses and whether alternative approaches can be envisaged. We address these issues with reference to two Latin American migrant groups – Colombians and Dominicans – in various European countries.[1]

Why focus on these Latin American groups in Europe? The existence of transnational processes has been widely documented by a large and growing body of literature about multiple migrant groups – especially of Latin American, Caribbean, and Asian background in the US. Documenting such processes in a European context is still rather novel and, except for the case of Spain, rarely includes Latin Americans. More specifically, we have chosen Colombian and Dominican migrants because recent studies in the US have documented their significant transnational connections with the countries from which they migrated, a central concern of our inquiry here. Finally, we are interested in discussing gendered cultural politics, migration and transnational processes in relation to Colombians and Dominicans because of the predominance of female migrants among these two groups in Europe.

We have chosen to build the analysis around six cases. These cases are not *representative* in the conventional sociological meaning of the term. Nevertheless, we claim that these cases are exemplary or typical of larger processes occurring as a result of contemporary migratory conditions. As such, the cases represent a variety of common experiences found during our comparative, multi-sited, and multi-year field work.[2] The cases are constructed by us based on the narratives of various migrants during long, in-depth conversations – some of which lasted several hours. The cases represented below are thus short summaries of larger and more nuanced accounts. We have made an effort to preserve the core experience of each case.

THE FEMINIZATION OF MIGRATION AND TRANSNATIONAL FAMILY RELATIONSHIPS

"Space invites movement", says Spanish writer Juan Goytisolo, who since the late 1950s has spent most of his life in exile, primarily in Paris and Marrakesh. Women and men may choose to move to whatever land they "deem appropriate", but they may also abandon their "native land" in search of a better life, for freedom, to make money, or out of necessity. Moving temporarily or permanently elsewhere does not necessarily mean that women and men are cut off from or themselves cut off social relationships to those left behind. On the contrary, Goytisolo continues, "Many migrants risk their lives to reach forbidden shores to be able to fulfill their family obligations: to provide for dependents and make living back home a possibility" (Goytisolo, 2004, my translation). That both women and men embark on migration to fulfill family obligations back home is of course a key insight. However, since most gender constructions privilege notions of masculinity and femininity that locate women in dependent roles to men, our argument throughout this article is that it matters a lot *who* in the family engages in transnational migration for the form and conditions under which their migration is socio-culturally and morally evaluated.

Current international migration, stimulated by uneven globalization and growing economic inequalities between northern and southern countries, has reversed the direction of traditional population flows and led to a growing complexity in migration practices and experiences. This complexity manifests itself in the *substitution of "old" migration destinations by new ones*, which in the present case means a redirection of Colombian and Dominican migration from the United States to Europe. This emerging complexity of migration is also observed in the growing social heterogeneity and *informalization* of migration, as migrants from the same source country increasingly include individuals of different class background who are often forced to enter the countries of destination surreptitiously (i.e. without the officially required documents or with forged ones) and often have to find work in an informal labour market. Finally, the complexity manifests itself in the *feminization* of particular streams. The increase in independent female migration has led to a renewed focus on the centrality of gender as a defining vector of migratory experiences and consequences for family structures, gender roles, and social organization in the source and destination countries of migrants. It has also led to various analyses of transnational family life, including work on transnational motherhood (e.g. Hondagneu-Sotelo and Avila, 1997), transnational childhood (e.g. Salazar Parreñas, 2003), and more recently transnational fatherhood (e.g. Pribilsky, 2004).

There is a general consensus in the existing literature according to which the concept of the family generally denotes a domestic group made up of individuals related to one another by bonds of blood, sexual mating or legal ties. The family is generally defined either in terms of the kinds of relations and connections encompassed by the institution (e.g. the domestic group or household, close kin who are not necessarily co-resident, and the wider network or deeper genealogy of kinship) or in terms of its functions (e.g. regulation of socialization, sexuality, labour and consumption). Within feminist theory, the family has moreover been conceptualized as a gendered unit of reproduction and cultural transmission or a space for gendered social relations (Anthias, 2000).

Within migration research, identification of the family with the domestic group has given rise to various analytical problems. First, many have seen family separation due to migration as potentially if not inevitably leading to family disintegration. Together with news stories and policy reports, scholarly work has repeatedly pointed to rising incidents of spousal abandonment, separation and divorce, male alcoholism, teenage pregnancies, children's poor school performance, delinquency and even high incidence of child suicide as a consequence of family separation due to migration (for a summary of such accounts, see Hochschild, 2003: 22). Second, the prediction of negative outcomes has been conspicuously salient in work dealing with migrant female mothers who leave husbands and children behind (for a critique, see Gamburd, 2000; Salazar Parreñas, 2003). However, as Pribilsky argues, the focus on disorganized households or family life totally misses the nuances surrounding men's (and women's) mobility; women's (and men's) reaction to it; the manifold ways migration transforms, reorients and reprioritizes conjugal relationships; as well as parent-child relationships in transnational social space (Pribilsky, 2004: 315).

In their rethinking of conventional wisdom on migration, Levitt and Glick Schiller (2004) approach transnational family life as social reproduction taking place across borders. They draw on Bryceson and Vuerela, who define transnational families as families that live some or most of the time separated from each other, but yet hold together and create a feeling of collective welfare and unity; a process they term "familyhood across national borders". Transnational families, Bryceson and Vuerela argue, have to cope with multiple national residences, identities and loyalties. Like other families, transnational families are not biological units *per se*, but social constructions or "imagined communities". And like other families, transnational families must mediate inequality amongst their members, including differences in access to mobility, resources, various types of capital and lifestyles (Bryceson and Vuerela, 2002: 3-7).

The forces that hold transnational families together may be stronger than the forces, both legal and physical, that separate individual family members. This is one of the central arguments that Herrera Lima (2001: 89) posits in reference to the fluid transnational social space that migrants have created between the Puebla-Tlaxcala region in Mexico and the New York City Metropolitan area. Transnational families, Herrera Lima argues, are buffered by extensive social networks, allowing transnational experiences to form a fluid continuum, rather than a radical divide compartmentalizing life into two separate worlds (Herrera Lima op cit: 91). Dispersed family members are brought together in one social space by emotional and financial ties. They stay in contact by modern means of communication and by occasional physical movement between sending and receiving societies.

Are there any grounds for thinking that transnational practices connecting Latin American and Caribbean families across the Atlantic would differ in any way from the Mexico-US experience described by Herrera Lima? In other words, are there reasons to believe that Europe-bound migration would provide a different context from which to evaluate gendered cultural politics, migration and transnational processes? To answer this question we would need to consider first the relationship between the feminization of migration and the position of women in the source countries (Ribas-Mateos, 2000). Secondly, we have to take into account women's labour incorporation into particular sectors of a given destination country's economy in order to be able to understand their social positioning and to discern their ability to maintain specific types of family relations and structures across borders (Anthias, 2000). Finally, the general circumstances of migration, in part shaped by the legal context provided by the source countries, should be considered as a contributing factor. For example, while the US has allowed continued immigration, however restricted it may be, most European countries have adopted a quite different take. Indeed, apart from family reunification, asylum, and work contracts in the service sector, most European countries have been virtually closed to legal migration since the early 1970s (Sørensen, 2002).

For the past several years, most labour demand in Europe has concentrated on the service sector, especially in domestic activities (from domestic labour to child and elderly care). These activities are conventionally conceived of as feminine activities. This partially explains why, in Europe, female Latin American migrants outnumber men by far. Not surprisingly, they tend to be particularly concentrated in domestic service and the sex/leisure industry, sectors that severely restrict living what most people would consider a "normal" family life. At the same time, their work makes possible the transformation of the subordinate role of women as unpaid family workers to paid family workers capable of providing for their family members living elsewhere. But while migrant domestic workers may have strong transnational family links and major responsibilities for providing for relatives left back home (Anthias op cit: 20; Gamburd, 2000; Sørensen, 2004), stricter migration controls and highly segregated migrant labour markets may not only limit "familyhood across borders" but also produce new and distinct transnational family relationships and structures. These include entering into marital relationships with European men in order to gain access to the continent in the first place through *matrimonio por residencia* (marriage for a visa, see Brennan, 2003), or, when in Europe, marriage to a European in order to legalize an undocumented status. Relationships *por amor* (for love) and relationships *por residencia* (for residence) may both result in distinct transnational family relations for which the country of origin no longer necessarily remains the prime point of reference. Given the complex array of possibilities, we therefore need to define what we mean by "transnational family relationships" – e.g. whether they only include family members sharing the same nationality of whom some reside abroad – before concluding what is "distinct" in such relationships and what may be a continuation of mobile livelihood strategies across international borders.

Dominican-Dutch-Indian family relations

The case of Lourdes,[3] who at the age of 19 migrated from the Dominican Republic to the Netherlands in 1988, is illustrative of the complexity of transnational family life. Lourdes' migration was facilitated by a Dominican woman who held Dutch nationality and claimed Lourdes to be her biological daughter. Lourdes left two young children in the care of her sister. When the Dutch authorities later found out that Lourdes was not blood-related to her sponsor, Lourdes lost her residence rights and had to begin the process of regulating her status all over again. This involved going back to the Dominican Republic to do the paperwork related to her own and her two young children's migration. Back in the Netherlands, Lourdes claimed welfare on the basis of being a single mother. She stayed on welfare for four years before taking up factory work. She then had her third child, the fruit of a relationship with a Dominican living in the Netherlands.

Lourdes met her current husband in the mid-1990s, the son of Indian migrants to Germany, now holding Dutch citizenship. His parents and siblings have all returned to India. In 1998, Lourdes and her Indian husband went to the Dominican Republic together. The purpose of the trip was to see whether they could establish themselves there permanently. Her husband was quite eager to establish a new family life in Santo Domingo, but Lourdes found it impossible to put up with local social conditions and low educational standards. The family moved back to the Netherlands after five months.

Over the years, Lourdes has facilitated the migration of a sister, an aunt and a cousin. Back in Santo Domingo, Lourdes still has her grandfather, her father, and four brothers to whom Lourdes and her husband send occasional remittances (to cover medical expenses in the case of illnesses). The family members in India are rather well-off and have no need for remittances. On the contrary, they have occasionally contributed to Lourdes' family economy in the Netherlands, not least since the birth of their granddaughter (Lourdes' fourth child) in 2002. Lourdes is currently applying for Dutch nationality. Although she finds life in the Netherlands very difficult, she has no plans of return.

The case of Lourdes illustrates that it is possible to maintain transnational family relations to family members in the Dominican Republic while simultaneously redefining the meaning of transnational family life. Over the years, Lourdes' family has come to consist of members living in more countries than those of "origin" and "destination". Her children moreover hold dual citizenships of various combinations.

Dominican-US-Scandinavian family relations

Other migrants may have broken the ties to an original country of origin. This is the case of Coco, a Dominican migrant to Denmark. Coco was only three years old when his mother, in the early 1970s, left the Dominican Republic for New York. His mother's situation in Puerto Plata had bean deteriorating steadily after the divorce from Coco's father, and news from Dominicans already established in New York City about readily available factory work convinced her that a better future was awaiting her there. Coco was left in the care of his *abuelos* until he, six years later, joined his mother in Queens. During Coco's childhood years, his mother succeeded in leaving sweatshop work behind. She re-married a US-resident, entered the university and, after graduating in advanced technology, found a well-paid job as a computer specialist. At the age of 21, Coco accompanied his mother on his one and only family visit to the Dominican Republic. It was a bad experience. In New York, he was considered an immigrant because of his Dominican ancestry. Back on the island, the locals – even his own family – called him immigrant because he came from New York.

After graduating in sign language, Coco worked with young deaf-mutes in Queens and Manhattan. He went to Spain, Norway, Holland and Italy, always returning to New York, where he felt he had his base. The trips abroad lasted three to six months and often involved overstaying a tourist visa. His stay in Norway resulted in a son born after his departure. Considered an African-American (though holding a Dominican passport) by local immigration authorities, Coco was never subject to the kind of problems fellow migrants (mostly North African) encountered. In 1998, he met a Danish woman in New York City. Together, they went to Copenhagen where the Danish girlfriend became pregnant. Given Coco's good career prospects in New York City, they decided that he should return, and that she should visit after giving birth to their daughter, to see if she could live there. She could not and went back to Denmark. In December 1999, Coco boarded a plane to Copenhagen with the intention of staying only six months. However, he found a relatively well-paid cleaning job, married (to secure his migrant status), began taking Danish classes, and through assistance from the Education Centre for Immigrants was able to enter an integration programme that paved the way to a job in an institution for deaf-mute children, a job he holds to the present. Coco currently lives with his nuclear family (wife and daughter) in Copenhagen. He maintains contact with his mother, sister and other family members in New York. When confronted with the migration researcher's question about remittances – one of the ways in which we as researchers try to establish the level of transnational relations between source and destination countries – he insisted that he is not sending remittances to anybody. Curiously, it turns out that Coco in fact remits monthly allowances to his son in Norway, with whom he maintains contact through visits.

Lourdes and Coco both live what we may consider transnational family life. They maintain links to family members, emotional as well as financial, but these family members are not necessarily located in their country of origin but rather dispersed in transnational space, including family members holding different nationalities. In Lourdes' case, this dispersal includes a sense of collective unity and welfare with family members in the Dominican Republic as well as in India; in Coco's case, money is sent from Denmark to Norway, while emotions flow in many directions. They represent their current family relations – the ruptures on the way notwithstanding – as no more nor less "harmonious" than conventional undivided families. They also both reject, in a rather non-nostalgic way, that the place in which they were born and grew up necessarily provides the best environment for unfolding family life.

CARE AND CHANGES IN GENDER RELATIONS DUE TO FEMALE MIGRATION

Much, albeit by no means all, literature on transnational migration has tended to concentrate on cases in which migration is generally described as being successful in maintaining family allegiances through a constant circulation of family members and in functioning rather smoothly across borders.[4] However, the emergent literature on "global care chains" takes a less sanguine approach, proposing instead that such relations are problematic, not only for marital life but also for the children left behind, who may suffer from a "care drain". The argument is that a growing wage gap between poor and rich countries, blocked social mobility, and an increase in female-headed households in developing countries have contributed to the feminization of migration. Demand for care-taking functions has risen in developed countries. As in conventional supply-push and demand-pull theory, global care chains are being created by the importation of care and love from poor to rich countries. In this process, the transfer of services associated with the wife/mother's traditional role leads to a "care drain" in the countries of origin (Hochschild, 2000; Ehrenreich and Hochschild, 2003). In other words, the labour demand for migrant women in caretaking functions has encouraged the emergence of "care-drained" transnational family forms, which appear to be somewhat distinct from those created by migration only a few decades ago when the demand was primarily for male workers.

In an attempt to formulate a general theory of global cultural processes without necessarily blaming the victim, Appadurai suggests that global diasporas involve immense strains on families in general and on women in particular. Women bear the brunt of "deterritorialized" family life, since "they become pawns in the heritage politics of the household, and are often subject to the abuse and violence of men who are themselves torn about the relation between heritage and opportunity in shifting spatial and cultural formations". However much dispersed family members may "enjoy the fruits of new kinds of earning and new dispositions of capital and technology", they have to "play out the desires and fantasies of these new ethnoscapes, while striving to reproduce the family-as-microcosm of culture" (Appadurai, 2003: 42).

But migration not only serves to re-orient and question conventional gender roles, family values and family functions. As Therborn's (2004) broad review of family forms in the 20th century – as well as numerous anthropological studies – have shown, the "family" covers a multitude of senses of relatedness and connections, among them mother-centered families in which the mother-child bond forms the affective and economic core and where the conjugal relationship is neither central nor necessary either to childrearing or to the family itself. This is relevant for the present analysis, since female-centred family forms are widespread throughout the region, based either on cultural valuing and centrality of the mother or in response to poverty and exclusion (for a summary, see Sørensen, 2004).[5] Although the cultural notions of "family" vary in the Colombian and Dominican cases (both between as well as within the two countries), we may say, with a somewhat rude generalization, that the two socio-cultural or economic processes of female-centred family forms mix. Given the further impoverishment generated by globalization, more female heads of households are forced to migrate.

Female-centered family relations … and the Italian novio

The mix of female-centred family forms and impoverishment may be illustrated by the case of María. María was born in urban Cali in 1961. She grew up in her parents' house, both employees with the railways. After marrying in the early 1980s, she moved with her husband to a small apartment where her daughter, Lupe, was born. The separation from her husband in

1986 coincided with the death of her father. She moved back to her mother's house, partly to support her during a difficult period, partly so that the mother could look after Lupe while María worked. Over the years, she managed to save a little money that she invested in a house of her own not far from her mother's.

Around 2000, María decided to migrate abroad, to any place that would allow her to make a better living. She contacted a local woman known for having helped Colombian women with travel arrangements to Europe. To be able to pay for the "travel agent's" services María took a loan in her house. She left Cali in April 2001 and boarded a plane from Bogotá to Madrid, and from there she travelled by train through Barcelona and Montpellier in France to La Spezia in Italy. The travel "package" included both initial boarding (in an apartment owned by a Dominican woman who made a living by renting out beds to newly arrived immigrants) as well as her first job (caring for an elderly Italian woman).[6] After two months she found a better paid job washing dishes in a restaurant. She met her current Italian *novio* (boyfriend) in the restaurant and moved into his apartment a couple of months later. The fact that he paid the rent and the daily living expenses enabled María to pay back her dept in Colombia within four months. After another eight months, she was able to sponsor her daughter's migration.

According to María, migrant women are obliged to establish relationships with Italian men. The two other alternatives – working as live-in domestics or working in the sex industry – are dead ends if one wishes to legalize or bring in other family members. Moreover, living with the Italian *novio* allows María and Lupe to remit around 600 euros a month for Maria's mother. Another 200 euros are spent on long-distance calls. Back in Colombia Maria's mother spends the money from Italy to add another floor to her house in Cali with the plan of supplementing her future income through rental. Marrying the Italian *novio* is not part of Maria's future plans. She intends to return to Colombia in a couple of years, while Lupe will stay in Italy. The plan is to establish Lupe as a self-employed *locutorio* owner, a migrant service business offering cheap international phone calls and other communication services. Both María and Lupe put a little money aside each month for the down payment for a small business place. Future business profits are meant to not only secure Lupe a better living in Italy, but also to enable her to remit money to María upon her return to Colombia.

Political insecurity in Colombia and stereotypes in Spain

Another case of female-centred family migration is represented by the Mejias, who in September 2002 were gathered in Josefina's apartment in Madrid. At the time of the interview, Josefina was 34 years old. She and her younger sister Celia were raised by Magaly, who became a single mother at the age of 20. When the daughters were old enough to contribute to the family economy, the three women began saving money for a family house, which they bought in the early 1990s in Medellín. By the late 1990s, however, they could no longer meet the down payments and had to sell the house.

The Mejías' migration history took off when Josefina a few years earlier had enough of the insecure living conditions in their hometown Medellín. Violence had made movement around the city a daily hazard. This had affected Josefina's school-age son to the extent that his psychological well-being was at risk, and had deteriorated the national economy to the extent that Josefina's wages – as an employee of a courier service – could no longer pay the monthly bills. With her mind set on migration, Josefina calculated the advantages of various countries. Visa requirements, language and currency value were seriously considered. To Josefina, Japan seemed a good option because of the yen, but then again very far away and difficult because of the language; USA, known to the family since a brother on Josefina's father's side migrated there in the 1980s, looked good in terms of wage opportunities but was a problematic choice in terms of obtaining visas; Costa Rica offered a more safe environment than Colombia as well as a shared language, but why go to another "Third World" country; and finally there was Europe. A sister of Magaly migrated to Switzerland in the mid-1980s, but from family visits, the three women knew that living expenses there were very high. Spain, on the other hand, offered a common language, relatively low living costs, and – perhaps most important – the possibility of entering without a visa.[7] After visiting Spain on a two-week tourist trip in January 2001 with Celia – an employee of Avianca with access to free travel – Josefina decided on Spain. Back in Medellín, Josefina sold her remaining belongings, boarded a plane to Madrid in April 2001, and left her son in the care of her mother.

Josefina started her migrant career in Spain as a sales agent for a Colombian textile firm. She then found employment in a cafeteria and supplemented her income by distributing information material for a computer firm during her time off. Later, she became an agent for a firm that promoted various products and was assigned to promote the sale of Kiwi fruit in Spain. Finding decent housing turned out to be more difficult than finding a job, since most rental offices or private renters backed out after learning that Josefina was Colombian. Luckily – and perhaps somewhat strategically – she met a Spanish man who signed the lease for an apartment into which they both moved. While her relationship to the Spanish *novio* paved the way to legalizing her status via marriage, finally having an apartment served the more immediate and pressing need to receive her son. By the end of 2001, Josefina reunited with her son in Madrid, who arrived accompanied by his grandmother Magaly.

Back in Colombia, Celia continued working for Avianca. To qualify for international travel bonuses – key to the female-centred family's future migration plans – she moved from Medellín to Bogotá. When in the autumn of 2002 she was eight months pregnant, she and her husband went to Madrid to visit Josefina and to ensure that their baby daughter would be a dual Colombian-Spanish citizen by birth. While they both intended to go back to Colombia, they were keen on securing a possible exit back to Spain for their daughter, a Spanish citizen by birth. They ignored, however, that Spain does not grant any immigration rights to parents of Spanish citizens, as the US does.

Contrary to María in Italy, Josefina seemed determined to marry her middle-aged Spanish boyfriend to legalize her status. Magaly, her good looking, 52-year old mother, played with the thought of following Josefina's example. Though Celia and her husband both held good jobs in Colombia, and actually returned shortly after delivery, the unstable and dangerous political and security situation in Colombia made it imperative to keep exit options open.

In both María and Josefina's cases, divorce occurred *before* migration, meaning that fathers and husbands were absent prior to the decision to migrate. Children were left behind for a relatively short period in the care of grandmothers who already participated in the children's caring and rearing. While we could expect an emotional drain on the part of children and mothers as a consequence of their temporal separation, these two cases illustrate that a "care drain" will not necessarily occur. Tactical relationships to European men were established either to enlarge the monetary flows to the homeland, to legalize migration status, or to find decent housing. Legal migration status can facilitate circular migration – as when María uses her legal status to reunite with a daughter in Italy in order to enable her own return migration – or serve as the grounds on which the entire family can relocate abroad in the future, as may be the case for the Mejías. The everyday tactics of these women must of course be understood as framed by structural factors that place migrants in a vulnerable position; the construction of Latina women in the minds of sometimes older, and often not particularly attractive European men, who may or may not take advantage of migrant women's vulnerability; and the use by migrant women of native men's needs/constructions to overcome their structural disadvantages.

Compadrazgo, domestic work and blurred family boundaries

In other cases, however, family members stay separated for extended periods of time. This has been the case of Fresa and her teenage daughters. Fresa was born in a rural village in the Dominican Republic, but was taken in by an upper class family in the capital when she was orphaned at the age of 13. It is not uncommon for poor Latin American families to establish fictive family bonds of *compadrazgo* to richer families. In Fresa's case, this bond involved working for her fictive kin as a live-in domestic. They treated her to some extent as "part of the family", but on the other hand, never allowed her the luxuries of their own children, e.g. to attend school or pursue any career. She waved goodbye to the family's children when they left for school in the morning and prepared their *bocadillos* and hot chocolate when they returned in the afternoon. At the age of 25, Fresa married a poor and honest man and moved from the upper class neighbourhood of her employers to one of Santo Domingo's working class barrios. Her husband treated her well and within three years their relationship resulted in two daughters. But it is not everyone's lot to live happily ever after. Shortly after the birth of her second child, Fresa's husband died. Left with no means of subsistence, Fresa returned to work for her former employers. She stayed until 1994, when she was offered to go to Panama and work for a Jewish family who were close friends of her Santo Domingo employers. She accepted the offer (the pay was substantially better than what she could earn in Santo Domingo), left her daughters in the care of her husband's sister, and boarded a COPA flight for Panama City. Her contract lasted two years, during which time she remitted most of her income for the daughters' education.

Back in Santo Domingo, she once again returned to work for her "old" family. When the family father in 2002 was stationed in Amsterdam, she was asked to join him. She signed a contract for domestic service, which paved the way for legal entry to the Netherlands. Shortly after her arrival, however, the by now old patriarch fell ill and died. His son, for whom Fresa served as a nanny during his childhood years, replaced him. Working for him, however, included much more than was stipulated in her contract (e.g. cleaning some of his friends' apartments); and he refused to pay the 1,200 Euros stipulated in her contract in addition to full board. Moreover, he insisted that her entire monthly wages be transferred to a bank account in Santo Domingo. This arrangement saved Fresa the Dutch income tax. The flip-side is, however, that Fresa needs to have money wired by Western Union from Santo Domingo to Amsterdam each time she has to pay her expenses.

Fresa wished to leave her job, but her legal status in the Netherlands depends on this particular contract. She contemplated finding herself a Dutchman. Last year, she met an older man, with whom she established a relationship. But he nevertheless left her for another younger foreign woman. She hopes to find another man, leave the unsatisfying domestic work behind, and establish herself as a Dutch housewife. By now her daughters in Santo Domingo consider the aunt to be their mother, and although this hurts Fresa's feelings, she maintains a sense of motherhood by contributing to their education *para que ellas tengan otra salida de la que he tenido yo*.

Fresa's experience is in many ways typical for many poorly skilled Dominican migrants of colour working in domestic service in Europe. Many of these women are poor, have migrated from rural to urban areas, and worked in domestic service prior to international migration. The consequence is long-term separation from their children. Marital instability is more acute amongst the poorer sectors of Dominican society, and many single women – whether divorced or widowed – leave their country in a search for social rights and services or at least better income opportunities. The family background of other migrants is matrilocal and based on serial monogamy (Sørensen, 2004).[8] While not necessarily improving their own lives and working conditions, international migration enables substantial economic contributions. In addition to emotional care and guidance from afar, these migrant mothers are able to pay for the education of the children they left behind, expecting to break the chain of poverty. While not denying the hardships migration places on such parent-child relationships, a focus on global care drain risks missing the nuances surrounding motherly love and ways of caring.[9]

TRANSNATIONAL MOTHERHOOD, FATHERHOOD AND CHILDHOOD

Migration serves to re-orient and question normative understandings of gender roles and ideologies by altering traditional roles, divisions of labour and other meaningful categories of gender and generational construction. With international migration, the task of cultural reproduction in intimate arenas such as husband-wife and parent-child relations easily becomes politicized and exposed to the "traumas of deterritorialization as family members pool and negotiate their mutual understandings and aspirations in spatially fractured arrangements" (Appadurai, 2003: 42). But as the previous examples have shown, they do not necessarily lead to disorganized families, spousal abandonment, divorce and emotional entanglement in the children left behind.

Approaching this issue of transnational family life from a different angle, namely that of fatherhood as it is played out in current male migration from Ecuador to the United States, Pribilsky (2004) sets out to examine conjugal relations, co-parenting, and family life. He takes issue with two commonly held views of transmigration, namely that spousal separation due to migration necessarily leads to family disintegration, and that gender studies focus on women's experience only. Based on interviews with male migrants in New York and their spouses in Ecuador, Pribilsky manages to "add" a gendered perspective on men's experiences and to present a more nuanced understanding of couples' work to redefine roles, relationships and family life across long distances and extended periods of separation.

While abroad, male migrants come to assume some traditional female roles such as cooking and cleaning, whereas women – in addition to handling remittances – come to take over tasks handled by their husbands before migration. Men's attention to the necessary domestic duties usher in "a new level of awareness of the gendered nature of work that otherwise might be routinely understood as natural and unchanging" (Pribilsky op cit: 319). Wives left in Ecuador are similarly brought into gendered spaces and positions previously associated with men (e.g. driving trucks and hiring day labourers). The level of social control nevertheless seems to differ. While infidelity may be a moral – if not an economic – possibility for men while abroad, women fear that even the slightest sign of impropriety may be reported by their in-laws to their husbands in the United States.

Why, then, do Ecuadorian women feel that they are "moving forward" even as their men reinforce their role as the primary breadwinners? According to Pribilsky, part of the answer lays in the qualitative difference between internal and transnational migration economies. When migrating internally, responsibility for both the generation and the allocation of income remains with those who migrate. When migration becomes transnational, migration not only tends to pay off better; the migrant also needs a "partner" to manage the economic gains. Remittance management invests "women with an authoritative language through which to make better claims for household needs" (Pribilsky op cit: 329).

In Pribilsky's analysis, it is not only relations between husbands and wife that change. Parental relationships to the couple's children are also altered. The argument goes as follows: In Ecuador, mothers are typically believed to foster relationships of trust (*confianza*) with their children, while fathers are expected to build such relationships through respect (*respeto*). Due to prolonged absences, men come to realize that if they want to have any relationship with their small children, they can no longer do it by exercising expectations of respect from thousands of miles away. Distance "made some hearts grow fonder" as Pribilsky puts it (Pribilsky op cit: 330). In addition, economically successful transnational migrant households can afford to relieve their children of their obligations to the family farm economy and send them to school. Providing "better" for the children is in itself an important index for relative success. Within the context of transnational parenting, the "transformation of children from 'economically worthless' to 'emotionally priceless' opens up new possibilities for the roles of father as well as mother" (Pribilsky op cit: 331).

Pribilsky's analysis is interesting on several accounts. Apart from showing that the migration of a parent is not always equal to a "broken home", his analysis also shows, however implicitly, that society's moral disciplining of transnational mothers and fathers varies to a great extent. Since fathers are supposed to be *absent* anyway, their migration abroad is in many ways a continuation of this absentee role. The current migration of Latin American women to Europe, however, goes against the grain of organic notions of *present* mothers, domesticity and morality, and culturally coded narratives of "family values" abound in the debate. As women are seen as symbolically representing the nation, there are strong sensitivities at play: within the sending state, within the national patriarchal community, and within the transnational community itself (Sørensen, 2004). The question nevertheless remains: Is the feminization of migration causing – or is it rather the conseq-uence of – volatile family relations? As our previous analysis has shown, marital separation may itself propel a single parent to travel abroad in search of a stable livelihood. So may exposure to violent family relationships.

INTERMEZZO: GENERALIZED AND DOMESTIC VIOLENCE

One of the world's most violent regions is Latin America. The most dangerous place for women and children in Latin America and the Caribbean may be their home, where most domestic and sexual violence takes place. Women and girls displaced by the continuing armed conflict in Colombia are furthermore vulnerable to violence perpetrated by armed actors. In Colombia, it is estimated that as many as 41 per cent of women are victims of violence at the hands of their husbands or partners. Statistics reveal that 5.3 per cent of women have been victims of sexual violence and that most of these women knew the perpetrator. In addition to gender-based violence within the family, Colombian women are also subjected to violence on account of the armed conflict. Not only are women and girls the majority of internally

167

displaced persons in Colombia, they are also particularly vulnerable to violence perpetrated by armed actors, who reportedly request that parents offer their girls to combatants for a weekend as a "community service" (Peacewomen, 2003).

A 2001 study of the prevalence of gender-based violence among female clients of PROFAMILIA and the public health services for teachers (SEMMA) in the Dominican Republic found that among the women attending these centres, 65.3 per cent reported emotional violence, 32.4 per cent reported physical violence, and 31.3 per cent reported sexual violence. The majority of these cases were perpetrated by a family member or someone known to the victim (Basta, March 2002: 3). The seriousness of domestic violence in the Dominican Republic is confirmed by the national police's death statistics. Between 1 November 2000 and 31 October 2001, 103 women were murdered in the Dominican Republic. 60 per cent of these murders were committed by a spouse. It is estimated that murder is the sixth cause of death among Dominican women aged 15-45, that one in six Dominican homes experience some type of family violence, and that 80 per cent of women who seek care do so as a result of domestic violence (CLAIHR, 2002).

The dangers of marrying for a visa

Among the experiences presented above, María and Josefina's migration decisions were directly affected by the situation of generalized violence in Colombia. None of the cases involves domestic violence. In the broader material, however, it is not uncommon that female migrants mention domestic violence as one among several reasons for deciding to migrate, and maybe even for choosing Europe over the US in order to escape a violent partner's wider social networks there. Prolongation of stay or postponement of return may be explained by reference to the problem of continuing political violence, the problem of *machista* violence within the family, as well as the problem of a tight European labour market not allowing Latino migrant occupational mobility and better earnings.[10] While some women may migrate with the understanding that family separation is temporary, many others may engage in transnational migration with the aim of *escaping the family* or relocating family members vulnerable to violence (domestic and political) abroad. Those entering into strategic relationships with European men may nevertheless find that the laws protecting European women from domestic violence may not apply to them.

This was the case for Patricia, who had her share of bad experiences with Colombian men before leaving Bogotá, first for New York City (2000-2001), then for Denmark (August 2003). Patricia, a lawyer by training and professional experience, found that in New York, a woman had to work her way up from bars and nightclubs before finding a more decent (but lower paid) job. In her own case, the nightclub work led to finding a North American *novio* and later to becoming a driver in his truck and trailer company. He promised to divorce his wife and marry her (to legalize her status), but before any action was taken the Twin Towers were attacked by terrorists, not only causing horror, death and grief among the people directly affected by the attack but also seriously deteriorating the life of undocumented migrants, who were suddenly seen as a security threat. Not daring any longer to walk the streets without papers – as well as feeling worried about her daughter, who she left in her grandmother's care in Bogotá – Patricia decided to return to Colombia.

Back in Colombia, Patricia posted her picture and a brief bio-statement on a dating website. A Danish man responded and went to Colombia to meet her in the spring of 2003. After three days, the couple married. Given the new Danish family reunification laws, the Danish authorities turned the couple's application for Patricia to enter Denmark down. Patricia nevertheless entered Denmark through a tourist visa to Sweden and was – after long and troublesome negotiations – allowed family reunification with her Danish husband only to find that he had a dark and hidden history of abusive relationships to foreign women. After a violent domestic fight, Patricia ended up in a crisis centre for battered women. Imagine her surprise when she learned that the "democratic" and "egalitarian" Danish society that was presented to her during Danish language and integration classes could not offer much to migrant women but deportation, if they divorce an abusive husband before they have been married for seven years!

ON FAMILY, NATION AND LEVELS OF INCLUSION

Migrants often interact and identify with multiple nation states and/ or localities, and their practices contribute to the development of transnational communities (Levitt, 2001) or a new type of social formation within trans-national social space (Faist, 2000). Such social formations are not static but transformed along the way. Existing studies of transnational migration have tended to look at larger processes of cross-border family relations, but have largely failed to address more closely micro-social processes – such as family formation and family transformation – beyond the simple description of continuous connections across borders. This is not least because the empirical research foci have remained concerned with the social ties that connect family members of the *same nationality* across nation state boundaries (for further critique, see Sørensen and Olwig, 2002). In order to further the discussion, it is necessary to let go of what Wimmer and Glick Schiller have termed methodological nationalism; that is, the assumption that the nation state is the logical, natural container within which social life – and by implication family life – takes place (Wimmer and Glick Schiller, 2003). Therborn's (2004) global analysis of geo-cultural family systems is a step in the right direction. However, due to this analysis' territorially defined optic, methodological nationalism is to a certain extent substituted with what we might call methodological regionalism.

Discourses on transnational family life in the age of feminization of migration have generally been framed in terms of gender relations within households or families. Relatively absent in these analyses are discussions of how state policies and programmes at both ends of the migration continuum influence family-level gender politics (Goldring, 2001) and the political economy of emotions (Sørensen, 2004). Such analyses run the risk of either victimizing or vilifying migrant women and of downplaying the valuable contributions these women make to those depending on them (and to their home countries' economies). As Salazar Parreñas has forcefully argued, questioning migrant women's role as mothers moreover promotes the view that a return to the nuclear family is the only viable solution to the emotional difficulties of children in transnational families (Salazar Parreñas, 2003: 52-53). One problem among others related to a nuclear family centred perspective is that this perspective is ethno- or Eurocentric, since the nuclear family is less wide-spread, even within our own societies, than habitually assumed (Therborn, 2004). It also overlooks how migrants transform the meanings of motherhood and fatherhood to accommodate spatial and temporal separations. Finally, it overlooks how migration and labour-market policies contribute to the spread of transnational families between source and destination societies as well as to the creation of new transnational family forms by marriage into and/or family formation with a wide selection of nationalities.

Of course, any definition of transnational families must be cognizant of differences between various migrant groups as well as of social, cultural and economic differences within distinct groups. At the same time, however, new transnational family alliances are formed *across* lines of national origin, race, ethnicity, class and sexuality. Nevertheless, migration research concerned with the family habitually takes for granted that transnational families consist of family members originating from the same national group.[11] While transnational analysis has vigorously shown how transnational social spaces emerge within the setting of international migration systems as well as within and beyond the specific legal and administrative framework of inter-state regulations, the focus on long-distance social ties may have reintroduced methodological nationalism in other guises, namely that family ties to fellow nationals are the most important and the only ones that count as "family". But whether women and men marry for love or for visas, enhanced border controls and strict migration policies are actively contributing to the formation of dual or multinational families.

The emergence of family structures and the shape they take across borders are not just the result of processes at the micro level. State regulations of inclusion and exclusion in host societies (through immigration policy, citizenship, integration, labour market regulations, social welfare policies, and so forth) – and in sending societies (through dual citizenship laws and the extension of certain social benefits to their extraterritorial co-nationals) – affect the everyday lives of those involved in the micro-politics of transnational family formation in its multifarious combinations and re-combinations. Transnational family life, therefore, should be seen as affected by complex and interconnected social, political and economic processes. The role of the state, and the policies associated with it, must inevitably be grappled with. So must the cultural and moral values forming the basis for family and migration policies. In Europe, transnational migration was not perceived as a threat to family life before the late 1980s, when the number of migrant women began increasing significantly. This suggests that changes to the gendered division of labour – in Europe as well as in the migrants' countries of origin – may play a much more decisive role in the emergence of transnational family life than hitherto acknowledged.

As the case examples provided throughout the paper have shown, there is a dire need for a reconstituted gender and family ideology (based on reality) and family policy (based on emerging transnational needs) in sending as well as receiving countries. A first step, in domestic as well as foreign policy, is to recognize the economic contributions women make to their families by redefining motherhood to include providing economically for one's family (Salazar Parreñas, 2003: 54).

A second step would be to approach not only problems pertaining to transnational motherhood but also to transnational fatherhood and childhood. The latest round of worries around transnational family life should be placed in historical context. Throughout the second half of the 20th century, transnational fathers and husbands provided resources, including human capital (skills, knowledge and traits that foster achievement in society), financial capital (money, goods, and experiences purchased with income), and social capital (e.g. family and community relations that benefited children's social development (Gills, 2000)). While there is no reason to believe that transnational mothers should not be able to do the same – or even "do the same better" – there are good reasons to critically scrutinize how changing migration legislation and job opportunities continually redefine the nation state by redefining the status of its inhabitants and their familial relations (paraphrasing Bryceson and Vuerela, 2002: 11).

An emerging policy area is care for the children of transnational families (see Hochschild, 2000; Salazar Parreñas, 2003). Calling for the return of migrant women will not necessarily solve the problems of being the main breadwinner, nor will it solve the problem of domestic violence plaguing families in the countries of origin or the violence mothers and children may suffer in their new "European" families.

Goytisolo (2004) reminds us of a central sentence in *A Thousand and One Nights*: "The world is the house of those who do not have a house". The world of human rights and the right to asylum nevertheless routinely discriminates against women by relegating the issue of domestic violence to domestic practices inside houses but outside the orbit of international protection. Letting go of ideal and unworldly idealist notions of the family as a harmonious social unit and realizing that migration can be caused both by a wish to sustain as well as a need to escape family relations seems to be a good feminist point of departure.

NOTES

1. The empirical examples presented stem from an ongoing research project carried out jointly by the authors among Colombian and Dominican migrants in Europe (Spain, Italy, the United Kingdom, Denmark and the Netherlands). The project has been partly funded by the Danish Social Science Research Council.

2. The larger project compares the mode of incorporation, transnational practices, and development effects of Colombian and Dominican migration to Europe. Data collection started in the summer of 2002 and finished in July 2005. It includes in-depth interviews with some 500 Colombian and Dominican migrants in multiple locations in Spain, Italy, England, Denmark and the Netherlands, and with around 200 returned, visiting migrants or family members in various locations in Colombia and the Dominican Republic. It also includes a probability sample of 821 Colombian and Dominican migrants in Madrid, Barcelona, Rome, Milan and London conducted between January and July 2005.

3. To protect the anonymity of informants, names used throughout the chapter are fictitious.

4. The cost of migration for Dominican family relations, in particular for children, was documented by Guarnizo (1997a, 1997b).

5. Migration induced by sexual orientation, that is, the migration of lesbian, gay and transsexual individuals, engenders other forms of relatedness and connections that may lead to new family forms.

6. The fact that María's migration was facilitated by a Dominican woman shows that transnational networks are not necessarily bound to the national migrant group. Dominicans established themselves in the Italian care industry before mass migration from Colombia took off. Their by now matured networks can be used by other national groups, often for a fee.

7. Spain did not require visas from Colombians until 2002.

8. We note this to underline that marital instability not necessarily and always is due to poverty but also may be the effect of culturally specific family forms.

9. As Steven Vertovec reminds us, emotional entanglements do not just relate to the children left behind. They may as well pertain to children who accompany their migrant parent(s) and may end up feeling "caught between two nations, educational systems and ways of growing up" (Vertovec, 2004).

10. There is lively debate over whether local labour market conditions or migrant's legal status determine migrant incorporation in host countries as well as their transnational practices. These two issues are hardly separable. Still, we maintain that states are capable of controlling social mobility (through regulation of the labour market), whereas their capability to control physical movement is rather limited. Thus, states do not control migration as such, but they do control the conditions under which transnational social relations are developed.

11. This is currently the case in Denmark where transnational families have become synonymous with some migrant groups' practice of finding a spouse in the country of origin. A new law introduced in 2002 requires that migrants living in Denmark must be over 24 years old to marry and bring their spouse to Denmark. The Minister for Integration legitimizes the policy by claiming that it prevents forced/arranged marriages.

REFERENCES

Anthias, F.
2000. "Metaphors of home: Gendering new migrations to southern Europe", in F. Anthias and G. Lazaridis (Eds), *Gender and Migration in Southern Europe: Women on the Move*, Berg Publishers, Oxford.

Appadurai, A.
2003 "Disjuncture and difference in the global cultural economy", in J. Evans Braziel and A. Mannur (Eds), *Theorizing Diaspora*, Blackwell Publishing, Oxford.

Basch, L., N. Glick Schiller, and C. Szanton Blanc
1994 *Nations Unbound: Transnational Projects, Postcolonial Predicaments and Deterritorialized Nation States*, Gordon and Breach, USA.

BASTA
2002 http://www.ippfwhr.org/publications/download/serial_issues/ basttta200203_e.pdf.

Brennan, D.
2003 "Selling sex for visas: Sex tourism as a stepping stone to international migration", In B. Ehrenreich and A.R. Hochschild (Eds), *Global Women: Nannies, Maids, and Sex Workers in the New Economy*, Granta Books, Great Britain.

Bryceson, D.F., and U. Vuerela
2002 "Transnational families in the twenty-first century", in D.F. Bryceson and U. Vuerela (Eds), *The Transnational Family: New European Frontiers and Global Networks*, Berg publishers, Oxford.

CLAIHR (Canadian Lawyers for International Human Rights)
2002 Current Projects: Dominican Republic, http://www.claihr.org/ projects_current_dominican.htm.

Ehrenreich, B., and A.R. Hochschild (Eds)
2003 *Global Women: Nannies, Maids, and Sex Workers in the New Economy*, Granta Books, Great Britain.

Faist, T.
2000 *The Volume and Dynamics of International Migration and Transnational Social Spaces*, Oxford University Press, Oxford.

Gamburd, M.
2000 *The Kitchen Spoon's Handle: Transnationalism and Sri Lanka's Migrant Housemaids*, Cornell University Press, Ithaca and London.

Gills, J.R.
2000 "Marginalization of fatherhood in western countries", *Childhood; a Global Journal of Child Research*, 7: 225-238.

Goldring, L.
2001 "Disaggregating transnational social spaces: Gender, place and citizenship in Mexico-US transnational spaces", in T. Pries (Ed.), *New Transnational Social Spaces: International Migration and Transnational Companies in the Early Twenty-first Century*, Routledge, London.

Goytisolo, J.
2004 *Metaphors of Migration*, Keynote Speech at the World Congress on Human Movements and Immigration, Barcelona, 2-5 September.

Guarnizo, L.E.

1997a "Going home', class, gender and household transformation among Dominican return migrants", in P.R. Pessar (Ed.), *Caribbean Circuits: New Directions in the Study of Caribbean Migration*, Center for Migration Studies, New York.

1997b "The emergence of a transnational social formation and the mirage of return migration among Dominican transmigrants", *Identities*, 4(2): 281-322.

Herrera Lima, F.

2001 "Transnational families: Institutions of transnational social space", in L. Pries (Ed.), *New Transnational Social Spaces: International Migration and Transnational Companies in the Early Twenty-first Century*, London, Routledge.

Hochschild, A.R.

2000 "Global care chains and emmotional surplus value", in A. Giddens and W. Hutton (Eds), *On the Edge: Globalization in the New Millennium*, London, Sage Publications.

2003 "Love and gold", in B. Ehrenreich and A.R. Hochschild (Eds), *Global Women: Nannies, Maids, and Sex Workers in the New Economy*, Granta Books, Great Britain.

Hondagneu-Sotelo, P.

1994 *Gendered Transitions: Mexican Experiences of Immigration*, University of California Press, Berkeley.

Hondagneu-Sotelo, P., and E. Avila

1997 "I'm here but I'm there: The meanings of latina transnational motherhood", *Gender and Society*, 11(5): 548-571.

Levitt, P.

2001 *The Transnational Villagers*, University of California Press, Berkeley.

Levitt, P., and N. Glick Schiller

2004 "Transnational perspectives on migration: Conceptualizing simultaneity", *International Migration Review*, (forthcoming).

Peacewomen

2003 Colombia's Humanitarian Crisis, http://www.womenwarpeace.org/colombia/colombia.htm.

Pribilsky, J.

2004 "Aprendemos a convivir: Conjugal relations, co-parenting, and family life among Ecuadorian transnational migrants in New York City and the Ecuadorian Andes", *Global Networks*, 4(3): 313-334.

Ribas-Mateos, N.

2000 "Female birds of passage: Leaving and settling in Spain", in F. Anthias and G. Lazaridis (Eds), *Gender and Migration in Southern Europe: Women on the Move*, Berg Publishers, Oxford.

Salazar Parreñas, R.

2003 "The care crisis in the Philippines: Children and transnational families in the new global economy", in B. Ehrenreich and A. R. Hochschild (Eds), *Global Women: Nannies, Maids, and Sex Workers in the New Economy*, Granta Books, Great Britain.

Sørensen, N.N.
2002 "New landscapes of migration? Transnational migration between Latin America, the US and Europe", in B.F. Frederiksen and N.N. Sørensen (Eds), *Beyond Home and Exile: Making Sense of Lives on the Move*, Roskilde University, Roskilde.
2006 "Narratives of longing, belonging and caring in the Dominican diaspora", in J. Besson and K.F. Olwig (Eds), *Caribbean Narratives,* MacMillan, London.

Sørensen, N.N., and K.F. Olwig (Eds)
2002 "Work and migration", *Life and Livelihoods in a Globalizing World*, Routledge, London.

Therborn, G.
2004 "Between sex and power", *Family in the World 1900-2000*, Routledge, London.

Vertovec, S.
2004 "Trends and impacts of migrant transnationalism", Centre on Migration, Policy and Society Working Paper No. 3, University of Oxford.

Wimmer A., and N. Glick Schiller
2003 "Methodological nationalism, the social sciences, and the study of migration", an Essay in Historical Epistemology, *International Migration Review*, 556-610.

Adios Peru: Persistence and Variation in Peruvian Transnational Engagement

Karsten Paerregaard

ABSTRACT

This chapter explores the migration experiences of eight Peruvians that in different ways elicit the circumstances that urge them to leave their country of origin. In particular, it examines to what extent migrants' decision to emigrate is influenced by their social and ethnic status in Peru that has been thrust upon them because of the migration histories of their ancestors. Moreover, this chapter examines how migrants' previous migratory experience (whether inside or outside the country) and economic and social status in Peruvian society influence their choice of destination and shape their current transnational engagement. In addition, this chapter examines how migrants construct different notions of home in response to the context of reception in their new settings as well as their previous migration experiences, and it discusses the ideas of belonging that these imaginaries give rise to. It concludes that Peruvian emigration is at variance with the migration practices described in the growing body of literature on transnational migration, and that a model of transnational engagement that takes into consideration people's previous migratory experiences and applies a global view of contemporary migration practices is warranted.

Ravenstein's attempt to formulate a law of migration more than a century ago was based on the assumption that population movements are the outcome of differences in economic and political development within and between nations (Ravenstein, 1885, 1889). The underlying premise of these laws is that migration occurs because people in areas where labour is abundant and capital is scarce move to areas where the reverse situation is prevalent (Kosinski and Prothero, 1975). From this perspective, then, migration is triggered by uneven patterns of development in different parts of the world, a rational response by society to counteract the emergence of relations of inequality and contribute to the welfare of the rich as well as the poor. However rational and consistent Ravenstein's theory may sound, world development in the 20th century demonstrates that the relations of inequality within and between nations do not automatically lead to increasing population movements, and that these, on the other hand, cannot be accounted for in pure economic and demographic terms.

Migration scholars influenced by the theories of modernization in the 1960s and 1970s recognize that people's decision to migrate is influenced by many variables (Lee, 1968). Thus, the push and pull theory claims that migration tends to increase not merely because people are attracted by better wages and life conditions in the area of destination, but also because they find the situation in the area of origin unsatisfactory (Eades, 1987). In other words, the circumstances that drive people to migrate are complex and may include relations that are not purely economic. The implication of the push and pull theory is that we regard migration as the outcome of a rational choice of what the migrant expects to gain and lose by moving to other locations. The variables that may influence such a decision can be material or economic, but other less tangible factors such as gender, ethnicity and political instability or the desire for modernity, education and individual freedom may play an important role as well (Safa, 1975).[1] An implicit supposition in these theories is that migrants feel a natural attachment to their place of origin, and that they continue to conceive of this as their "home" even after they have migrated. Similarly, they rest on the assumption that migration is an act of uprooting and moving away from a place of origin towards unknown and remote horizons and that the act of return, by contrast, is a movement that in both time and space brings the migrant back to where the migration process was initiated – "home".

This chapter argues that rather than viewing population movements as a one-way process in which people who migrate pull up their cultural roots and thereby turn their back on what is assumed is their "home", as is implied by the modernist paradigm implicit in the push-pull theory, we need to understand migration as multi-directed with multiple time movements in an extended process of movements that may take many directions and can continue over time, even over several generations. In effect, migrants may construct many different notions of home in response to the context of reception in their new settings, as well as to their previous migration experiences. The theoretical implication of such a view is that geographical mobility is conceptualized as an integral aspect of social life and an important resource in creating new livelihoods and achieving social mobility that people draw on when the opportunity occurs (Olwig and Sørensen, 2002). It also implies that we regard transnational engagement as an activity that is not only caused by macroeconomic and demographic changes but may vary in form and meaning depending on migrants' social and ethnic status in their country of origin. Rather than reducing the determinants of migration to structural conditions (whether economic or demographic factors) or individual decision making, this chapter argues that the causes of transnational engagement are complex and should be searched for in different realms of social life, including migrants' personal trajectory as well as family and ethnic history. In other words, social and ethnic groups may respond very differently to the same structural changes and opportunities to migrate, and such variations may be the result of larger migratory systems shaped by historic conjectures (Kritz and Zlotnik, 1992).

To study such migratory systems, the experiences of eight migrants are explored, that in different ways elicit the circumstances that urge Peruvians to leave their country of origin. In particular, the chapter examines to what extent migrants' decision to emigrate and choices of destination are influenced by their previous migratory history (whether inside or outside the country) and the social and ethnic status in Peru that has been thrust upon them because of the migration histories of their ancestors (Paerregaard, 2002). The data vary considerably from the observations made by recent attempts to theorize transnational migration mainly based on the studies of Caribbean and Mexican migrants in the United States (Portes, Guarnizo and Landolt, 1999), which suggest that a model of transnational migration must account not merely for the ties and relations that migrants create between one or two places of settlement and their country of origin (Rouse, 1995; Levitt, 2001; Glick Schiller and Fouron, 2001), but also for the global networks that emerge from dispersed migration patterns as practiced by Peruvians and other migrant groups (Axel, 2001; Salazar Parreñas, 2001).

The eight migrant experiences were gathered during field research among Peruvians in the United States, Spain, Argentina and Japan, and represent a broad selection of migrants in terms of not only gender and age as well as the economic and social stratification of Peruvian society. The ideas and imaginaries that migrants create of "home" are explored, and the identities that they give rise to are discussed. In a similar vein, I examine how migrants' previous migratory experience and economic and social status in Peruvian society influence their choice of destination and shape their current transnational engagement. For this purpose, I have indexed the eight migrant experiences in four groups according to migrants' position in Peru's national and ethnic ideology. This classifies Peruvians according to their class position as well as their migratory history and racial origin, thus conflating economic status with ethnic identity. As a result, the country's population is divided into two opposite segments: (1) the dominated classes synonymous with either Peru's ethnic minorities comprising the rural indigenous population scattered in the Andean highland and the descendants of former population movements such as the enslaved Africans imported to Peru in the colonial period, the labour migrants from Asia that arrived in the early republican period, or the rural-urban migrants of Indian descent living in the shantytowns of the country's major cities (the so-called *cholos*); and (2) the dominating classes identified as Peruvians of either European or mixed (*mestizos*) descent. The two segments are ranked in a social hierarchy that pictures the indigenous population together with the ethnic minorities and the *cholos* as an obstacle to progress and development and associates Peruvians of European descent and the *mestizos* with modernization and Western civilization.

Whereas the indexation of the eight narratives explored in this chapter recognizes the stratification of the Peruvian society into two opposite social classes, it also differentiates each of these in two subcategories according to ethnic classification, thus operating with a total of four groups: (1) ethnic minorities, who either belong to the country's indigenous population or are descendants of Japanese (so-called *nikkeijin*), Chinese or African migrant workers or slaves, (2) *cholos* (urban migrants of indigenous descent), who have moved to Peru's cities where they make up the bulk of the country's working class, (3) *mestizos*, who represent Peru's urban middle class, and (4) descendants of European immigrants from the country's upper class.

THE EIGHT MIGRANT EXPERIENCES

Nicario

Nicario was born in Alqaminka, a Quechua-speaking peasant community in the department of Ayacucho, in 1957. He was raised in a group of seven siblings. In 1968, he moved to Huamanga, the capital of the department of Ayacucho, together with his family, the first move in a long chain of migrations that eventually brought him to Lima and finally to the United States. In Huamanga, he finished elementary school and began to receive training as a folk artisan in accordance with the family's tradition. As both his father and grandfather were *retablistas*, Nicario learned to make *retablos* or rectangular wooden boxes with two painted doors, which contain small figures representing people and animals engaged in social and ritual activities, such as agricultural work, cattle-herding, trade and exchange, and religious celebrations of mostly Christian events.

In the early 1980s, the political violence in Ayacucho forced Nicario to migrate to Lima with his family, where he found a place to live in Comas, a shantytown in the northern part of the city. A few years later he was invited by a North American historian to lecture about his work as a folk artisan at one of Miami's universities, and in the following years, Nicario continued travelling to United States to participate in academic events. Simultaneously, he started to show his works, produced at his workshop in Barranco, at local art exhibitions in Florida. When he was granted a temporary residence visa in 1997, he decided to move permanently to Miami, bringing one of his daughters with him.

While lecturing in Miami, Nicario changed his notion of what it means to be a *retablista*. He learned that the distinction between folk art and true art is very fuzzy, and that his *retablos* are valued not only because he manufactures them according to an Andean folk art tradition, but also because of his

Adios Peru: Persistence and Variation in Peruvian Transnational Engagement

own individual ingenuity and creativity. This rethinking of his own identity as an artisan encouraged Nicario to engage in what he considers a personal struggle to win recognition as an artist, not only within the Peruvian community in Miami, but also at the official art exhibitions throughout the United States. In 1997, he established a workshop in a rented flat in Miami, which served as his main base for producing *retablos*. He later moved the workshop to Naples in West Florida, where he currently lives with his daughter. Periodically, he travels all over the United States to display his works at art festivals, which over the years has won him numerous prizes and opened the doors to the North American market. Yet Nicario does not feel that his works have won the recognition they deserve. When I interviewed him in Miami in 1998, he said, "They always try to place me in a special section of folk art, and they gave me all those prizes. But I wanted them to recognize my work as real art. So I ask them to place it in the section for art. Sometimes they let me do it. See, they think I'm a folk artisan because I'm Peruvian and make *retablos*. But I want them to understand that I'm an artist."

Nicario moves within a transnational network that allows him to renegotiate his role as a folk artisan in Peru and to redefine the meaning of folklore and art. In Lima, his wife and son continue to exhibit his *retablos* as folk art at a gallery in Barranco that also serves as a vehicle to promote the works of other Andean artisans. Nicario himself, however, invests most of his time exhibiting *retablos* at art festivals in North America, thus winning recognition as an artist. At the same time, he acknowledges the cultural roots of his *retablos* and the continuity between the traditional Cajón de San Marcos and his own creations by displaying his works together with the works of his grandfather, father and children. These fluid and apparently contradictory identities as traditionalist, rural folklore artisan and modern artist emerge from a migratory process through which Nicario links Alqaminka to Lima and Miami and a transnational network that connects him to artists and academics in the United States, folk artisans in Lima, and fellow villagers in Ayacucho. Nicario says, "I feel at home in many places. Today I live in Florida. Tomorrow I may live somewhere else."

Silvia

Silvia was born in Sarayka, a Quechua-speaking village in Peru's Andean highland where she grew up together with her family. When she was 18, her father sent her and Andrea, her older sister, to Lima, Peru's capital, to stay with one of their aunts. Silvia soon found a job as an assistant at a dental clinic in San Isidro, an upper class residential district, and she started to make plans for the future. These included a dream to *progresar* (to make progress); that is, get an education, make money and establish a life of her own. Two years later, Peru's violent conflict forced the rest of the family out of Sarayka to take refuge in Lima, where Silvia and her siblings offered them shelter and took care of them. Although Silvia and Andrea felt relieved that the family was reunited in Lima, they were now forced to spend all their earnings on maintaining their newly arrived parents, who were unemployed, and their sisters and brothers, who were too young to work. To make things worse, Silvia's boyfriend, Fredy, was pressuring her to accept, formalizing their relationship and become his future wife. In effect, she felt that her plans to save money in order to study, make a future career as a dental technician, and create a life for herself in Lima were hanging by a thread.

One year later, Andrea, Silvia's older sister, migrated to Miami in the United States, where an aunt offered her economic support and help to find a job. Andrea's departure left Silvia as the sole breadwinner in the family, and in 1992, she too left Peru and travelled to the United States overland as an undocumented immigrant. In Miami, Silvia soon found a job as a waitress and a place to live. However, Silvia's prospects of creating the kind of life she had dreamt of before migrating looked rather gloomy because of her illegal status. Hence, when a friend introduced Silvia to Danny, an American who was willing to marry her in return for US$ 3,000, she decided to accept. In 1996, the couple contracted marriage, which they planned to last for five years until Silvia would be entitled to receive a permanent green card. The arrangement, however, complicated Silvia's life considerably. The couple had trouble communicating because of language problems. Danny, who originates from the Midwest, hardly knew a single word of Spanish at the time when they married, whereas Silvia's proficiency in English was still rudimentary. Moreover, Danny's mother, who was getting worried about her son's sudden marriage, moved into the small flat the couple shared in north Miami Beach, creating further tension in the marriage.

Although over the years Danny has become involved emotionally with Silvia and wants to establish a permanent relationship, she continues to regard the marriage as a temporary solution to her problems. She says that she is counting the days until she finally can start on a life of her own and tell her family in Lima about her new life in the United States. After three years, Silvia obtained a temporary work and residence permit, and when I interviewed her in 1998 and asked her what she felt about her new life in the United States, she replied "Well, I feel more Peruvian now," and added, "I never liked Lima. I never felt at home. In the United States, people look at me as a true Peruvian. Here, I am more distant from my family and more independent. And people accept me here and respect my wish to make progress." And when I asked her whether she ever thought of returning, she said, "No, why should I? Of course, I miss my family and Sarayka but I can always go back to visit them. I feel as much home here as in Lima."

Antonio

The son of Japanese immigrants in Peru, Antonio identifies himself as a *nikkeijin*, that is, a descendant of Japanese emigrants. Encouraged by a Japanese contractor, who offered them a loan to finance the trip and helped them find work on Peru's sugar plantations, his parents left Japan in 1934 on the same boat to Peru as former President Fujimori's parents. Antonio's father laboured hard during his first years in Peru to pay off their debts, but was then successful in saving enough capital to buy land in Huaral, north of Lima. As Huaral at that time had a large colony of Japanese settlers, Antonio and his five brothers and sisters were brought up in an environment that was still strongly influenced by the customs and values of their parents' place of origin. Antonio recalls that his oldest brother, who was born before World War II, was the most "Japanese" of the six siblings, the others being more "Peruvian". He also remembers that when the family had visitors, their mother instructed her children carefully in their responsibilities. To his mother, Japanese visits had to be "perfect".

World War II radically changed the situation for Peru's Japanese colony. It reminded many *nisei* and *sansei* (second- and third-generation Japanese immigrants) that the ties that their parents and grandparents maintained with Japan and the exclusive identity as an ethnic minority that they claimed before the war was placing their position in Peru in jeopardy, and that their own future lay in the country where they were born. As a result, all Japanese schools in Peru were closed after the war, and the post-war generation of *nikkeijin* were given European names and learned to speak proper Spanish. This shift in orientation away from their nation of origin and towards their country of residence is reflected in the fact that since 1945, Japanese immigrants in Peru have married outside their own ethnic group to a much greater extent than *nikkeijin* in other South American countries, such as Brazil. Unlike their parents and older siblings, who grew up with the idea that they were real Japanese and therefore were going to return to Japan one day, the generations born after the war increasingly identify themselves as a mixture of Peruvian and Japanese cultures.

Antonio is painfully aware of the impact that World War II had on his life. Not only did the authorities confiscate his father's properties when Japan and Peru suddenly became enemies, but the family was forced to hide on the farm of a Peruvian friend to avoid deportation to prison camps in the United States. After the war, his parents became less insistent on maintaining Japanese traditions, which allowed Antonio and his younger siblings to become much more familiar with the Peruvian way of life and to integrate into the surrounding society than their older brother. He relates that they particularly enjoyed the freedom to go to parties in the Peruvian style, which they found spontaneous and open to individual initiative. Eventually, they all defied their parent's wishes and entered marriages with non-Japanese Peruvians.

In the 1950s and 1960s, Antonio's father went to Japan to visit relatives a number of times. At that time, Peru was experiencing a period of economic boom, and Antonio's family's business prospered. Thus, his father was received as a hero in Japan. Antonio says, "My father left Japan as a poor man looking for work in Peru. And he came back a rich man. In Peru, he gave each of his nephews a gold necklace that was worth a car in Japan in those days". However, the relationship between the two countries was reversed in the following three decades.

After finishing school, Antonio found a good job at the office of Nissan's Peruvian branch in Lima. However, as he wished to make a career in the car industry and his father knew of a Japanese *contratista* looking for workers from Peru, Antonio decided to try his luck in Japan, where a new immigration law in 1990 allowed foreign-born *nikkeijin* to work temporarily in the country. In Japan, he visited two sons of one of his father's brothers, who invited him to stay with them and take a job in a small company they owned together. However, Antonio declined the offer because he lacked proficiency in Japanese and because he felt estranged from the cousins. He says, "I didn't feel they understood my situation. I only wanted to make money and return to Peru as soon as possible." His Peruvian wife had just passed away and their three children were living in Peru. He continues, "I had a good job in Peru making US$ 500 a month. I only went to Japan because the *contratista* had promised that I could improve my skills and make good money. In the contract, I was promised work similar to what I had in Peru."

To his regret, he ended up as a factory worker in Japan's "bubble" economy together with thousands of other *nikkeijin*, not as a white-collar worker as he had been promised by the *contratista*. The *enganche* practice has changed little since his father migrated to Peru almost seven decades ago. Today, after five different factory jobs in Japan, Antonio has retired at the age of 48. He bitterly adds, "They only want young people today, preferably women". Yet Antonio has no intention of returning home to Peru. His Peruvian wife died several years ago and his three children, who all emigrated from Peru during the 1990s, now live with him in Japan. He declares, "My children do not feel Japanese as I do. They were raised as Peruvians. To them, Japan is not home. They don't understand me when I insist that they are Japanese. Maybe they're right. After all, we don't feel welcome here in Japan."

Goyo

Goyo is the grandson of Chinese emigrants who travelled to Peru in the 1920s to work. The family later settled in Nazca, a city on the Peruvian coast south of Lima, where Goyo's father married a local woman and became a successful businessman. Despite the family's economic wealth and social status, however, the father constantly reminded his 13 children that their family name, Li, and physical appearance would determine their ethnic identity as *chinitos* wherever they went. Goyo recalls that when one of his older brothers asked for the family's consent to enter Peru's military school, their father refused. He said, "No one called Li will ever be accepted in the Peruvian army". Not surprisingly, Goyo and his siblings had mixed feelings about their dual identity as Chinese and Peruvian.

At the age of ten, Goyo migrated to Lima to later study at one of the city's many universities. A few years later, he graduated as an engineer and set up a small printshop. However, because of the economic and political crisis that affected Peru in the late 1980s, Goyo had to close his business and leave the country. He recalls that he decided to emigrate after a bomb placed by one of Peru's terrorist groups exploded two blocks from his workshop in Lima. He says, "They could have killed me as well. The workshop they blew up was no different from mine. Next time it could be me". However, Goyo's decision to emigrate was triggered not merely by Peru's political crisis, but also by the problems caused by his marriage to a Peruvian woman. In 1978, Goyo's oldest brother, who was identified as the principal heir in the family's will, had also married a Peruvian woman without his father's consent. As a result, the father sent him to Los Angeles, where a business contact of his promised to look after him. When Goyo also defied his parents' wishes and married a woman outside the family's ethnic group, he too was forced to emigrate. Thus, in 1989, Goyo travelled to the United States on a tourist visa together with his wife and two children. With the help of a friend of his brother's in Los Angeles, he found a job in a small company that was looking for engineers, and after a while managed to obtain a so-called H-9 visa, which allowed him to stay in the United States and work. Today, he owns an import/export company together with his brother.

Ironically, Goyo feels more Peruvian in Los Angeles than in Peru. He says, "Maybe I look Chinese, and that's probably why people here in the United States believe that I'm Asian. But I always say that I'm Hispanic. I don't feel Chinese here but Peruvian or Latino". Goyo's mother still lives in Lima, although his father is now dead. A number of his siblings also live in Peru. However, Goyo has no plans to return. He says, "The Hispanic community here in Los Angeles is so big, so why should I go back?"

Pedro

Pedro was born in La Victoria, one of Lima's largest and oldest working-class neighbourhoods, and raised as one of a family of eight children. His parents were both Peruvians and originated from Peru's African population, which was brought to Peru in the colonial and early republican period to work on the coastal plantations as slaves.[2] His father made a living as a blue-collar worker, while his mother worked as a street vendor. Because of the family's economic situation, Pedro's and his siblings' opportunities for studying and making a traditional career were few. Hence, Pedro, who was known as Pelé among his age mates because of his ability to kick a football, decided to try and make a living as a professional soccer player. After a couple of years, he succeeded in obtaining a contract in a local soccer club, but when Peru's economic situation deteriorated in the mid-1980s, he was forced to find another way of making a living. In 1985, Pedro married an Afro-Peruvian woman, and the couple decided to set up their own restaurant in La Victoria. As Pedro's wife is a good cook known for her *tamales* and *criollo* food, the business was quite successful. However, as Peru's economic crisis deteriorated in the late 1980s, it became increasingly difficult to keep the business going. Eventually, Pedro decided to emigrate to the United States. That was in 1987.

As Pedro had no relatives or friends outside Peru, he travelled alone and did not know what his final destination was going to be. He recalls that he first went to Mexico by air and then continued to the United States on land together with a small group of Peruvians he met on the way. After crossing the US-Mexican border as undocumented immigrants together, they continued to Los Angeles, where they split up. Pedro says that although he ended up staying in Los Angeles, he had no idea where to go when he arrived. He recalls, "I might as well have ended up in New York or New Jersey. In fact, I don't even remember why I ended up in Los Angeles. But this was where I arrived." In Los Angeles, Pedro had no one to help him, and he spent several months all by himself before he ran into a fellow Peruvian migrant and established contact with the Hispanic community. Later, his family followed.

In Los Angeles, Pedro's wife set up a new business selling *tamales* and Peruvian food. Her customers came from within the city's huge Hispanic

Living Across Worlds: Diaspora, Development and Transnational Engagement

community. Pedro, meanwhile, established himself as the manager of a local association of Peruvian soccer teams, while also working as a sports reporter for one of the Peruvian newspapers in Los Angeles. Indeed, the couple has been quite successful economically and is famous within the Peruvian community. By combining soccer and food, they seem to have touched the cultural essence of what many migrants identify as Peruvian and what they associate with home. As Pedro points out, "When I arrange a soccer match, my wife always comes by selling *tamales*. And people always buy them. That makes them feel like they were in Peru. Later, I write about the event in the newspaper using my nickname Pelé." When I asked him whether he has ever thought of returning to Peru one day, Pedro replies, "We're doing fine here. In Peru, people always looked on me as Black. Not that it really bothered me, but in the United States I feel more Peruvian."

Maritza

Maritza, 40, was born and raised together with her six siblings in the shanty town of Canto Grande in Lima. Her parents were both rural-urban migrants who moved from their natal Andean villages in Arequipa and Ayacucho to Lima before they married. Because the family could not afford to pay for her studies, Maritza was forced to find work after finishing school and marry at an early age. After marrying, she and her husband, a local police officer, moved into their own house not far from where she was raised. Later, Maritza got a job in a state prison in the neighbourhood (Luringancho) where she lived, and for a while the couple did quite well economically. However, the economic crisis of the early 1990s forced them to change their plans for the future, and in 1993, they decided that Maritza should go to Argentina, where a distant cousin had been living for several years with her husband.

Maritza entered Argentina on a tourist visa, which she later overstayed. One of her sisters had already left Peru with the help of the cousin and had been living in Argentina for a couple of years. Through the cousin and her husband, who were working as cook and gardener for a rich Bolivian family, Maritza soon found a job as a nanny for the family's children. After obtaining a work permit with the help of her employer and thus becoming a legal immigrant, she returned to Peru with all her savings (US$ 1,800) to see her husband in Lima, who had promised to come to Argentina once she had found a job and a place to live. However, to her surprise, the man had found another woman, and instead of following her to Argentina, he asked for a divorce. In Peru, the sister of one of her in-laws who had emigrated to Italy but was home for a short visit, tried to encourage Maritza to come with her to work as a domestic servant in Milan, where she was living. Maritza recalls, "For a moment, I thought that I might as well use my savings to go to Italy to work there. But then I thought, no I would rather spend the money on my family and on living a good life in Peru. So I didn't go."

Maritza eventually went to Argentina for a second time to work for the same family that she had worked for before returning to Peru. Later, she met an Argentine man whom she wanted to marry. However, he left her for another Peruvian woman who needed to marry an Argentine citizen in order to obtain a legal residence permit. In her current job, she makes US$ 700 a month as a live-in nanny and spends the weekends in a flat she shares with her sister and two cousins. She says, "It's a very good salary. My sister only makes US$ 450, because she doesn't work as a live-in domestic." However, Maritza is not content with her current life. "I don't like the Argentineans. They are too cold. I'm only here because of the work, and because I can send money home to my family every month. Of course, I could have gone to Italy, but I don't regret not doing so. It's much easier to go to Peru from here. I go there every year to visit my family and spend my savings. I miss Peru, but I have nothing to go back to."

Ana

Ana, 57, was born in Lima, where she worked for 24 years as a school-teacher. Her father also came from Lima while her mother was born and raised in Callao, Lima's port. Ana's husband, who is 60, is also from Lima and used to work in the city's transport company as a manager of the public bus system. The couple has three children. Because Peru's economic and political crisis in the late 1980s made it increasingly difficult for Ana and her husband to maintain the family and pay for their children's education, they started to explore the possibilities of emigrating. A friend of the family who had an uncle in New York was preparing to leave for the United States, and she suggested that Ana's oldest daughter join her on the trip by land through Central America and Mexico. However, the daughter was afraid of travelling illegally and decided to wait and apply for a tourist visa. In 1989, Ana and her daughter both obtained tourist visas for the United States and left Peru. When they arrived in New York, the friend who had left a year earlier helped them to find a place to live. After three months, Ana returned to Peru, but her daughter overstayed her tourist visa and became an illegal immigrant in New York. Since her daughter had studied electric engineering in Lima, she found work in a factory producing electronic devices with help of their friend. Later, she married a Puerto Rican man, which gave her the right to American citizenship. She then moved to Kearney, NJ, where the man was living.

In 1993, Peru's economic crisis reached its peak, and Ana's husband was fired because the company had to cut down its activities. The couple then decided to leave together, and later their two younger children and Ana's mother could follow. The same year, they both obtained tourist visas for the United States and left for Kearney, where their oldest daughter and her husband were waiting for them. After three months, Ana returned to Peru to take care of her two youngest children, leaving her husband in Kearney as an undocumented immigrant. In 1993, she travelled to the United States for a third time, now through the family reunification programme, having been invited by her daughter, who had become an American citizen. The daughter also applied for a green card for her father, which he obtained after a few months. Moreover, Ana, who is now an American citizen, has invited her mother to come the United States through the family reunification programme, together with her two youngest children, who are studying in Lima.

Ana and her husband have both found work in Kearney and continue to send money back to Ana's mother and their children, who live on the allowances that her husband received after he was laid off from his former job in Lima. Their plan is to reunite the entire family in the United States. Although this plan seems close to being fulfilled, they are not content with their new life. Ana says, "My husband doesn't like living here. He works in a factory in Kearney and has no hope of finding other jobs. He was better off in Peru. I would like to go back to Peru, too. We had a good life there. We still have our house there. But our children can have a better future here. We told them to study professions they can use in the United States". She adds, "Look at my husband's nephew. He left for Chile to find work two years ago. He sells handicrafts there. That's where people go now. I prefer to be in the United States."

Roberto

Roberto, 50, was brought up in Miraflores, an upper-class neighbour-hood in Lima. His family belongs to an exclusive group of upper-class Pe-ruvians who claim descent from European immigrants and invoke this to distinguish themselves from the rest of the population. He went to school in Leoncio Prado, a famous military school for boys. Although the school's main function is to provide new recruits for Peru's armed forces, it also serves as educational institution for the children of the country's middle and upper classes. After finishing school, Roberto underwent training to become a pi-lot, hoping to make a career in one of Peru's airlines. However, because of the political changes that followed the military coup against the democratic government of Belaúnde in 1968, these plans never materialized. The new regime installed by the military introduced a reform policy that gave land and voice to Peru's marginal and powerless rural population at the cost of the dominant upper class of European descent, who felt that their privileges were being threatened and their traditional position of power undermined. As a result, Roberto and his family decided to emigrate.

In 1968, Roberto travelled by air to Los Angeles on a tourist visa, which he then succeeded in converting into a student visa. He recalls, "I didn't have any close family in Los Angeles, only a couple of friends who offered me a place to stay. They also told me how I could get a job to make money to get started." His first job was as a parking assistant, but after a few years, he man-aged to obtain a license to fly and obtain work in a commercial air company. Later, he married a Mexican woman, with whom he had four children, all American citizens. In 1978, Roberto became an American citizen, which al-lowed him to bring his brothers and sisters to California. He also brought his parents to Los Angeles before they died. In fact, his entire family has now left Peru. Roberto also started his own business, and now he has his own tourist and travel agency in Hollywood. Moreover, he has become a respected per-son in the Peruvian community in Los Angeles and is currently the president of the local chapter of the national association of Peruvian organizations in the United States.

For Roberto, home is no longer in Peru. Indeed, Roberto's family is scattered all over the world. Several cousins in Europe and others have taken up residence in the United States. But Roberto's sense of being a diasporic Peruvian is not only a product of his family's global network; it is also shaped by his identity as a *leonciopradino*, that is, a former pupil of the Leoncio

Prado School in Lima. Migrants who graduated from Leoncio Prado have formed associations to support each other in various parts of the world. The aim is to create a global network of ties based on solidarity and the exchange of favours. Roberto says, "We're part of one family, and we always support each other to get jobs and get along, wherever we travel or migrate. I don't think I'll ever go back to Peru. I feel at home here in Los Angeles, but maybe I'll go to Europe one day. Who knows?"

DISCUSSION

The eight migration histories illustrate that the economic crisis and political conflict make up two major push factors in contemporary Peruvian emigration. They reveal that, first, the political reforms introduced by the military government in the late 1960s and 1970s prompted members of the country's ruling class to emigrate (Roberto) and, secondly, the economic crisis and the violent conflict that haunted Peru in the 1980s and early 1990s instigated Peruvians from the urban middle and working class to emigrate as well (Ana and Maritza). In effect, the data suggest that Peru's exodus resembles Latin American migrations, e.g. the Cuban (Pérez, 1992), which also took the form of waves of migrants from particular social classes that emigrate in response to economic changes and political shifts in the country of origin. However, the histories also suggest that structural causes alone cannot account for the recent emigration of between one and one-half and two million Peruvians. They indicate that Peruvians from the country's minorities are particularly inclined to migration and that their transnational engagement is often triggered not merely by economic and political changes but also the previous migration experience of earlier family members and the social status that they have been entrusted as descendants of former slaves or contract workers.

Although Antonio had no personal migration experience himself before going to Japan, transnational engagement is present in his family history. Nicario and Silvia, on the other hand, who spent their childhood in the rural Andes and moved to the city before coming of age both regard Miami as just another destination in their search for social mobility and struggle to change social status. In a similar vein, although transnational engagement is not present as an active memory in the personal or family trajectories of Goyo and Pedro, the two men clearly consider emigration as an important resource to escape the ethnic discrimination that they suffered in Peruvian society due to their ancestors' status as contract or slave labourers and to achieve mobility in the United States. In other words, to Antonio, Nicario, Silvia, Goyo and Pedro, who all belong to Peru's ethnic minorities, geographical mobility and social mobility are two sides of the same coin.

Peruvians who are descended from Peru's indigenous population but live in shantytowns of the country's major cities generally take great pains to distance themselves from their Andes past and gain recognition as Spanish-speaking, western-oriented *mestizos*. However, because they notoriously are classified as *cholos*, these migrants are constantly reminded of their family's

Living Across Worlds: Diaspora, Development and Transnational Engagement

rural roots and migration practice; an identity that is further evoked by the transnational relations they maintain to remote family members living in the Andes. During the economic and political crisis of the past two decades, the deteriorating prospects of escaping poverty and achieving social mobility have prompted large numbers of these rural-urban migrants classified as cholos to reconsider their family's migration practice and livelihood strategies and use this experience to emigrate and search for new ways of making a living outside Peru. Maritza initially entered the new country of residence on a tourist visa but overstayed this and became an undocumented immigrant once the visa expired. Arguably, the stigmatization that she suffers in Argentina as ostracized illegal subject reminds her of her previous experience as *cholo* in Peru. And although she acknowledges that she has improved her living conditions compared to the situation before emigration and has managed to legalize her presence in Argentina by gaining a work contract, she still claims to be subject to discrimination and exclusion. Hence, much like Peruvians belonging to Peru's indigenous population and minority groups, Maritza draws on their families' previous migratory experiences. However, unlike Nicario, Silvia, Goyo and Pedro, who claim to feel more Peruvian after emigrating, but much like Antonio, Maritza expresses little hope that her life as immigrant will lead to an improvement of her social status, suggesting that the context of reception in new countries of residence plays a critical role in migrants' incorporation and subsequent transnational engagement.

Unlike Peru's peasantry or working class, who either belong to and or descend from the country's indigenous population, and the urban middle class descending from African or Asian immigrants, Peruvians descending from Europeans immigrants or classified as *mestizos* point out that they emigrate due to political instability and economic crisis rather than racial discrimination or ethnic prejudices. However, the experiences also indicate that emigration serves very different means for the two groups. Thus, while middle-class *mestizos* (whether from provincial cities like Huancayo or the capital of Lima) regard migration as a temporary strategy to regain lost economic opportunities and social status in Peru and possibly return to what they consider their home country (Ana), Peruvians of European descent tend to view it as a way to strengthen their economic and social position, not merely in Peruvian society but also within existing diasporic networks of the country's economic and ethnic elite (Roberto). In other words, whereas middle-class *mestizos* migrate because they feel that their economic and social position is jeopardized, Peruvians of European descent regard it as a strategy to confirm existing relations of control and power.

GLOBAL NETWORKS

Although the eight migration histories represent individual experiences, they are exemplary for a large sector of Peruvian migrants insofar as they have been selected among a wide range of migrant experiences in terms of gender, class and ethnic origin; similarly, they have been collected in a variety of countries and cities of settlement, which allows for a comparison of the different contexts of reception that Peruvians encounter when migrating. The eight histories suggest that although economic crisis and political instability constitute critical push factors in contemporary Peruvian emigration, these changes cannot account for the complexities and varieties that shape this practice. In order to understand the migration patterns of particular economic and social groups within Peruvian society, their previous migratory trajectory and current ethnic status need to be taken into consideration. By the same token, the narratives show that Peruvian transnational engagement is the outcome of a century-long migration practice among not merely the descendants of the country's immigrant groups but also its indigenous population that have engaged in rural-urban migration to achieve social mobility throughout the 20th century. This migration experience (internal as well as international) has given rise to a geographical hierarchy of emigration that prompts Peruvians from different social classes and ethnic groups to migrate to particular cities and countries and thus make use of already existing networks and livelihood strategies (Paerregaard, 2002). Hence, considering that Peruvians migrate not just to one or two but many destinations in the world, including several major cities in the United States as well as South America and Japan, it can be argued that Peruvian emigration is at variance with the migration practices described in the growing body of literature on transnational migration (based primarily on studies of Caribbean and Central American migration to the United States). Rather than developing strong two-way transnational relationships between the country of origin and of settlement, Peruvians create global networks that link migrants not merely to relatives in their country of origin but also to migrants in other parts of the world, suggesting that a model of transnational engagement that takes into consideration people's previous migratory experiences and applies a global view of contemporary migration practices is warranted.

NOTES

1. Similarly, scholars have become increasingly aware that migration is an issue that is influenced by but also influences policy planning (Castles and Miller, 1993).
2. Today, most of the country's African minority lives in Lima and the southern coastal towns of Cañete, Chincha and Ica, and belong to Peru's impoverished urban working class.

Adios Peru: Persistence and Variation in Peruvian Transnational Engagement

REFERENCES

Axel, B.
  2001 "The Nations' tortured body", *Violence, Representation and the Formation of a "Sikh" Diaspora*, Duke University Press, Durham.
Castles, S. and M. Miller (Eds)
  1993 "Age of migration", *International Population Movements in the Modern World*, MacMillan, London.
Eades, J.
  1987 "Anthropologists and migrants – changing models and realities", in J. Eades (Ed.), *Migrants, Workers and the Social Order*, ASA Monographs 26, Tavistock, London, 1-16.
Glick Schiller, N. and G. Fouron
  2001 "Georges woke laughing", *Long-distance Nationalism Among Haitians in the United States*, Duke University Press, Durham.
Kosinski, L., and M. Prothero
  1975 "Introduction: The study of migration", in L. Kosinski and M. Prothero (Eds), *People on the Move – Studies in Internal Migration*, Methuen and Co., London, 1-17.
Kritz, M., and H. Zlotnik
  1992 "Global interactions: Migration systems, processes, and policies", in M. Kritz and L. Lim (Eds), *International Migration Systems: A Global Approach*, Clarendon Press, New York, 1-16.
Lee, E.
  1968 "A theory of migration", in D. Heer (Ed.), *Readings on Population*, Prentice-Hall, New Jersey.
Levitt, P.
  2001 *The Transnational Villagers*, University of California Press, Berkeley.
Olwig, K.F., and N.N. Sørensen (Eds)
  2002 *Work and Migration: Life and Livelihoods in a Globalizing World*, Routledge, London.
Paerregaard, K.
  2002 "Business as usual: Livelihood strategies and migration practice in the Peruvian diaspora", in K. Olwig and N. Søresen (Eds), *Work and Migration: Life and Livelihoods in a Globalizing World*, Routledge, London, 126-144.
Pérez, L.
  1992 "Cuban Miami", in G. Grenier and A. Stepick III (Eds), *Miami Now! Immigration, Ethnicity, and Social Change*, University Press of Florida, Gainesville, 83-108.
Portes, A., L. Guarnizo, and P. Landolt
  1999 "Introduction: Pitfalls and promise of an emergent research field", in Special Issue of *Transnational Communities – Ethnic and Racial Studies,* 22 (2): 217-237.
Ravenstein, E. G.
  1885 "The laws of migration", *Journal of Statistical Society,* XLVIII, Bobbs-Merrill Reprint, no. S-482.
  1889 "The laws of migration", *Journal of Statistical Society,* LII, Bobbs-Merrill Reprint, no. S-483.

Rouse, R.

    1995 "Questions of identity: Personhood and collectivity in transnational migration to the United States", *Critique of Anthropology,* 15(4): 351-380.

Safa, H.

    1975 "Introduction", in H. Safa and de Toit (Eds), *Migration and Development*, Mouton, Paris, 1-16.

Salazar Parreñas, R.

    2001 "Servants of globalization", *Women, Migration and Domestic Work*, Stanford University Press, Stanford.

Conclusion
– Thoughts for Policymakers and Practitioners

Ninna Nyberg Sørensen

The previous chapters have challenged the received wisdom on international migration and have invited a fresh perspective on diasporas, development and transnational engagement. Drawing on the geographically wide range of documentation, this concluding discussion identifies common themes and insights that emerged from the previous case studies with the aim to indicate relevant analytical approaches for policymakers and practitioners in the field.

Several themes stand out and converge across the individual case studies. First, all contributions suggest that a simple typology of diasporas and the assumption that migrant identities remain the same over time seriously narrows the outlook on diaspora contributions to development and blurs the distinction between migrants who move to better their economic position, those who seek safety from political or civil conflicts, migrants fleeing natural disasters, or those attempting to diversify their livelihood resources and improve their social mobility prospects.

A second important theme evolves around the new "development mantra" of remittances (Kapur, 2004). Whether material or social remittances are concerned, the case studies show that such transfers are not to be seen in isolation from their historical context. As such, their usefulness and actual use by the recipients will depend on many personal variables and social determinants and will themselves vary with the underlying conditions over time. They are neither uniform nor constant. Therefore, to treat remittances migrants send home as a national development resource, national and international development agencies not only risk to reduce these transfers to a cost-free source of national income (Hernandez and Coutin, 2006), but also to overlook the complex and manifold forms diasporic capital may take.

Third, the case studies underline that while return migration and repatriation may sound relatively simple in policy formulations, a final return is rarely a sustainable migratory practice. Successful return often depends on continued links to diasporic or transnational networks, as well as remaining well connected to local power structures while away. Moreover, ideas and practices of return relate to gender and status in complex ways that, just as in the case of emigration, may result in the dispersion of family members over prolonged periods. Curiously, successful return migration may actually turn out to be of a more circular and temporary nature than the original movement. Moreover, circular and temporary movements may, however symbolically, be the only way to hold together dispersed family members who have developed their own various notions of what development means – and where future development can be achieved.

Diaspora and migrant groups play an important but sometimes also controversial role in the development in their countries of origin. A fourth point of convergence across the various case studies is that most diasporas or migrant collectives are internally divided as concerns their time and cause of arrival, different social and political backgrounds, and different experiences and varying positions in the host countries. Diasporas often harbour ongoing political projects that continue to be disputed, contested and destabilized.

As platforms for politics, diasporas are potentially locations of change, but as a extra-territorial political arena diasporas also suffer from a certain time lag in relation to ongoing political developments in the country of origin. As such, diasporas may cultivate conservatism, historical and political fractions and antagonisms.

Finally, the case studies reveal that migration may lead to many different forms of diasporas, and distinct household and family arrangements within them. Although women have always migrated, they now increasingly do so independently as breadwinners or heads of households. Transnational families have to mediate among their members, including their different access to mobility, resources, labour markets and social acceptance. They must also respond to different migration policies, which in turn may transnationalize family life even further. Much as bridges that cross class divisions in the diaspora may contain the potential for socio-economic and democratic development eventually being remitted to the home countries, bridges spanning nations and transnational communities may enable such democratizing potentials to be truly global in scope. The research presented in this volume reveals that it is seldom the simple act of migration, but rather the conditions under which migration takes place which determines the developmental impact of the migration experience. Therefore, instead of normative discussions whether migration and remittances should contribute to development, whether to promote return, or whether development cooperation should aim at collaborative efforts with migrant and refugee diasporas, the following recommendations focus rather on the questions policymakers and practitioners should consider when background analyses for such decisions are made.

ENGAGED DIASPORAS
– ENGAGING DIASPORAS

The concept of diaspora seems well suited to account for the global networks that emerge from dispersed migration patterns that include more than one migration destination. Diaspora formations are not only related to population dispersal. They may also result from border redefinition. Most diasporas are internally differentiated. However, to become important players in homeward oriented national politics, some links between the different social layers within a diaspora must exist. Therefore, a first premise for engaging diasporas is to understand the contexts shaping diaspora formation. As several authors in this volume argue, a context analysis must involve:
- the degree of internal division within diasporas;
- the basis for such divisions (e.g. class, ethnicity, political affiliation);
- the degree of community, elite or activist consciousness regarding the need for a link to the home country, including attempts to reconcile internal divisions;
- the actors involved when active links to the home country are established, the direction and nature of their actions and the dynamics which may result therefrom.

When the notion of diaspora enters home country vocabulary, expectations tend to rise. A context analysis must therefore also encompass:

- the degree to which the home government encourages such links;
- whether such encouragement goes beyond capturing remittances and the migrant vote;
- the perception of emigrants and refugees by the home society and communities;
- whether organized diaspora groups are representative of broader development goals encompassing the transnational social field of home country interests.

Migrants engage in transnational activities only when they have the social and financial resources to do so. If and when they do, their involvement may be directed towards the family, the community or the social or political level. The physical and social mobility of diaspora members may constitute their most important resource in their attempts to establish such links. This has led some observers to suggest that allowing continued transnational mobility seems to be the best and most durable solution to post-conflict situations (Van Hear, 2003). The argument seems to be valid for development situations in poor countries in general.

REMITTANCES

Any assessment of the impact of remittances needs to take account of the complexity in which such transfers occur. Or, as recently put by Arjan de Haan, "a key issue appears to be not migration itself, but the conditions under which people leave, and conditions for development generally, which determine the impact of migration" (de Haan, 2006: 11).

The case studies included in this volume show that remittances do contribute to the development of both state-centred efforts, such as Somaliland independence, and community-oriented efforts, such as those presented for some Central American countries, and to individual efforts to position oneself better than before migration. They also show that productive investment potentials are often exaggerated, as many home societies either cannot or are hesitant to provide the necessary recognition, communication or dialogue forums for possible mutual agendas, or that the parallel social and economic development investments from home governments are not forthcoming. The recommendation to facilitate recognition and forums for dialogue is therefore implicit.

The case studies also show that a solely economic remittance definition is too narrow to grasp the complex and manifold ways in which migrant transfers influence local development. Many of the changes induced by migration are not the result of monetary remittances only. Other kinds of processes are also at work, among them social remittance processes. Social remittances include the ideas, practices, identities and social capital that flow from receiving to sending country communities. They are transferred by migrants and refugees, or they are exchanged by various forms of communication. They often affect family relations, gender roles, class and race identity, and they may have a substantial impact on political, economic and socio-cultural participation: At times, social remittances potentially strengthen peace, development and democracy. At other times, these transfers contribute to long-distance nationalist support for sustained conflict.

Social remittances constitute a so far neglected counterpart at local level to macro-level global monetary and cultural flows, although they are essential to understanding how migration modifies the lives of those who remain behind (Levitt and Sørensen, 2004). So do collective transfers made by hometown associations. Assuming a broad definition of development that includes economic, social, community and political development, a first premise for mobilizing remittances for pro-development efforts is to understand that *different types of remittances* contribute to *different aspects of development*. A key difference between individual and collective remittances has to do with the institutions that mediate the transfer and use of the funds (Goldring, 2004). It may therefore be argued that although collective remittances may not be nearly as important in economic terms as family remittances, the extra-economic social dimensions of organization and experience that accompany them represents an under-theorized and under-utilized development potential. The squatter incident discussed by Nauja Kleist in the Somaliland case shows that such a potential is not straightforward. Together, the case studies suggest that any analysis of remittance practices should include such questions as:

- What is being remitted?
- For what purposes?
- Through what channels?
- Under what conditions?
- In what form?
- To what extent are such flows related to global constructions of migrants bearing responsibility to remit so as to belong or count as contributors to development?

RETURN OR PARTICIPATION FROM THE DIASPORA

The concepts of return and repatriation share many of the same sedentary notions that underlie development theory. Yet, several contributions suggest that the revolving returnee as discussed by Peter Hansen, may be a far more common figure than a large part of theory and policy would have it. In order to be able to return, returnees must be well connected to local and transnational networks, and to the West. Their return not only requires the ability to be able to sustain themselves, but often also to provide for numerous – and at times distant – family members. Part of their reinsertion in local or national life depends on the portable credentials or transnational skills that they developed in the diaspora. If such credentials or skills are absent, or if returnees cannot meet the financial demands made on them, they may face social exclusion from relatives as well as the state. Rather than receiving empty-handed returnees, many developing countries prefer to keep successful migrants in the diaspora, where they can work for homeland goals. Coming home with nothing means just another drain on scarce resources. The difference between repatriated refugees from camps in neighbouring countries and returnees from the wider diaspora is illustrative of this point. Ultimately, a western passport and the acquisition of dual or foreign citizenship seem to be central conditions for the risk-taking involved in return.

The historical optic applied in the case studies also suggests that separate waves of migrants from particular social classes have migrated in response to economic changes and political shifts over time. It is therefore to be expected that eventual returns – be they permanent or revolving – will reflect the opportunity structures for these different social classes in source and destination countries. Moreover, differences in class and ethnic positions, as well as different political affiliations, seem to be crucial to understand possible diaspora contributions to development from abroad.

As was the case with remittances, the question of what determines return/repatriation varies and is primarily determined by three factors:
- Diaspora mobilization and the returnee's connectedness (to family, community, nation and state).
- Whether or not the home country provides social, economic and institutional spaces for the returnees to use their economic and social diasporic capital.
- In the case of refugee repatriation, but also in the case of labour migration from ethnically or politically divided countries, an additional factor is a political climate that facilitates the working together by former adversaries. Or, put differently, the level of domestic solutions to conflict.

Thus, owing to the complexity of migration flows and the concomitant diversity of returnees, the issue of return needs to be disaggregated in the same way as remittances, if we are to understand who returns, when and why, and why some returnees become development actors in particular social, institutional and structural circumstances, whereas others are less likely to play a developmental role. The types of migration experiences gained abroad have a certain bearing on the various levels of potential capacity to contribute to development. It is therefore not enough to focus exclusively on the voluntary dimension of return. By including diaspora mobilization and connectedness, emphasis is put on the returnees' ability to gather tangible and intangible resources before, during and after return takes place. The level of connectedness corresponds directly to the returnees' ability to mobilize resources and is a precondition for contributing to development. At the same time, resource mobilization may be determined by involvement in the dynamics and maintenance of cross-border economic and social networks.

TRANSNATIONAL FAMILY LIFE

Migration affects family life. Some families pool money to send their oldest, unmarried children abroad. In other families, fathers or mothers migrate, often for an intended shorter period of time, in order to settle a debt, save money for a particular family project, to construct a house, buy land, invest in a business, or simply provide for left-behind family members. In this process, grandmothers or older siblings become mothers to children left behind, spouses are separated, and children become separated from their fathers or mothers. Depending on context, gender and generational roles are either reinforced or changed. Finally, remittance practices, return and diasporic engagements seem to be gendered, although not in a uniform way.

Throughout the book, family and transnational family life have been explored from different vantage points, including the ties sustained to family members in the homeland; the family ties broken, not only after but also before and during migration; the gendered visions of family life that circumscribe imagined and actual returns; older family ties to foreign nationals facilitating migration to former colonial powers, or distant migration destinations such as Japan; and the new and distinct transnational family relations resulting from love as well as from a need to legalize an undocumented migration status.

The final point of convergence across several of the case studies evolves around the problems, challenges and possibilities involved in extending family life across borders. As argued by several authors, mobility is an integral part of social life, including family life. At times, families stretch their economic, social and cultural functions over several countries and/or continents in order to create new livelihood possibilities. At other times, the urge for such stretching may stem from a wish or a need to escape the given family condition, including domestic violence. The family may well function as a collective social unit. However, this does not mean that power hierarchies are not at play. Focusing on individual family members' social status within the wider family unit turns attention to the hierarchical dynamics and levels that individual family members are embedded in, as well as on the gendered social orders structuring migration. To detect such orders, a first step is to ask the following analytical questions:

- Who migrates?
- Who stays behind?
- In what circumstances?
- For what purposes?
- What are the consequences?
- Does this change over time?

Whether women or men initiate the migration process seems to be intimately related to the position of women and men in the source countries. Labour market demands in specific destination countries constitute another determining factor. In addition, as shown in Sørensen and Guarnizo's case study, the legal as well as the labour market context in destination countries

Conclusion – Thoughts for Policymakers and Practitioners

have a strong bearing not only on the kinds of family life that can be lived but also on the new family forms that may result.

The losses and emotional consequences of long-distance transnational family life should not be minimized. Nor should it be taken for granted that family breakdown necessarily follows from migration. Thus, there cannot, nor should there be, theoretical closure on the themes raised around transnational family life. As the case studies have shown, social reality is more complex and subject to unanticipated outcomes than any analytical model is able to predict. At a relational level, however, it might be worth studying in more detail the emergence of large groups of children and young people who, due to their parents' migration, grow up with a definition of development equivalent to being *anywhere but* in the developing country in which they are born, at the same time as they increasingly find their mobility restricted. Perhaps one of the most severe problems facing developing countries is the fact that entire new generations have stopped believing in local development prospects and therefore refrain from directing their socio-cultural, political and educational practices towards such ends. Some may lack access to the resources generated by migration, others may live on their families' remittances. But they all now live in a context where it has become the norm to consume goods and pursue careers and other future aspirations beyond their reach. Coupled with decreasing prospects of ever being able to leave this may prove a sour cocktail.

REFERENCES

De Haan, A.
 2006 "Migration in the development studies literature: Has it come out of its marginality?", Research paper No. 2006/19, World Institute for Development Economics Research.

Hernandez, E., and S. Bibler Coutin
 2006 "Remitting subjects: Migrants, money and states", *Economy and Society,* 35(2): 185-208.

Kapur, D.
 2004 "Remittances: The new development mantra?", G-24 Discussion Paper 29, UNCTAD, Geneva.

Levitt, P., and N.N. Sørensen
 2004 "The transnational turn in migration studies", *Global Migration Perspectives,* 6: 2-13.

Van Hear, N.
 2003 "From 'durable solutions' to 'transnational relations': Home and exile among refugee diasporas", Working Paper Nr. 83, UNHCR, Geneva.

List of Contributors

Luís E. Guarnizo is Associate Professor of Sociology at the Department of Human and Community Development, University of California, Davis. He holds a PhD in sociology from the Johns Hopkins University. He has worked on contemporary transnational migration, immigrant entrepreneurs, comparative development and citizenship, involving various Latin American migrants to the United States and Europe. His current research focuses on Colombian and Dominican migration to Europe.

Department of Human and Community Development,
University of California, Davis
One Shields Avenue, Davis, CA 95616
+1 530 752-3558
leguarnizo@ucdavis.edu

Peter Hansen is a Post Doc Fellow at the Danish Institute for International Studies. He holds a PhD in Anthropology. His PhD research focused on return migration among Somaliland transmigrants. His areas of interest include the formation of political identities among transmigrants, the socio-cultural dynamics of financial and social remittances, the gendering of transnational migration and the theoretization of return migration within a transnational analytical framework.

Danish Institute for International Studies
Strandgade 56, DK-1401 Copenhagen K
+ 45 32698787
pha@diis.dk

Nauja Kleist is a Post Doc Fellow at the Danish Institute for International Studies. She holds a M.A. in International Development Studies and History, and a PhD in Sociology. Her PhD research focused on linkages between transnationalism and integration among Somalis in Denmark, in particular transnational political mobilization and organization in relation to diasporic identification, marginalization and processes of recognition.

Danish Institute for International Studies
Strandgade 56, DK-1401 Copenhagen K
+ 45 32698787
nkl@diis.dk

Manuel Orozco is Director of remittances and development and the Inter-American Dialogue, conducting policy analysis and advocacy on issues relating to global flows of remittances. He also heads the Central American Program. In addition to his work at the Dialogue, he is Senior Researcher at the Institute for the Study of International Migration at Georgetown University. He holds a PhD in Political Science and his areas of interest include Central America, globalization, democracy, migration, conflict in war town societies, and minority politics.

Remittances and Rural Development Programme
Washington, DC
+ 202 463-2929
morozco@thedialogue.org

Karsten Paerregaard is Associate Professor at the Institute of Anthropology at Copenhagen University. He holds a PhD in Anthropology. The topic of Paerregaard's current research is the relation between development and transnational migration. This research draws on data gathered among Peruvian migrants in the US, Italy, Japan and Chile and compares the development impact of rural and urban migrant networks in Peru's Andean highland and urban centres.

Department of Anthropology, University of Copenhagen
Øster Farimagsgade 5, DK-1353 Copenhagen K, Denmark
+45 35323486
karsten.paerregaard@anthro.ku.dk

Ninna Nyberg Sørensen is Senior Researcher at the Danish Institute for International Studies, Copenhagen. She holds a PhD in Anthropology. She has worked on Dominican, Moroccan and Colombian transnational migration, the developmental impact of remittances, internal displacement and repopulation in Peru, and diasporic gender and family politics. Her current work focuses on democratization, human rights and anti-corruption in Central America.

Danish Institute for International Studies
Strandgade 56, DK-1401 Copenhagen K
+45 32698787
nns@diis.dk
nnyberg@dinamarca.guate.net.gt

Pia Steen is a Research Fellow at the Institute for International Development Studies at Roskilde University and at the Danish Institute for International Studies. She holds an M.A. in Cultural Sociology, and a PhD in International Development Studies. Her PhD research focused on the Nicaraguan diaspora in Costa Rica and the United States and transnational political participation.

Danish Institute for International Studies
Strandgade 56, DK-1401 Copenhagen K
+45 32698787
pst@diis.dk

Simon Turner is Senior Researcher at the Danish Institute for International Studies, Copenhagen. He holds a PhD in International Development Studies. He has worked on diaspora and conflict, refugees, youth and globalization, conspiracy theories related to violent conflict and genocide, and gender and ethnic conflict with particular emphasis on masculinities. His work has focused on Burundi, Rwanda, Congo and South Africa.

Danish Institute of International Studies
Strandgade 56, DK-1401 Copenhagen K, Denmark
+45 32698787
stu@diis.dk

List of Contributors

Fiona Wilson is Professor of International Development Studies at Roskilde University, Denmark. She holds a PhD in geography. She has worked on 19th and early 20th century in Latin America as well as on the analysis of contemporary social and political change especially in Central Mexico and Andean Peru. Her current research focuses on Andean citizenship in the context of post-conflict Peru.

International Development Studies
Building 8.1, Roskilde University, DK 4000 Roskilde, Denmark
+45 46743210
fiona@ruc.dk